SEC
The Disruption of the A

By
James A. Rawley
Carl Adolph Happold Professor Emeritus of History
University of Nebraska

AN ANVIL ORIGINAL

Under the general editorship of
Louis L. Snyder

ROBERT E. KRIEGER PUBLISHING COMPANY
Malabar, Florida

1990

Original Edition 1990

Printed and Published by
ROBERT E. KRIEGER PUBLISHING CO., INC.
KRIEGER DRIVE
MALABAR, FLORIDA 32950

Library of Congress Cataloging-in-Publication Data

Rawley, James A.
  Secession : the disruption of the American republic, 1844–
1861 /
by James A. Rawley.

  p. cm.
  "An Anvil original."
  ISBN 0-89464-249-9 (alk. paper)
  1. United States—Politics and government—1845–1861.
2. Political parties—United States—History—19th century.
3. Secession. 4. Sectionalism (United States) 5. Slavery—United
States—History. I. Title.
E415.7.R39 1989
973.6—dc19   89-2505
                                                                          CIP

10   9   8   7   6   5   4   3   2

TO
Asae, Gay, Jane, and Marit

CONTENTS

TABLES

MAP

PREFACE AND ACKNOWLEDGMENTS

The present book continues a long-held interest in Civil War era politics. Earlier works include a biography of a Northern political figure, a book about the impact of "Bleeding Kansas" upon national politics, and a study of Northern politics during the Civil War.

This book affords an opportunity to look afresh in the light of subsequent scholarship at some of the works earlier done. It also fills a gap in my writing between the end of the Kansas book in 1858 and the beginning of the wartime politics book in the spring of 1861. And it enables me to dwell more fully than before on the South, which was my home for ten years.

In writing this book I have incurred heavy academic debts. The dean and staff of the University of Nebraska-Lincoln Libraries have been invariably helpful. Professor Hans Trefousse at Brooklyn College of The City University of New York encouraged me to write the book. Professor Benjamin G. Rader, chairman of the history department at the University of Nebraska-Lincoln, graciously provided photocopying and typing help. Sandra Pershing and Joan Curtis of the administrative and secretarial staff have been of great assistance and Linda Ernstmeyer has my warm thanks for typing the manuscript. My colleagues, Peter Maslowski and Kenneth J. Winkle, generously took time to read and comment on the manuscript. They have improved the work, but must be absolved of any blame for shortcomings. Finally, my wife, Ann, has been patient and sympathetic during the writing of this work.

INTRODUCTION

Secession in United States history meant the withdrawal of a state from the central government. Asserted as a basic principle of the American Revolution, the idea gained strength in successive interpretations of the Constitution. James Madison wrote: "Our governmental system is established by *compact*, not between the Government of the United States and the State Governments but between the STATES AS SOVEREIGN COMMUNITIES, stipulating EACH with THE OTHER. . . ."

From the time of the making of the Constitution to the Civil War both Northerners and Southerners claimed the right to secede. Not until the presidency of Andrew Jackson did the view appear that the Union was permanent. Talk of secession accompanied but was not a part of the Virginia and Kentucky Resolutions (1798–1799), the Hartford Convention (1814), the Missouri Compromise (1820), and South Carolina's nullification of the tariffs of 1828 and 1832.

The talk grew more ominous in mid-century. John Quincy Adams believed that the free states would secede in the event Texas were annexed. The threat became louder at the time of the Compromise of 1850, and from then on resonated throughout the decade. Though Northerners at times invoked the right, increasingly Southerners uttered the doctrine, with such frequency many Northerners dismissed the threat as mere rhetoric or blackmail. But in the fifties the conviction grew among Southerners that the Constitution was a compact of states, from which a state could withdraw through a state convention and popular ratification—a mode resembling the making of the Constitution. This means of protecting minority rights became an article of faith in the slaveholding South.

Slavery, its preservation and expansion (and the two became inseparably linked), emerged as the principal right to be protected against the free North, rapidly growing in numbers and hostility to the South's peculiar institution. Slavery in the states, most Americans acknowledged, could not be tampered with, because it enjoyed the protection of both state and property rights.

The territories, not having reached statehood and being under congressional authority, had a different status. As early as 1787 the Congress of the Confederation prohibited slavery in the Northwest Territory, later affirmed by the Congress of the United States. In 1820 amidst heated controversy Congress exercised the right to prohibit slavery in the territories by drawing a line through the Louisiana Territory at 36°30', banning slavery "forever" north of the line. Events at mid-century, as this book shows, stirred a pot that had previously come almost to the boiling point.

Where does the narrative of secession begin? With the American Revolution, the Constitution, the Virginia and Kentucky Resolutions, the Missouri Compromise, the Compromise of 1850? Many narratives of the 1860–1861 crisis start with the Compromise of 1850. This book chooses none of these. Concentrating on the breakup and re-forming of political parties as a way to understand secession in 1860–1861, it begins in 1844 with the question of annexing slaveholding Texas and the consequent splintering of parties on sectional lines.

This book differs in another major respect from previous accounts. Historians customarily have divided the United States into sections, North and South—the line being drawn between free and slave states, and East and West—the line being rather imprecise. In this book we emphasize a more complex United States. The North remains a section of freedom, but a line roughly at the 41st parallel separates the Upper North from the Lower North. The Upper North gave birth to the Free Soil and Republican parties, strongly favored the personal liberty laws protecting the rights of allegedly fugitive slaves, gave vigorous support in Congress and elsewhere to anti-extension of slavery, played a role in the Lincoln-Douglas debates, and tended to favor the presidential candidacy of William H. Seward in 1860. The Lower North gave a less emphatic, but still strong, endorsement to anti-slavery issues.

The historians' South of 1860 comprised fifteen slave states. Many writers have striven to show the undoubted variety among these states in such matters as the economy, slaveholding, ownership of land, and politics. The argument has great credence when one generalizes about all fifteen states, but loses force when one distinguishes three Souths. The Lower South com-

prised the seven states that seceded before Lincoln's inauguration: South Carolina, Mississippi, Florida, Alabama, Georgia,
Louisiana, and Texas. Four states forming the Upper South—
Virginia, Arkansas, Tennessee, and North Carolina—seceded
after Lincoln summoned militia to quell insurrection in the
seven sister states. The Border South—Delaware, Maryland,
Kentucky, and Missouri—remained in the Union.

This book argues that generalizing about "the South," including the Border states, distorts understanding of secession.
From the 1840s on, if not earlier, the eleven states that formed the
Confederacy possessed elements in common—a high proportion of slaves in their populations, a high proportion of plantations, and a preference for the Democratic Party. In these particulars a large degree of cohesiveness characterized the future
Confederate States of America. This book seeks to examine that
unity through the lens of party behavior until secession in 1860–
1861.

PART I

THE PATH TO SECESSION

CHAPTER 1

THE YOUNG REPUBLIC

THE STATES UNITED. At the opening of the 1840s the United States of America had existed for only two generations. Though young it stood out among the world's nations. It was a republic, contrasting with Europe where the republican idea was in disfavor and an experiment in republicanism had failed in France. Monarchy was the dominant form of government, and the notion that man could govern himself was looked upon suspiciously abroad.

The United States not only was a republic, it also had a written constitution, not amended since 1804. Its durability lay partly in its capacity for change without amendment. By 1840 the nation had developed a system of party government outside the Constitution that organized voters, provided mass participation, and afforded smooth transitions from administration to administration. The party system organized voters into only two parties, avoiding the splintering of votes and power; each party was national in reach, binding together the immense republic that extended from the Atlantic Ocean to the Rocky Mountains and from the 49th parallel to the Gulf of Mexico. East and West, North and South, divided their votes between the two parties as they took part in electing presidents and congresses.

The prize of the presidency animated political parties, which by 1840 had discovered the magnetism that military heroes exerted on voters. Even so, distinctive principles separated the parties. The Democrats, the older of the two, favored states' rights, a low tariff, and a liberal public lands policy, and opposed a national bank and federal aid to internal improvements. The Whigs had sprung into being in the 1830s, opposing Democrat Andrew Jackson's policies, and favoring a broad construction of the Constitution that enhanced the power of the national government. With Henry Clay as their spokesman, they stood for a protective tariff, keeping the public lands as a revenue source, a national bank, and federal aid to internal improvements.

SECTIONAL STRESS AND ECONOMIC DEVELOP-MENT. Beneath the surface of national unity, suggested by a durable constitution and a two-party system, simmered sectional differences that caused the Whigs in 1840 not to adopt a platform but to rely for victory upon hero-worship of a military figure and symbols of republican simplicity. In the presidential election "Old Tip," General William Henry Harrison, the aging hero who had defeated the Indians at the Battle of Tippecanoe in 1811, was presented to voters as a man who loved the simple life represented by log cabins and cider, and scored a decisive upset of the Democrats, who had adoped a platform stating their principles. Voter participation attained a new high as four of every five eligible voters went to the polls.

Foremost among sectional differences was the institution of black slavery. Introduced in the seventeenth century, it had existed in all the original thirteen colonies until the American Revolution. Through state and national action it had become sectionalized, and by 1840 abided only in the states south of the Potomac and a line drawn through the Louisiana Purchase at 36°30' latitude. Importation of slaves had been banned by Congress in 1808, and with the dividing line drawn through the federal territories, slavery seemed contained. Organized opposition to slavery was a cloud on the national horizon no larger than a man's hand. In 1840 a tiny band of abolitionists, vouching "every consideration of duty and expediency" required "Christian gentlemen" to organize a Liberty party, put forward a candidate who polled merely 7,609 votes—all in free states—of 2,400,000 cast. (*See Reading No. 1.*)

Offsetting this sectional stress and adding to national unity were American churches, which though divided by denominations, in the main shared a heritage of Protestantism and evangelicalism. The leading religious body was the Methodist Church, growing rapidly toward a million members, followed in numbers by Baptists and Presbyterians. A schism among Presbyterians had developed over both doctrine and slavery, but it had not divided the church between North and South. On the whole, in 1840 the large denominations were not sectional but national. Common religious ideas, party spirit, and pride in the republic bound Americans to one another.

Growth was a striking trait of the America of the forties.

Census takers decade after decade discovered an increase of about one-third in population totals. Between 1830 and 1840 the new nation grew by 4,200,000 to 17,000,000, and it would swell by another 6,000,000 in the forties. The population changes lay not only in scale but also in the ethnic composition of a heretofore Anglo-Saxon nation.

Beginning in 1840 substantial numbers of immigrants arrived from Ireland and the Germanies, the Irish quadrupling in numbers of annual arrivals in the decade and the Germans more than doubling. These new citizens settled principally in the northern states, adding to a sectional population imbalance that dramatically favored the North. In 1860, 87 percent of the foreign-born population resided in the free states. The new ethnic groups shaped partly alignments. The Democrats gained the support of almost all Roman Catholics, both Irish and German, while the Whigs won adherents among Protestants, the less numerous in the migration.

The size of the national domain and the distribution of population markedly changed in the forties. At the beginning of the year 1845 the United States comprised 1,788,000 square miles; less than four years later it boasted 2,992,747 square miles. Four states entered the Union during these years, the two slave states of Texas and Florida, and the two free states of Iowa and Wisconsin.

As Americans moved west the Mississippi Valley grew in importance in the nation's councils. In the Deep South, Mississippi, Louisiana, and Arkansas enjoyed phenomenal growth. In the free West population shot up from about three to five million. The trans-Mississippi West was luring emigrants. Of special significance was the striking growth of free Iowa and slave Missouri, exerting pressure, as the "westering" spirit surged, to organize the nearby territory in the Louisiana Purchase.

While pioneers were pushing westward, other migrants and immigrants were swelling American cities. New York, the nation's largest city, exploded by 200,000 inhabitants to a figure of over half a million in 1850. Brooklyn, Buffalo, and Cincinnati more than doubled in size in the decade, St. Louis grew fivefold, and Chicago sixfold. New Orleans, the only large city in the Deep South, made a modest gain, slipping from the nation's fourth largest city to the fifth. Overall, in the 1840s the percentage of Americans living in cities (defined as centers of 8,000 or more) doubled.

Farming remained the way of life for most Americans. As the population grew, new lands were put under the plow. The number of farms rose by one-third in the 1850s; improved agricultural techniques drove up productivity. The corn crop more than doubled in the forties and shot up by more than 40 percent in the fifties. The cotton crop more than doubled in the forties and again in the fifties.

Agricultural abundance encouraged urban and industrial growth; farmers could feed city-workers and at the same time furnish raw materials for manufacture. As in the instance of farming, technological change improved productivity. The leading manufacturing industry in the nation was the making of cotton cloth, which more than doubled in value in the two decades after 1840. The value of woolen manufactures tripled in these years, and that of machinery grew fivefold. Observing the vast growth of cotton production and cotton making, the head of the U. S. Census in 1860 said, "The growth of the culture and manufacture of cotton in the United States constitutes the most striking feature of the industrial history of the last fifty years."

REGIONALISM. In this far-flung, geographically diverse nation, regional specialization characterized the economy. The Northeastern states increasingly engaged in commerce, both domestic and foreign; and adopting the corporate form of business organization, with its legal and financial advantages, held the lead in manufacturing. Together New England and the Middle states accounted for four-fifths of the capital invested in manufacturing in 1860.

The free states of the West produced foodstuffs, particularly wheat, corn, and livestock. From the forties on they helped to feed the Northeast, western Europe, and the South. They accounted for about one-fifth of capital invested in manufacturing in 1860. The steel plow, the mechanical reaper, the threshing machine, and improved transportation all contributed to the concentration of foodstuff production by western farmers.

The South, especially those eleven states that were to form the Confederate States of America in 1861, was doubtless the nation's most distinctive region. Rural and relatively sparsely populated, it consisted of large plantations as well as small and mid-size farms. Here agriculturists concentrated on growing cotton, tobacco, sugar, and rice—staple crops for sale in distant markets. Cotton cultivation was a prerogative of the Lower South. Requiring a long, warm growing season and favorable soil, it flourished in a belt of states stretching from Georgia to Texas. Less than 1 percent of all cotton was grown outside the future Confederacy. In 1849 the leading cotton states were, respectively: Alabama, Georgia, Mississippi, and South Carolina.

The plantation was more than an efficient method of agriculture. True, it proved to be the most lucrative way to grow staple crops with slave labor. But beyond that, it represented an ideal; though later overblown in fiction and on the screen, it dominated Southern life. The plantation symbolized wealth, political power, and social status. The large middle class—the Southern yeomanry—looked up to planter society and aspired to join it. Planters wielded power disproportionate to their numbers in local, state, and national affairs. At the same time they developed a sense of paternalism toward both less favored whites as well as to blacks. The planters were a distinct minority in the entire slaveholding South, and were concentrated in the cotton-growing Lower South, where two thirds of them lived. (*See Table 1.*)

Speaking in the Senate in 1844, George McDuffie of South Carolina conceived of three separate confederacies—"one consisting of the Middle and Eastern States, another of the Western and Northwestern States, and the third of the Southern and Southwestern States—denominated, respectively, the manufacturing, the farming, and the planting confederacies." (*See Reading No. 2.*)

PARTY RESPONSE TO SECTIONALISM. Varied regional economies in previous years had led to crises that racked the republic, created the Whig Party, and left politicians wary of waging campaigns based on sharply defined principles. A Northeastern proposal to restrict the sale of public lands in 1830 had provoked strong opposition from the West and South. Two years later a Northern-backed protective tariff infuriated South Carolina, which nullified the law and threatened secession. Worried

Table 1
Plantations in 1850*

State	Cotton	Sugar	Rice	Tobacco	Hemp	Total
Alabama	16,100					16,100
Florida	990	958				1,948
Georgia	14,578		80			14,658
Louisiana	4,205	1,558				5,763
Mississippi	15,110					15,110
South Carolina	11,522		446			11,968
Texas	2,262	165				2,427
			Lower South subtotal (67%)			(67,974)
Arkansas	2,175					2,175
North Carolina	2,827		25			2,852
Tennessee	4,043			2,215		6,258
Virginia	198			5,817		6,015
			Upper South subtotal (17%)			(17,300)
Delaware						0
Kentucky	21			5,987	3,520	9,528
Maryland				1,726		1,726
Missouri					4,807	4,807
			Border South subtotal (16%)			(16,061)
			Slaveholding South (100%)			101,335

*Source: J. D. B. DeBow, *Statistical View of the United States* (Washington, 1854), p. 178.

statesmen worked out a compromise. But in the same year a bill to recharter the Bank of the United States, favorable to some Northern interests, aroused deep disfavor among debtors in the South and West. President Andrew Jackson, a Tennessean who personified both South and West, vetoed the bill. Soon after this, Jackson removed government deposits from the Bank, but only after dismissing two secretaries of the Treasury, who opposed removal. The Senate struck back by passing resolutions censuring Jackson. By 1834 a coalition of anti-Jackson forces and followers of Henry Clay had formed the Whig Party. Formation of a two-party system, nearly equally balanced between South and North, was a force for national unity.

If a vigorous two-party system existed in the Old South, exception must be taken to historians' assertion that the Whigs held a slight majority, with states moving back and forth between parties. The assertion is true if one contemplates all the slaveholding states; and it usefully dispatches the myth of a one-party Democratic South. But the view is different if one focuses on the eleven states that formed the Confederacy.

They were Democratic in their party faith. Instead of the Whigs scoring a majority of the popular vote in three of the five presidential elections from 1836 through 1852, in the future Confederate states the party won a majority of the popular vote only twice, in 1840 and 1848, excluding South Carolina where the legislature elected the members of the electoral college and where the electoral vote was Democratic. Instead of states shifting back and forth between the two parties, five states were Democratic, including South Carolina's anti-Jackson vote in 1836, which ignored both the Democratic and Whig party nominees. One state, Tennessee, was steadfastly Whig. Georgia and North Carolina voted Whig three times, Louisiana twice, and Mississippi and Florida once. In 1852 Tennessee was the only state to vote Whig. The view that a slight Whig ascendancy prevailed in the Old South does not apply to those states that seceded in 1860–1861. (*See Table 2*.)

REGIONAL INTERDEPENDENCE. A two-party system, functioning North and South, however, did exist, furthering national unity; in addition a regional economic interdependence promoted unity. Southerners sold cotton to New England mill owners, bought insurance and manufactured wares from the North, exported cotton to England on Northern-owned ships, and to an extent exaggerated by past historians purchased foodstuffs from the Northwest. Northeasterners benefited from the above activities, and as they increasingly turned to manufacturing looked West for foodstuffs for themselves and for export. Westerners produced foodstuffs for both sections and bought manufactures from the East.

Regional interdependence gained greatly from technology, a Supreme Court decision, and construction of a network of canals and railroads for domestic trade. The application of steam power to transportation speeded up commerce by water and rail. The rapid running of steamboats upriver, i.e., against the current, startled a generation. The Supreme Court in 1824 struck down private monopolies in interstate shipping, giving an impetus to steam navigation on rivers, harbors, and bays. The Hudson

Table 2
Electoral Vote, 1836–1860*

	1836	1840	1844	1848	1852	1856	1860
Lower South							
Alabama	D	D	D	D	D	D	SD
Florida	/	/	/	W	D	D	SD
Georgia	W	W	D	W	D	D	SD
Louisiana	D	W	D	W	D	D	SD
Mississippi	D	W	D	D	D	D	SD
South Carolina	AJ	D	D	D	D	D	SD
Texas	/	/	/	D	D	D	SD
Upper South							
Arkansas	D	D	D	D	D	D	SD
North Carolina	D	W	W	W	D	D	SD
Tennessee	W	W	W	W	W	D	U
Virginia	D	D	D	D	D	D	U
Border							
Delaware	W	W	W	W	D	D	SD
Kentucky	W	W	W	W	W	D	U
Maryland	W	W	W	W	D	A	SD
Missouri	D	D	D	D	D	D	ND

*Source: *Historical Statistics of the United States*, II, 1076
Key: D = Democrat; SD = Southern Democrat; ND = Northern Democrat; W
= Whig; AJ = anti-Jackson; U = Constitutional Union; A = American

River, the Great Lakes, the Mississippi, Ohio, and Missouri
rivers became busy routes for passengers and freight. Artificial
waterways were constructed in great abundance in the quarter
century before 1850. The Erie Canal connecting the Atlantic
port of New York with Lake Erie is only the most celebrated of a
series of canals that linked the interior with tidewater and sea-
ports. In the Northwest, canals tied together the Great Lakes
with the Ohio and Mississippi rivers. The Illinois and Michigan
Canal fostered the phenomenal growth of Chicago by connecting the Illinois River and Lake Michigan.

A mania to build railroads overtook America after 1830. By
1840 when all Europe had 1,818 miles of tracks, the United States
boasted 3,328 miles. In that year the entire nation had about an
equal number of miles of canals and railroads. During the next
decade canal mileage grew by fewer than 400, while railroad

mileage shot up by more than 5,500. About three-fifths of this gain was in New England and New York. The South, possessing a good river system that did not freeze over in the winter, had only a small share in this construction, although Georgia, Virginia, and South Carolina built substantial segments. At mid-century the future Confederacy had only one-tenth the canal mileage of the entire nation, and five of these states had none. Two states had no railroads and the whole region could claim only one-fifth of the nation's tracks.

BLACK SLAVERY. If on the whole in the early 1840s political and economic forces seemed to be uniting the nation, one glaring dissimilarity stood out: the presence of black slavery in one section. Casually begun in the seventeenth century, racial slavery sank deep roots in the next century. By 1780, one-fifth of the American population was black, of whom 85 percent lived in only four of the thirteen states.

Despite the Declaration of Independence's ringing statement that all men are created equal and have a natural right to life and liberty, and the Constitution's intention to secure the blessings of liberty to ourselves and our posterity, slavery survived. Still, Northern states abolished slavery within their borders and the Confederation Congress prohibited it in the Northwest Territory. By the turn of the century, slavery, once continental in scope, had become sectionalized, lawful only south of the Mason-Dixon line, except in those Northern states where gradual emancipation was taking place. Stunted in the North, slavery flourished in the South. By 1850 nine slave states had been added to the Union. Large concentrations of slaves lived in the new Gulf states extending from Florida to Texas.

Nine of every ten (88 percent) slaves dwelt in the future Confederacy. Those states that took the lead in the Southern rights movement of the 1850s contained unusually high proportions of slaves: over half the populations of South Carolina and Mississippi, and nearly half those of Louisiana and Alabama. In these four states could be found the largest slaveholdings. And in the Cotton Kingdom, three of every four plantations in the nation were situated.

Slaves were unevenly distributed both in geography and ownership within the fifteen slave states. Generally speaking, few slaves could be found in the mountains and upcountry. The western Virginia counties that became the free state of West Virginia during the Civil War had few slaves; and eastern Tennessee, which produced a Southern president of the Union who completed Lincoln's second term, also had few. Most Southern families, in fact, did not own slaves; perhaps only a quarter held slaves. Beyond all this, most slaveholders owned only a few slaves. Of the 347,525 slaveowners listed by the census in 1850, only 254 owned more than 200 slaves. Half of all slaveowners held only five or fewer slaves.

The influence of slavery reached beyond these numbers. Each slaveowner was the head of a family averaging five members, accounting for about one-fourth of the South's white population. In the future Confederate states the proportion was much higher, directly involving nearly one-third of the white population in slavery. In these states the holders of twenty or more slaves existed in far larger proportions than prevailed in the four Border slave states. In the seven states that first seceded and formed the Confederacy the percent of the slaveholding population to the total free population ranged from 29 to 52; and by 1860 the proportions were even higher.

Owners of twenty or more slaves and two hundred or more acres formed a planter aristocracy. At the apex of a pyramidal social structure they wielded formidable influence in economic, political, and social life. Persons below them looked up to this elite as an ideal for which they strove. And the tendency of the 1850s was toward greater concentration of slave ownership.

ANTI-SLAVERY. Slavery—the South's "peculiar institution"—divided the nation between freedom and servitude, North and South. In the 1830s that division was sharpened by the rise of anti-slavery and pro-slavery sentiment. In 1831 a youthful journalist, William Lloyd Garrison, launched *The Liberator*, an abolitionist paper that stridently, uncompromisingly demanded immediate emancipation. Never enjoying a wide circulation, *The Liberator* saw its articles frequently reprinted in other papers. Garrison's extremeness and eccentricity put off many Northerners, who disliked not only his advocacy of women's suffrage and prohibition, but also his call for the North to secede from the Union. A host of anti-slavery warriors sprang into action, including a number of blacks. Of these perhaps the most striking was Frederick Douglass, a slave who escaped to freedom; in 1845 he published his autobiography which recited the cruelties of his youth and bore impressive testimony to the intellectual capacity of a black abolitionist, writer, and orator. (*See Reading No. 3.*)

In the South, thinking about slavery and blacks' capacities was moving in the opposite direction. The same year that Garrison began *The Liberator*, a black preacher and mystic, Nat Turner, organized a rebellion that killed sixty whites in Virginia. The largest slave revolt in American history, it sent shock waves throughout the South.

When anti-slavery sentiment in the North had resulted in a flood of petitions to Congress urging abolition in the District of Columbia and in the South, a senator from the Lower South, John C. Calhoun, shot back in a speech defending slavery and degrading blacks. (*See Reading No. 4*). "I hold that in the present state of civilization," he declaimed, "where two races of different origin, and distinguished by color, and other physical differences, as well as intellectual, are brought together, the relation now existing in the slaveholding States between the two, is, instead of an evil, a good—a positive good." Calhoun's bold assertion that slavery was a positive good rejected an earlier Southern outlook that apologized for the peculiar institution. His view emphasized the growing divergence between free and slave states over the morality of slavery.

In spite of the forces for national unity one section was difficult to fit into the national mold. Historians in recent years have been at pains to demonstrate diversity in the Old South in its agriculture, distribution of slave ownership, economy, and politics.

However, if one critically examines those eleven states that formed the Confederacy, one finds, certainly from the 1840s on, a distinctive region. It grew nearly all the nation's cotton, owned nine of every ten slaves, held three of every four plantations, was intensely rural, had poor canal and rail connections, was more homogeneous in its population than the rest of the nation, and favored the Democratic ticket. Moreover, what was portentous for the future, it was determined to preserve its way of life based on black servitude.

CHAPTER 2

THE TEXAS QUESTION

THE ELECTION OF 1844. Like a fire in dry, piney woods, the Texas question raged in the South in the spring of 1844. It had been smouldering for years, and now was threatening to spread widely, checked only by the fire wall Northern abolitionists had erected against it.

Texas, populated mainly by Americans, had declared its independence from Mexico in 1836, but had been rebuffed in its hopes of being annexed to the United States because of Northern, largely Northeastern, antagonism to adding another slave state to the Union. As the presidential election loomed, southern leaders believed the annexation issue would unite the South and West and bring victory to the party that espoused expansion.

Southerners exerted great pressure to make the question a national one. They persuaded Andrew Jackson, who as president had drawn back from annexation, to issue a public letter favoring acquisition. "His Accidency" John Tyler of Virginia, elevated to the presidency by the death of William H. Harrison, believed the issue might garner him the presidency in his own right. His secretary of state, John C. Calhoun of South Carolina, also hopeful of a presidential nomination, negotiated a treaty of annexation with Texas.

The sectional clash resounded loudly in April as the nominating conventions drew near. Calhoun, in a most unwise note, reasserted his belief in Negro inferiority, praised slavery as a beneficial institution for blacks, and defended annexation as a means of combatting British efforts to effect emancipation in Texas. Declaring emancipation would imperil the Union's security and prosperity, he made slavery the crucial issue.

Cooler heads took a different view. The titular leaders of the two major parties saw only trouble in making annexation a public question. On the same day, each issued a public letter opposing annexation. Ex-president Martin Van Buren of New York, "the Little Magician," and Jackson's hand-picked successor, took his stand against Jackson and annexation. Denied a second term as president during the depression year 1840, he

15

believed he could regain office now that prosperity had returned by keeping the divisive question out of politics.

Henry Clay of Kentucky, the enormously popular "Harry of the West," a founder of the Whig Party and for a score of years aspirant for the presidency, agreed with Van Buren's view that annexation might lead to war with Mexico, which had not recognized Texan independence, "and was dangerous to the integrity of the Union." Both leaders insisted that the integrity of the Union hinged upon the annexationist issue.

Clay, four days later, unanimously won the Whig nomination. A resolution that substituted for a platform defined the campaign issues as a protective tariff, distribution of the proceeds from sales of public lands to the states (as a means of promoting internal improvements without giving direct, and allegedly unconstitutional federal aid), and a single term for the presidency. The resolution avoided the sensitive issues of a national bank and annexation of Texas.

The Democrats did not convene until a month after the antiannexationist letters had been published. Van Buren's repudiation of Texas annexation stunned Southern Democrats. Though Van Buren led on the first ballot, Southern insistence upon a two-thirds majority blocked his bid for the prize. Not until the ninth ballot did a divided and feverish convention unite upon a "dark horse" candidate, a Tennessee slaveholder and expansionist, "the bosom friend of Old Hickory." James K. Polk, the nominee, had not even been proposed until the eighth ballot.

Robert J. Walker, wily senator from Mississippi, now executed a strategy intended to unite the party's southern and northern wings. Cleverly combining the South's desire for Texas and the Northwest's for Oregon, jointly occupied with Great Britain, he persuaded the convention to adopt a platform deceptively (as though the United States had previously annexed and occupied these areas) calling for the "reannexation" of Texas and the "reoccupation" of Oregon.

The platform on other issues reaffirmed the Democratic Party's belief in strict construction of the Constitution: opposition to a protective tariff, federal support of internal improvements, a national bank, and to abolitionist efforts to have Congress interfere with slavery. A third party, the Liberty men, had met in 1843, renominating James G. Birney and calling for "the divorce of the General Government from slavery."

The idea of "manifest destiny" braced the expansionist Democratic platform. The phrase originated in a magazine called the *Democratic Review*, which in 1844 proclaimed America's "Manifest Destiny to overspread the continent allotted by Providence for the free development of our yearly expanding millions." This joining together of God, nationalism, freedom, and expansion exerted a strong appeal in a proud, growing nation. It particularly fitted the needs of the Democratic Party.

In a spirited canvass the issues of Texas, the tariff (for Pennsylvanians), and the ethnic vote figured prominently. Calhoun's treaty to annex Texas was brusquely rejected by the Senate, every Whig except one Mississippian voted against it and seven defiant Democrats joined them. The Missouri Democrat, Thomas Hart Benton, charged that the Texas movement aimed to dissolve the Union. An adroit letter by Polk, its contents suggested by Walker, reassured many Pennsylvanians that Polk was safe on the tariff. Many immigrant voters, believing the Whigs hostile to the foreign-born, favored the Democrats.

To many people Texas was the overriding issue. "It is the greatest question of the age," exclaimed an Alabama expansionist, "and I predict will agitate the country more than all the other public questions ever have." Alarmed to see his strength waning in the South because he opposed annexation, Clay waffled and declared, "I should be glad to see it, without dishonor, without war, with the common consent of the Union, and upon just and fair terms." The preservation of the Union, he said, was the key to his policy, but his straddle satisfied neither Southerners nor Northerners. (*See Reading No. 5.*)

Polk became a minority president, with his tariff letter winning Pennsylvania, Birney's candidacy garnering enough New York votes to snatch from Clay the support of the nation's largest state, and the South strongly supporting the expansionist. In the future Confederate states, staunchly Whig Georgia voted for Polk, and Mississippi and Louisiana, which had gone Whig in 1840, gave him their votes. Only North Carolina and Tennessee voted Whig, but the Democrats made substantial gains in both states. One Southern Whig wailed, "For the present the Whig party in the South is dispersed."

The election of 1844, revealing the influence of slavery in American politics, held its lessons for the future: an anti-slavery third party movement was emerging in the United States; the

South could force the Democratic Party to adopt its views and a Whig candidate to trim his; and the Lower South could unite in favor of slavery. While Liberty men could rejoice over a ninefold increase in their votes, Clay's forces were disheartened and Van Buren embittered. The election exposed weaknesses in the Union's political fabric.

CHURCHES DIVIDING. The religious fabric was even weaker. The great national denominations were not immune to the growing anti-slavery agitation. The largest of these, the Methodist Church, at the time of its organization in 1784 had taken measures to exclude slaveholders and slave traders from membership. As slavery spread it relaxed its stand, until in 1843, ministers and members owned over 200,000 slaves. The General Conference in 1836 on the one hand had conceded the evils of slavery and on the other condemned "modern abolitionism."

Opposition to slavery rose among Northern Methodists, and a crisis rocked the church in 1844 over the holding of slaves by the bishop of Georgia. The General Conference by an overwhelming sectional vote asked the bishop to "desist from the exercise of his office" so long as he owned slaves. Southern delegates promptly proposed a friendly secession, which brought almost unanimous agreement. The next year the Methodist Episcopal Church South was organized; the largest denomination had split fifteen years before the Civil War sundered the nation.

In the same year the Baptist Church, second largest denomination, divided over the same issue of slaveholding by members. The Home Board in 1844 had refused to appoint a missionary nominated by the Georgia Baptist Convention, and said to be a slaveholder. Soon after, the Foreign Board, when asked by the Alabama Baptist Convention about its appointment policy, took the same ground. Delegates from nine states gathered in Georgia in 1845 to found the Southern Baptist Convention.

Like the Methodists, the Presbyterians, third in members, had early taken a stand against slavery, in 1818 condemning it as inconsistent with the law of God, pledging to strive for its abolition, and recommending annual collections for support of the American Colonization Society. In 1837, a time of strenuous agitation in Congress over slavery, a schism developed between Old School and New School Presbyterians. The former, strong in the South, believing in the sinfulness of man's nature and predestination, expelled the New Schoolers, strong in the North, believing in the basic goodness of man and free will. For two decades Presbyterians remained divided between Old and New School believers, with members in both the North and the South.

In 1857 after the New School General Assembly repudiated the notion that slavery was divinely ordained, the Southern members withdrew and formed their own church. In May of 1861, after a shooting war had started, when the Old School General Assembly professed loyalty to the Union, the Southern members withdrew and formed the Presbyterian Church South. The two Southern groups joined together in 1864.

Observing how the political and religious cords that "bind the States together" were snapping, Calhoun in 1850 lamented, "to this extent the Union had already been destroyed by agitation, in the only way it can be, by sundering and weakening the cords which bind it together." On the eve of his death in 1852, Henry Clay, the great architect of compromises, cried, "I tell you, this sundering of the religious ties which have bound our people together I consider the greatest source of danger to our country."

TEXAS ANNEXED. The Texas issue, which had divided political parties in the campaign, now found a champion of expansion in President John Tyler, a states'-rights Democrat in Whig clothing. Advancing the dubious claim that the election had shown that "a controlling majority of the States have declared in favor of immediate annexation," he urged Congress to annex Texas by a joint resolution. This device, requiring only a simple majority of both houses, he hoped would overcome the Constitution's mandate of a two-thirds Senate consent to a treaty.

The resolution passed the Democratic-controlled House by a vote that split parties; 112 Democrats and 8 Whigs voted aye and 70 Whigs and 20 Northern Democrats voted nay. The Senate, which had defeated Calhoun's treaty in the earlier session, was another matter. The Southern strategist, Robert J. Walker, introduced an amendment allowing the president the option of a treaty or a joint resolution. In this form the resolution passed the Whig-controlled Senate by the narrow margin of 27 to 25 and the House by virtually a party vote.

The amended resolution became law five days before Polk's

inauguration. Tyler, for whatever reason, thought time was of the essence. Senator Benton had voted for the measure in the belief that the issue would be handled by Polk, who would negotiate a treaty. On the day before his term expired, Tyler, seizing the alternative of a joint resolution, invited Texas to join the Union. Polk acquiesced in this act and before the year was out a huge slaveholding state had become a member of the Union.

The annexation of Texas had been executed with a guile that exceeded the usual shuffle of politicians. The Democratic Party platform had artfully called for "reannexation" of Texas; Tyler had pretended the election was a mandate for annexation and circumvented the Constitution's requirement of a two-thirds vote on treaties by resorting to a joint resolution. The favorable Senate vote on the joint resolution had been maneuvered by Walker in a manner giving an impression that President-elect Polk would negotiate a new treaty, subject to a two-thirds rat-ification. With unseemly haste Tyler had then invited Texas to join the Union. Such proceedings left a cloud of suspicion and mistrust hovering on the horizon. The skies would darken in the next administration.

POLK DIVIDES HIS PARTY. The new president, James Knox Polk, was not truly a "dark horse." He had been a congressman and member of Jackson's "kitchen cabinet," speaker of the House of Representatives for four years, and governor of Tennessee. Short in stature but erect in bearing, he was a determined, if secretive man, who gave onlookers the impression of strength, as tight-lipped he gazed at them through his steel-gray eyes. He was reserved if not rigid in manner, devious though superpatriotic, on occasion hot-tempered and blustering, but capable of compromise. Above all, he knew what he wanted.

Though the election of 1844 was anything but a mandate, Polk set out to attain four goals. His record of achievement was remarkable and of enduring importance, but in the end he left a badly fractured party. Polk confided to a friend his four objec-tives: to lower the tariff, reestablish the Independent Treasury, settle the Oregon boundary dispute, and acquire Texas.

With the Democrats controlling both houses he began by proposing to lower the tariff. The measure passed the House

114–95, with 18 Democrats voting no; and the Senate by 28–27, squeaking through with the votes of the two new Texas senators. Slave state support of a low tariff fostered antagonism toward slave interests in the Northeast where protectionism was favored.

In logrolling for the new low tariff Southern Democrats had assured northwestern Democrats of their support for internal improvements measures in return for support of the tariff. They had not consulted with the president, who slapped his veto on a river and harbor bill much desired by the Northwest. The following year a River and Harbor convention in Chicago, attended by over 10,000 people, roundly condemned "Polk the Mendacious." The alienation of northwestern Democrats from a party seemingly dominated by Southerners had begun.

The president next signed the Independent Treasury bill, reestablishing an institution begun by Van Buren, separating the government from private banking. Reestablishment won the ex-president's approbation but did not lead to a reconciliation.

THE OREGON COMPROMISE. Polk made his most enduring contribution in the field of foreign policy, and at the same time suffered the deepest criticism from his contemporaries. The popularity in the Northwest of the platform plank calling for the reoccupation of Oregon had offset the Southern cry for the "reannexation of Texas." "54°40′ or Fight" became a slogan to rally northwesterners around the Southern president's policy toward Oregon.

Polk had fostered this belligerent stance not only by announcing in his inaugural that the American title to all of Oregon was clear and unquestionable, but also in his first annual message repeating this claim. He recommended Congress terminate the joint occupation agreement. "The only way to treat John Bull," he said privately, "was to look him straight in the eye."

He softened his belligerency early in 1846 when he learned that Great Britain was making military preparations including construction of more than thirty naval vessels. Though these were probably intended for a possible war with France, Polk did not want a war with Great Britain.

Polk not only backed down on his earlier fighting posture, but he also abandoned the usual responsibility of a president in handling foreign policy. Customarily a president negotiates a treaty and then submits it to the Senate for advice and consent. Polk encouraged Great Britain to prepare the treaty and let the Senate discuss the draft, and if appropriate later ratify the treaty. His conduct caused one eminent historian to brand him "Polk, the buck-passer."

Polk prepared his path to retreat. He instigated three Southern Democratic senators to speak in favor of compromise. Robert Toombs of Georgia, a Whig leader, voiced further Southern support of compromise, saying, "I don't care a fig about *any* of Oregon . . . . The country is too large now . . . ." By the time the draft treaty had arrived from Great Britain, Polk had involved the nation in a war with Mexico, and without a recommendation he sent it to the Senate for advice.

Few persons wanted to risk carrying on two wars at the same time. The Senate advised the president to accept the British draft; he then signed it and returned it to the upper chamber for ratification. The treaty yielding the American claim to the territory north of the 49th parallel passed amidst cries of betrayal from northwesterners. Polk's policy, statesmanlike in results but deceptive in means, deepened disaffection among Democrats in the Northwest.

WAR WITH MEXICO. California was the key to Polk's expansionist policy. His primary aim was not acquiring land for farmers, but ports on the Pacific for mercantile interests with an eye on the trade of Asia. His willingness to compromise in Oregon rested partly on the fact that the settlement gave the United States access to the Juan de Fuca Strait with its splendid harbor. California boasted two magnificent harbors: San Francisco and San Diego. Polk proceeded to foster revolt in California where about one-half the population was American.

All the while Polk was following a more honorable course. Believing that Mexico, which had broken off diplomatic relations after Congress passed the resolution annexing Texas, was willing to negotiate, he dispatched the Louisiana politician John Slidell on a secret mission to Mexico. Slidell's instructions included securing an agreement upon the Rio Grande as the southern boundary of Texas, in exchange for assumption by the United States of claims against Mexico held by American citizens. He had authority to offer $5 million for New Mexico and up to $25 million for California.

No Mexican government could accede to these demands, and Mexico refused to receive the American commissioner. The door to negotiation seemed shut. Polk next took a provocative step, ordering General Zachary Taylor, commander of American forces in Texas, to advance into the disputed borderland between the Nueces and Rio Grande rivers and to take his stand near the mouth of the Rio Grande. Smarting under Slidell's rejection and invoking the matter of unpaid claims, Polk told his cabinet at a Saturday meeting that he was planning to ask Congress for a declaration of war the following Tuesday.

At six p.m. Polk received news that a Mexican force had crossed the Rio Grande and skirmished with American forces, killing eleven Americans, wounding five, and capturing the rest of a reconnoitering party. The Mexicans had played into Polk's hands. On Sunday the president went to church, and though he disliked to break the Sabbath, completed work on his war message.

Congress heard it at noon the next day. Polk recited American grievances against Mexico, going on to charge that Mexico had spilled American blood on American soil. He threw the war guilt upon Mexico, asserting, "war exists, and notwithstanding all our efforts to avoid it, exists by act of Mexico herself." He asked Congress to recognize the existence of war, and to give him the means to wage it. He promised to reopen negotiations whenever Mexico seemed ready to talk. (*See Reading No. 6.*)

Many Congressmen mistrusted Polk's actions, but the president was too adroit for them. Administration forces drafted a bill appropriating $10 million and authorizing the president to call out 50,000 volunteers. These provisions were intended to rescue and strengthen the American forces in Texas. They were presented to the House in a debate limited to two hours. As the time was expiring a preamble was added, declaring "by the act of the Republic of Mexico a state of war exists." By the vote of 123 to 67 the House accepted the preamble. It cleverly linked "rescuing" Taylor and declaring war, making it difficult for some congressmen to vote against war. In the end the House swallowed its objections and approved the measure, 174–14, with Southern Whigs supporting the president. But 20 representatives refused to vote; and during the debate the Kentucky Whig from Henry Clay's district charged, "it is our own president who began this war."

Senate approval of a war declaration encountered the opposition of two Southern members of the president's own party.
Benton of Missouri told Polk on Monday morning that he opposed "an aggressive war." Calhoun of South Carolina in-
formed the Senate, "it was just as impossible for him to vote for
that preamble as it was to plunge a dagger into his own heart, and
more so . . . ." Benton contrived to postpone action and Calhoun to refer it to committee consideration.

Polk's forces lost no time; they sent one of Benton's friends to
tell him, he "must stick to the war party or he was a ruined
man." To the surprise of the peace men, Polk's forces brought
the bill out of committee the next day and in a cohesive bloc
systematically defeated peace amendments, 20 to 26. In the end,
weary of the struggle and aware of the public's patriotic approval
of war against Mexico, the Senate declared war by a vote of 40 to
2 (both Whigs) with 3 abstentions (including Calhoun but not
Benton).

A close examination of the congressional declaration of war
demonstrates that the final vote of only 14 negative votes in the
House and 2 in the Senate is deceptive. Opposition sank under
administration pressures and public patriotism. Within a short
time the president again was having difficulties with Congress.
He sent the House a message, anticipating "a cession of territory
. . . may be made" by Mexico, for which the United States
should pay a fair equivalent," and asking for an appropriation of
$2 million with which he might negotiate.

THE WILMOT PROVISO. David Wilmot, a Pennsylvania
Democrat, fired what may be called the opening salvo of the
Civil War. He proposed an amendment whose principle formed
the central theme of political debate through 1860. It provided
"as an express and fundamental condition to the acquisition of
any territory from the Republic of Mexico . . . neither slavery
nor involuntary servitude shall ever exist in any part of the
territory. . . ."

Historians have spilled a great deal of ink in debating
Wilmot's motives. One thing is clear: he did not act out of
concern for blacks—what he described as a "morbid sympathy
for the slave." He flatly declared he was concerned about white
men. "I would preserve to free white labor a fair country, a rich

inheritance, where the sons of toil, of my own race and own color can live without the disgrace which association with negro slavery brings upon free labor."

Wilmot's proviso was a turning point in the history of political parties and of sectional relations. To this time the two major parties had sought to evade the issue of slavery. Whigs had kept their silence, and Democrats in 1844 had merely denounced abolitionists for trying to interfere with Congress. The historic arrangement about the territories had seemed satisfactory: divide the territories between North and South, between freedom and slavery. That principle was implicit in the Democrats' yoking together of Oregon and Texas.

Wilmot's strident cry dismissed the old principle of compromise and demanded *all* of the territories for freedom. To some Southerners the demand was unnecessarily provocative, if not foolish, because they believed much of the territory in the southwest was not suitable for slave expansion. Others saw political extemism creeping into American politics, and branded the move as an act of Northern aggression. Southerners perceived a Hydra-headed threat to national unity, the South's right to govern its own affairs, a barrier to expansion, and a wound to Southern honor.

The alignment in the House on the Proviso was, indeed, alarming. Fifty-two Northern Democrats favored the amended bill at the same time as fifty Southern Democrats and four Northerners opposed it, thus demonstrating a sectional fracture of the Democratic Party. The Senate adjourned without acting on it. The Proviso came before Congress a few months later, fomenting a heated debate. This time the House adopted it by a vote of 115 (with only one slave state vote) to 106 (with only eighteen free state votes). The Senate now defeated it, with only one slave senator favoring it and only five free state senators opposing it. The Proviso would come before Congress many times, never passing, but it became the principle of first the Free-Soilers and then the Republicans.

DEMOCRATIC PARTY DIVISIONS. Within a short time major views of how to cope with the expansion of slavery came into focus. President Polk furiously noted in his diary that the Proviso was "a mischievous & foolish amendment," intended to embarrass him in his negotiations with Mexico. He would veto it, if it should pass both houses. As "this firebrand," as he termed it, continued to blaze, he held a full discussion of it in a cabinet meeting. Everyone agreed that if territory should be acquired the old principle of dividing it at a line drawn at 36°30' should be followed.

If Wilmot's proviso represented an uncompromising Northern position on how to treat slavery in the territories, resolutions which Calhoun introduced into the Senate outlined an equally uncompromising southern posture. Calhoun boldly claimed that the territories did not belong to the national government. They were the common property of the states and Congress had no right to prohibit slavery in the territories. The Wilmot Proviso, therefore, was unconstitutional. He foresaw a threat of civil war in a shift in the national balance between the South and the North, and turning from his earlier emphasis upon states rights he now called for unity of the Southern states.

The South, Calhoun said portentously, should merge its political parties into a single party to defend southern rights. He did not press the Senate to act on his resolutions, but several Southern legislatures endorsed them. They became known as the Platform of the South.

The great Democratic Party was now split into three elements: followers of Polk and a compromise line through the territories; adherents of Wilmot and congressional prohibition of slavery; and supporters of Calhoun and his common property doctrine, denying power to Congress. Alarmed by the fragmentation of his party, jeopardizing his presidential ambitions and the Northwest's interest in expansion, Lewis Cass of Michigan formulated a different compromise solution.

Cass tried to defuse the threatening detonation by emphasizing the frontiersman's traditional reliance upon local self-government. He announced he was "in favor of leaving the people of any territory which hereafter may be acquired, the right to regulate it [slavery] themselves, under the great general principles of the Constitution." (*See Reading No. 7.*)

Popular sovereignty cut the ground from each of the other three positions, denying both the national government and the states' authority over slavery in the territories. Moreover, the doctrine was marvelously ambiguous, allowing Southerners to believe voters in territories could exclude slavery only in their state constitutions and Northerners to believe voters in the territories could abolish slavery in forming a territorial government.

The question of how to deal with slavery in the territories seriously split the Democratic Party many years before the party schism of 1860. The outcome of the Mexican War, with its probable addition of territory to the nation, would bear heavily upon both party and national unity.

CHAPTER 3

THE CRISIS OF 1850

While politicians were formulating their positions with respect to slavery in the territories, American military forces in Mexico were gaining ascendancy over the Mexicans and inadvertently shaping the political future.

THE MEXICAN WAR. The Mexican War brought military fame to future presidential candidates. Zachary Taylor, "Old Rough and Ready," Whig nominee in 1848, won a victory over the Mexicans at Monterrey. Winfield Scott, "Old Fuss and Feathers," Whig nominee in 1852, captured Mexico City. Franklin Pierce, Democratic nominee in 1852, won modest fame for his generalship. John C. Frémont, "The Pathfinder," Republican nominee in 1856, participated in the conquest of California.

Alarmed by a movement to acquire all of Mexico that further aggravated the question of the status of slavery in the territories, Polk had dispatched an emissary to negotiate a peace. The terms agreed upon in a suburb outside Mexico City, Guadalupe Hidalgo, changed the future of both nations. Mexico was dismembered, relinquishing its claim to Texas and the immense domain formed by Upper California and New Mexico (from which four states and parts of three others were later formed). The United States area made a quantum leap of nearly 1,200,000 square miles (including Texas). The United States agreed to pay $15 million and take over the claims of its citizens against Mexico. The southern Texas boundary was set at the Rio Grande River.

THE WAR'S UNPOPULARITY. Though the terms were unsatisfactory to those who wanted all of Mexico as well as to those who feared the consequences of acquiring potential slave territory, the Treaty of Guadalupe Hidalgo won Senate approval. Voting for ratification were 26 Democrats and 12 Whigs, against 7 Democrats and 7 Whigs. An effort to tack the Wilmot Proviso to the treaty failed, 38 to 15.

If the Senate was unwilling to vote against peace and a vast and valuable acquisition, the war had been a very unpopular one. Opposition was sectional, political, philosophical, and religious. The Northeast furnished only a small portion of volunteers for the army. The Massachusetts legislature passed a resolution charging, "It is a War to Strengthen the 'Slave Power.' " (*See Reading No. 8.*) James Russell Lowell in colloquial verse cried,

"They jest want this Californy
So's to lug new slave-states in"

Whigs in general opposed the war. Illinois Congressman Abraham Lincoln introduced resolutions asking whether the first blood had been shed on Mexican or American soil. Horace Greeley's *New York Tribune*, the most influential newspaper in the nation, hammered away at "Mr. Polk's War." Among Democrats, Calhoun spoke repeatedly against the war, urging that not "one foot of territory" should be acquired by a war of aggression.

Philosophers, pacifists, and men of letters spoke out against the war. Henry David Thoreau in his famous essay on "Resistance to Civil Government" accused the government of abusing and perverting the people's will. "Witness the present Mexican war," he wrote, "the work of comparatively a few individuals using the standing government as their tool; for, in the outset, the people would not have consented to this measure."

Churchmen divided over the war. Southern Baptists, Methodists, and Roman Catholics supported the war; but Quakers, Unitarians, and Congregationalists opposed it. A leading Unitarian minister avowed that if he enlisted in this "damnable war," it would be on the Mexican side. Frederick Douglass, the black abolitionist, decrying the war as one of plunder and murder, appealed, "let petitions flood the halls of Congress by the million, asking for the instant recall of our forces from Mexico."

THE ELECTION OF 1848: THE DEMOCRATS. The danger of dissolution of the Union became apparent in the presidential contest of 1848. Coming immediately after conclusion of the war it revealed that slavery was a sleeping dragon, which experienced politicians did not want to arouse. The Democrats, a party divided, were the first to meet to nominate a candidate. Anti-slavery elements from New England to Ohio favored the Wilmot Proviso, anathema to Southern Democrats. In New York the party had two factions, Barnburners, Wilmot Proviso devotees who critics said would burn down the barn to get rid of rats, and Hunkers, administration supporters who were said to "hunker" after public office. Many thought that Democratic ex-president Martin Van Buren, though defeated for renomination in 1844, was the only man who could unite the Northern Democrats. In the Northwest Cass, author of the popular sovereignty doctrine was popular, but he was at odds with the Wilmot Proviso men. Calhoun, opposed to both the Wilmot Proviso and popular sovereignty, maneuvered to keep South Carolina out of the Democratic nominating convention. The great Georgia Whig, Robert Toombs, thought the Democratic Party was being "denationalized," on the verge of becoming a sectional party.

The outset of the convention was disquieting. Barnburners and Hunkers sent delegates, each faction claiming New York's seats and votes. Rejecting a proposal to divide the seats, both sides sat out the convention, but the Hunkers promised to support the nominee. Thus, the nation's largest state did not take part in the proceedings. In the absence of the Barnburners, Van Buren was not nominated. Cass led on the first ballot and cleared the hurdle of the two-thirds rule to win the nomination. Some Southerners refused to make the nomination unanimous. William O. Butler of the slave state of Kentucky won the nomination for vice president. Both men held the title of general; the Democrats were conscious of a military title's appeal.

Sixty-five years of age, Lewis Cass presented himself as a candidate who stood on Jacksonian principles, supported the temperance movement, joined in baiting Britain, and above all, walked in the middle of the road on the slavery dispute. Experienced in public life, intelligent but indolent, he could be masterful in debate when aroused. His cold manner, ponderous weight, and sad manner could not endear him to voters.

The platform repeated most of the planks of 1840 and 1844, including the 1840 avowal that Congress had no power to interfere with questions of slavery in the states and the denunciation of abolitionists as a danger to the Union. The Alabama "Fire-eater" William L. Yancey unsuccessfully sought to add planks guaranteeing federal protection of slavery in the new territories and rejecting any candidate whose position allowed the exclusion of slavery from any territories. The Alabama Platform, so-called, won endorsement by the legislature of Georgia as well as Alabama and Democratic state conventions in Florida and Virginia. But the national party evaded the burning issue of the hour and sought to hew a middle path.

THE ELECTION OF 1848: THE WHIGS. When the Whigs met in early June in Philadelphia the prospects of nominating another military hero, if a political innocent, were bright. The press had exaggerated Taylor's military prowess, and Polk's treatment of him made him appear a persecuted victim of an ungrateful and ambitious chief executive. Taylor was a Southern slaveholder, popular in the North because of the victories at Monterrey and Buena Vista. Never having held civil office, he had offended no one, unlike Clay and Webster. Clay envied Taylor's reputation as a military figure, and reportedly said, "I wish I could kill a Mexican."

As for Taylor he would have accepted nomination by either party, or best of all, by public acclamation. Even so, in April he announced, "I am a Whig but not an ultra Whig" and would accept the will of Congress on matters of tariff, currency, and internal improvements.

Like the Democrats the Whigs were a divided party, having anti-slavery followers in the same geographical belt from New England to Ohio. In Massachusetts and New York, Whigs were split between "Conscience Whigs," friendly to the Wilmot Proviso, and "Cotton Whigs," friendly to the South. Though the Northern delegates held the majority and could have imposed Clay, Webster, or Scott on the convention, the risk of sundering the party was too great. On the fourth ballot, sixty-nine Northerners joined with Southern Whigs to nominate the Southern slaveholder and national war hero for the presidency. On the second ballot Millard Fillmore, a New Yorker identified with the Cotton Whigs, prevailed over Abbott Lawrence of Massachusetts for the vice presidential nomination. New York was vital for a Whig victory.

As in 1840 the Whigs offered no platform, thus ignoring not only the old economic issues but also the new territorial issue. Taylor's noncommittal acceptance letter left the nagging question, was he a true Whig? On the advice of supporters who helped the ungrammatical general write a public letter, he gave assurance that those who had served with him in Mexico knew that he was a Whig in principle.

THE ELECTION OF 1848: THE FREE-SOILERS. Evasion of the territorial issue brought fervent anti-slavery adherents together in a convention held in Buffalo in August. The anti-slavery movement was gathering strength; 18 states were represented, including three slave states in the Upper South. Barnburner Democrats, Conscience Whigs, Liberty Party men and others united in forming a third party. The Free-Soil Party nominated for president a former Democratic president, Martin Van Buren, now at odds with Polk over patronage and policy about slave expansion.

The platform lashed out at the major parties, at the Democrats for "stifling the voice of a great constituency," and at the Whigs for "abandoning . . . distinctive principles for mere availability." The Free-Soilers appealed to northwestern voters with planks favoring river and harbor improvements and free homesteads, and with the flat avowal "No more Slave States and no more Slave Territory" set at defiance the South and those who would shun the slavery issue. The platform memorably promised the party would fight under the banner, "Free Soil, Free Speech, Free Labor, and Free Men."

SIGNIFICANCE OF THE ELECTION. The outcome was notable. Success again came to the Whigs by nominating a war hero and avoiding a platform. Taylor was elected president of the United States. He carried the largest state, New York, with its 36 electoral votes to garner a total of 163 electoral votes, as against Cass's 127 votes. Without New York, Taylor would have lost the election and the twelfth president would have been Lewis Cass. Van Buren had cut into Democratic columns there and captured more votes than Cass. In 1844 and again in 1848 the anti-slavery vote in New York had been pivotal in electing a president.

The Whigs won a majority, albeit a slight one of 51 percent,

South Carolina not included, in the future Confederacy. The Democrats stood firm only in Virginia and saved Alabama and Mississippi by thin margins of 700 votes in each state. The Democratic reversal may be attributed in large degree to the popularity of a Southerner who was a slaveholder and a military hero, and to the failure to vote by many Democrats. Voter participation throughout the nation fell off from a national average of 78.9 percent in 1844 to 72.7 percent. In these circumstances Whig strength peaked in 1848.

The election revealed the deterioration of the two-party system. Not only had Cass failed to carry the South, but Taylor would be a minority president. He faced a Congress in which the Democrats controlled the Senate and thirteen Free Soilers held the balance of power in the House. One of every ten voters had given his suffrage to a third party anti-slavery candidate. In the late canvass, Taylor and Cass spokesmen in the North each assured voters that their candidate was committed to "the principle of no new Territory to be annexed to our Africa." Southerners had cast their ballots in the belief their candidate would safeguard slavery interests. The voters had erected an unsteady structure threatened by angry gales blowing from South and North.

The president-makers of '48 had tried to avoid the slavery question as a national issue, but it would not disappear. States'-righters and popular sovereignty men insisted that slavery was a local issue, but from the states, the District of Columbia, and the territories sprang problems demanding national attention.

CONGRESS AND CRISIS. When the Thirty-first Congress met on December 3, 1849, neither major party held a majority in the House. For three weeks the business of the House was paralyzed while sections and factions fought over election of a speaker. Here was the first of three pre-Civil War crises over the speakership, each demonstrating the weakness of the old two-party system. Southern Whigs refused to support the previous speaker after the party caucus rejected an attempt to pledge opposition to the Wilmot Proviso. They found incongruous support from the Free-Soilers, wielding the balance of power, who believed the speaker had not been sympathetic to anti-slavery spokesmen. In the course of the struggle the Georgia

Whig, Robert Toombs, thundered "in the presence of the living God," that if the North sought to exclude slavery from the territories, *"I am for disunion."* (*See Reading No. 9.*) The debate further separated Southern and Northern Whigs. The House adopted a rule allowing a plurality rather than a majority to elect a speaker.

Thus the crisis passed, but not until on the sixty-third ballot the House chose a moderate Southerner, Howell Cobb of Georgia, who believed that a united national Democratic party was a better safeguard for the South than a sectional party. Paralysis in the House had meanwhile prevented the president from delivering his annual message on the state of the Union.

When Taylor did send his message its contents shocked Southerners and sidestepped urgent issues. The new southwestern territories, which he had helped wrest from Mexico, were still under military rule, that is, without civil government. Moreover, nine days before Mexico signed the Treaty of Guadalupe Hidalgo ceding California to the United States, Americans had discovered gold in the region. The great gold rush of 1849 commenced, almost overnight filling California with enough population to become a state.

Taylor recommended that California and the remainder of the Mexican Cession be formed into two states, by-passing the normal territorial stage, and be admitted to the Union. Southerners were horrified by the prospect of two more free states, for that undoubtedly would be their status. At present with fifteen slave and fifteen free states, each section enjoyed equality in the Senate. In the House the free states already had a majority.

The census to be taken in 1850, as Calhoun anticipated, "would add greatly to the decided preponderance of the North in the House of Representatives and in the electoral College," further upsetting what he termed the equilibrium of the two sections. The census would, in fact, show that the fifteen slave states had fewer than one-third of the nation's people.

Taylor's message distressed many persons because he refrained from considering other urgent matters. Texas was advancing a claim that would have widened its panhandle all the way west to the Rio Grande, cutting in half the present state of New Mexico, and enlarging an already immense slave state. A boundary war threatened in the Southwest.

AN ALARMED SOUTH. For years anti-slavery forces had petitioned Congress to abolish the slave trade and slavery in the District of Columbia, an area under congressional control. In the preceding session the Whig-controlled House, with the help of northwestern Democrats had passed a bill to abolish the slave trade in the District. This move, perhaps a prelude to even stronger action against slavery, greatly alarmed Southerners who immediately called a bipartisan caucus in the Senate chamber to discuss the threat.

An "Address of the Southern Delegates," written by Calhoun at the caucus's request, not only denounced the bill, but as well recited a list of Southern grievances. It conjured up the spectre of eventual emancipation, a race war, and black supremacy over white Southerners. This fresh effort to create Southern unity and dispense with party division in the South failed. (*See Reading No. 10.*) Only 69 of the 118 Southerners in Congress attended the caucus; only 48 signed the "Address," of whom only 2 were Whigs. Cobb was among the Democrats who declined to sign; instead, he issued his own address calling for a national Democratic party.

Southerners felt outraged by a turn just taken in enforcement of the fugitive slave law. Though the Constitution guaranteed return of fugitive slaves, the Supreme Court had recently ruled in *Prigg v. Pennsylvania* that no state had an obligation to enforce the federal law. The ruling unintentionally encouraged Northern states to pass personal liberty laws, which assured free blacks that they would not be kidnapped, and withdrew state assistance for removing blacks to slavery. Calhoun denounced these laws as "one of the most fatal blows ever received by the South and the Union."

The Wilmot Proviso ever hovered over the Congress. Southern legislatures girded themselves to act should the Proviso be passed. In that eventuality Virginia provided for a special meeting of her legislature, and Georgia for a state convention. Other legislatures were considering cooperation with sister states, and in October 1849 a Mississippi convention, prompted by Calhoun, issued a call for a general Southern convention to meet in the Upper South at Nashville in June 1850. Ever striving for a united South, he hoped the convention would issue an ultimatum to the North. The years since the introduction of the Wilmot

Proviso had converted many Southerners from the belief that secession was treason to the nation to the notion that it was a constitutional right.

Taylor hoped to circumvent the Proviso by immediate admission of California and early admission of the rest of the Cession as New Mexico, making impossible establishment of slavery. The previous summer he had assured a Pennsylvania audience, "The people of the North need have no apprehension of the further extension of slavery." So far as the other issues were concerned, he advised, "Congress should abstain from the introduction of those exciting topics of sectional character which have hitherto produced painful apprehension in the public mind." Recognizing the many threats to the Union, the old soldier belligerently declared, "I shall stand by it and maintain it in its integrity."

This attitude of their slaveholding president alarmed Southerners. Deepening their alarm was the winning of the president's ear by a Northern anti-slavery Whig, William H. Seward of New York. Henry Clay, a close observer of Congress for more than a third of a century, noted, "The feeling for disunion among some intemperate Southern politicians is stronger than I supposed . . . it could be." He feared the Southern masses "may become influenced and perverted."

COMPROMISE PROPOSED AND DEBATED. Returned to the Senate by the unanimous vote of the Kentucky legislature, Clay now seventy-two years of age, bald, gaunt but genial and conciliatory as ever, rose in the Senate chamber a little more than a month after Taylor offered his "non-action" policy to present a comprehensive settlement. The Great Compromiser of 1820 and 1832 proposed that (1) California be admitted as a state without restriction as to slavery; (2) the other area acquired from Mexico be organized as territories without restriction as to slavery; (3) the boundary between Texas and New Mexico be adjusted by a compromise under which Texas would relinquish its extreme claim in exchange for assumption by the United States of the public debt owed by Texas at the time of annexation; (4) the slave trade (but not slavery) would be abolished in the District of Columbia; and finally, (5) a more effective fugitive slave law be enacted.

Over the next several weeks occurred one of the most exciting and dramatic debates in the Senate's history. The scene was an American *Götterdamerung* (a twilight of the gods), as the three great, aged sectional leaders, Clay, Calhoun, and Webster, gave stirring orations memorized by later generations of school-children. Clay pleaded for "mutual forbearance" and conces-sion. Calhoun, a dying man, wrapped in flannels, "sore-baffled statesman," as Whittier described him, listened while a col-league read his speech for him.

Calhoun recounted the shrinking of the South to a minority within the Union, described the relationship between the two races in the South as "a vital portion of her social organization," reviewed Northern efforts to destroy that relationship, recited the events shaping the cords of the union, and rejected both the Taylor and Clay plans. "How can the Union be saved?" he asked. By only one way, Calhoun said, for the North to concede to the South an equal share in the territories, do its duty in returning fugitive slaves, cease agitation of the slave question, and agree to a constitutional amendment that would guarantee protection to the South. "The responsibility of saving the Union rests on the North," he concluded in a sad, uncompromising speech.

Daniel Webster, though sixty-eight, was as magnificent in appearance as ever, erect, his brow massive, his dark eyes deep-set, his voice sounding like blasts from a trumpet. He "looked like a cathedral," an English observer said of "the God-like Daniel." On the seventh of March the great orator addressed a crowded Senate chamber. "I speak today for the preservation of the Union," he pronounced.

As to the territories including California, geography dictated slavery could not flourish there, he said. The Wilmot Proviso was an unnecessary provocation of the South; both sides should back off and allow "an ordinance of Nature" to prevail. As to secession, "Peaceable secession is an utter impossibility," he cried. He described the problems of two rival republics trying to live side by side, and hoped the Nashville convention would "adopt conciliatory counsels." He acknowledged Northern fault in failing to enforce the fugitive slave law and in antagonizing the South with its abolitionist agitation. Webster ended with an emotional appeal for the preservation of "a great, popular, constitutional government."

The old generation of leaders was passing, giving place to new. New York had sent the former Whig governor, William H. Seward, to the Senate. Elected governor at the age of thirty-seven, he had stood out from other governors by being reelected and by being friendly to Roman Catholics. Destined to become one of the foremost leaders of political anti-slavery, he was a versatile figure, ambitious and devious, given to making extremist statements, and incurring distrust among his contemporaries. Though a new senator he had quickly won favor as a close adviser to the guileless new president. Short in stature, red-haired, and craggy in features, he now rose to dash cold water on compromise. A phrase he uttered in his speech sent shivers down the spines of persons who believed the Constitution was the shield and protector of slavery. "There is a higher law than the Constitution," he orated, while branding compromise a surrender of conscience.

Lines were hardening in Congress and emotions rising. Mississippi Senator Henry S. Foote, feeling threatened one April day, whipped a pistol from his coat and pointed it at Missouri's Thomas Hart Benton. Colleagues intervened, but the incident revealed how sharp personal feelings were. The old soldier at the opposite end of Pennsylvania Avenue remained adamant, talking to a visitor of embargoes, blockades, and personally leading a military force to keep Texans from taking New Mexico territory.

Southern Whigs, in particular, were agitated by the obstinacy of their president. The national party as well as the nation were in peril. Striving for party unity through acceptance of Clay's compromise, a secret caucus of Southern Whigs sent Toombs and two others to remonstrate with the president. Taylor coldly declared he would not sacrifice the nearly ninety Northern Whigs for the sake of fewer than thirty Southern Whigs.

COMPROMISE ACCEPTED. Peacekeeping forces were fortunately at work. The nation was enjoying great prosperity, which now was endangered by the political crisis. Gold was pouring out of the sluices and mines of California; railroads were linking regions together; farmers were selling grain in the market newly opened up in the United Kingdom by repeal of the tariff barriers; and Texas securities' holders were feverishly lobbying to make their investment secure. The threat of a united

South faded when the Southern rights convention called by
Mississippi met and adjourned after mildly recommending solv-
ing the territorial question by extending the old Missouri Compromise line to the Pacific Ocean. Shunned by Whigs, it attracted only fifty delegates, fourteen of them from Tennessee.

As in a Greek drama a *deus ex machina*—a god from a
machine—appeared to solve the superhuman difficulties. On a
hot and humid Fourth of July, President Taylor attended patriotic
exercises under the intense sun. When he returned to the Executive Mansion thirsty, he called for iced water, chilled milk, and
cherries—risky because of an epidemic of cholera, a dreaded
epidemic disease during the nineteenth century. That night he
fell ill and on July 9 succumbed to what doctors described as
cholera morbus.

The president was dead, succeeded by the mild, flexible new
president, Millard Fillmore, who announced he would accept
any compromise passed by Congress. Another redoubtable
leader of the new generation took a hand at managing a compromise. He was Stephen A. Douglas, "the Little Giant" from
Illinois, no less ambitious and energetic than Seward. Historians
long considered the Compromise of 1850 a Whig achievement,
but Douglas, a Democrat, from early on had believed the om-
nibus bill, a package of measures, could not enlist majority
support. He disentangled the proposals and pushed them through
the Senate one by one. In the House, with strong support from
Speaker Cobb and Democrats, the proposals also passed. (*See
Reading No. 11.*)

Fillmore signed the bills incorporating Clay's plan. The danger of disunion was averted. Secession did not take place in
1850. But the compromise contained ominous features. In the
pattern of congressional voting only once and only in one house
did both Northern and Southern majorities occur, that is to say,
on nearly every vote a sectional majority opposed it. The compromise, it has been suggested was but an armistice.

Another shadow on the future was the new fugitive slave law.
Severe in its provisions, it allowed federal commissioners to
summon citizens to assist in enforcing the law, denied captives
claiming to be free the right of trial by jury or to testify for
themselves, and paid the commissioner a $10 fee if he handed the
black over to a claimant and $5 if not. Extenuated on the ground
that the former ruling required more paper work than the other,

the notorious provision looked like a downright bribe to abolitionist eyes.

A third source of potential discord was the solution to the
territorial question. The familiar formula of a geographical line
had not been followed; nor had the Wilmot Proviso won acceptance. Rather, the new formula of popular sovereignty had been
adopted. But what did popular sovereignty mean? Could the
people of a territory outlaw slavery, as the Northerner Stephen
A. Douglas insisted; or did the people of the slave states have the
right to take slaves into territories and hold them in slavery until
a decision was made at statehood, as the Southerner Robert
Toombs insisted? The anti-slavery senator from Ohio, Salmon P.
Chase, prophesied, "The question of slavery in the territories
has been avoided. It has not been settled."

The nation sighed in profound relief. The trauma was over, the
Union preserved. But the crisis of 1849–1850 underscored the
weakness of the old two-party system. The Whigs, in particular,
suffered severely, as events witnessed the split between Taylor
on one side and Clay and Webster on the other; between Seward
and Fillmore in the important state of New York; and above all,
between Southern and Northern Whigs. Discord between these
last had brought on the speakership imbroglio, and vast differences marked their voting on the issues of slavery in the District
of Columbia, the fugitive slave law, and admission of California
as a free state. Overall, Southern Whigs favored compromise,
while one-third of Northern Whigs opposed it. The compromise
dealt a nearly mortal blow to the Whig party.

As for the Democrats, in voting on the fugitive slave and
California measures, they, too, had divided, revealing a serious
North–South schism. Southern members of the party had sponsored a movement for Southern unity, which would eliminate a
two-party South. When the adjourned convention met in November it was attended by one-third as many as in June. Though
the South ignored its recommendation for another Southern
convention, the commitment to Southern nationalism had subtly
deepened during the crisis.

Political skills, national prosperity, and dread of disunion and
civil war had saved the Union in 1850. Old Daniel Webster
believed that Providence too had played a part: "if General
Taylor had lived," he said, "we should have had civil war."

CHAPTER 4

PIERCE AND PROSPERITY

A year and a half before the 1852 presidential conventions, President Millard Fillmore had sounded the keynote of the coming campaign. In his annual message of 1850 he had urged Congress to adhere to the Compromise as "a Final settlement." But the Compromise neither sealed over the political fractures that had developed in the 1840s, nor stilled the moral and emotional differences evoked by the distinct, yet related issues of slavery and slavery expansion.

AN UNEASY ARMISTICE. The dissonance of political parties, however, could not be fully muted. In New York, anti-Seward Whigs defected from the party; and the Democrats, as rife with factionalism as ever, divided offices between Barn-burners and Hunkers and managed to endorse the Compromise. In Georgia a special state convention adopted a platform that perhaps best represented the view of the Lower South. The Georgia Platform announced that the Union was "secondary in importance only to the rights and principles it was designed to perpetuate," that while Georgia did not wholly approve of the Compromise, it "will abide by it as a permanent adjustment of this sectional controversy"; and that it would disrupt her ties to the Union should Congress go beyond the Compromise in acting against slavery. "Upon the faithful execution of the Fugitive Slave Bill by the proper authorities, depends the preservation of our much loved Union," it warned. (*See Reading No. 12.*)

All the while, the new Fugitive Slave Law, intended to be an instrument of harmony, was inflaming passions both in the North and in the South. Vermont, in November 1850, enacted a more stringent personal liberty law. The arrest in New York City of James Hamlet, the first person apprehended under the new law, touched citizens' hearts; and after the federal commissioner had sent him back to slavery, they made up a purse and bought his freedom. In Boston an armed mob of blacks rescued Fred Wilkins, known as Shadrack, and hastened him on his way to freedom in Canada. President Fillmore, responding to a demand from Henry Clay, issued a proclamation calling upon "all well-disposed citizens to rally to the support of the laws of their country." But open contempt for the law flared in many Northern communities.

THE ELECTION OF 1852: THE DEMOCRATS. Less battered by the winds of controversy than the Whigs, the Democrats enjoyed a resurgence of strength in the congressional elections of 1850, capturing 140 of 233 House seats. They looked forward to a return to power in 1852. Cass of Michigan, standard-bearer in 1848, hoped for a renomination, his popular sovereignty doctrine having been incorporated in the Compromise. Douglas of Illinois, a principal architect of the Compromise, also aspired to the party's honor. James Buchanan of Pennsylvania, who had scored the second highest number of ballots in the first round of nominations in 1848, now sought first place. "A Northern man with Southern principles," he had the South's support. The South had no candidate of its own to put foward, but it plainly did not want an advocate of popular sovereignty.

None of these three could surmount the hurdle of the two-thirds majority requirement, which gave the South a veto. On the thirty-fifth ballot the name of Franklin Pierce of New Hampshire appeared for the first time. A former member of both houses of Congress, a brigadier under Scott in the Mexican War, a pleasant man, he had offended no one by asserting principles. A weary convention on the forty-ninth ballot acquiesced in the nomination of Pierce for president. The Deep South took satisfaction in the nomination of William R. King of Alabama, a friend of Buchanan, for the vice presidency.

In their platform the Democrats pledged to abide by the Compromise, singling out the touchy fugitive slave law, and to resist all attempts to renew agitation of the slavery question. They reaffirmed traditional Jacksonian stands on banks, tariff, internal improvements, and states' rights. They spoke a friendly word to immigrants whom they envisioned as prospective Democratic voters. By the end of the convention the Democrats had pulled together by nominating a minor military hero, free from party strife, and adopting the keystone principle of popular sovereignty that had sustained the Union in 1850.

THE ELECTION OF 1852: THE WHIGS. "The Whigs are as much at sea as our side," an old-time Democrat told Van Buren in late 1850. Observers in 1852 waited to see whether the Whigs could go as far as the Democrats in bringing their vessel to a safe mooring. The Whig Party tossed on the troubled seas of "Finality." Many Northern Whigs could not accept the Compromise as the final answer to the slavery question; and when a finality resolution came up at a Whig congressional caucus, Northern Whigs opposed it and Southern Whigs walked out.

President Millard Fillmore, who had approved the Compromise and called for finality, aspired for his party's nomination. He had the support of Southern Whigs, but the enmity of William H. Seward, who together with the crafty president-maker Thurlow Weed, was plotting to nominate General Winfield Scott of Mexican War fame. The two New Yorkers remembered that the party had won the presidency twice before with military heroes, in 1840 and 1848, and only with military heroes. With Scott they faced the problem of muzzling the outspoken old general, who by blurting out his support of finality might alienate Northern Whigs. They managed to keep him quiet until the convention. The third leading candidate was the venerable Daniel Webster, supported by some Southern Whigs but anathema to Northern Whigs for his brave Seventh of March speech in favor of compromise.

The poet Whittier reviled him in these lines:
"So Fallen! So lost! the light withdrawn
   Which once he wore!
The Glory from his gray hairs gone
   Forevermore!"

A fortnight after the Democrats chose Pierce, the Whigs met in the same convention hall in Baltimore to name a candidate. Anxious Southerners insisted on drafting a platform first, and then installing a candidate on it. Finality was their concern; and they won approval of the Compromise, with specific mention of the fugitive slave law. Maintenance of the Compromise, the platform stated, was "essential to the nationality of the Whig party, and the integrity of the Union." Though this plank passed with a comfortable majority, all of the negative votes were cast by Scott men.

The Democrats in this stressful year of intra-party clash had balloted forty-nine times before coming to an agreement on a nominee. The Whigs, more fragmented, had even greater difficulties. At first, Fillmore led the balloting, but he could not gain a majority. The convention seemed deadlocked. Then Scott broke the silence imposed on him by Weed and Seward; and without consulting them sent word that he would endorse the platform with its affirmation of finality. On the fifty-third ballot Scott won the nomination, but on an ominously sectional vote. He had received only eleven votes from the future Confederate states, as against seventy-six for Fillmore. Eight of those votes had been cast by delegates from his native Virginia.

Like Taylor, General Scott was a political innocent. Years before he had written an unfortunate letter, now held against him in Irish and German districts, expressing sympathy with the anti-foreign movement. Though he had a splendid military record, he was vain about his appearance and stiff in manner. Standing six feet three, weighing 230 pounds, bright of eye, he was an impressive figure; but punctilious about his military uniform, he had earned the nickname "Old Fuss and Feathers." Southerners suspected he was Seward's tool.

Though the convention had named a Southerner, William A. Graham of North Carolina, as his running mate, Scott failed to win support in the South as well as in the North. Toombs told the House that Scott was "unfit for the office under any circumstances." Democrats taunted Whigs, "We Polked you in 1844, we shall Pierce you in 1852."

The Free-Soilers met in Pittsburgh, where they adopted an eloquent platform that condemned the fugitive slave law and called for "a total Separation of the General Government from Slavery." While washing clean the hands of the national government, they put the "sinful" institution wholly in the hands of the slave states. The Free-Soilers nominated John P. Hale of New Hampshire for president and George W. Julian of Indiana for vice president.

SIGNIFICANCE OF ELECTION. Without sharp definition of issues by the major parties, the campaign lacked luster. The only real excitement had been in the bruising Whig convention battle nominating Scott. Voter participation fell to the lowest percentage (69.6) in the years from 1840 to 1860. In Springfield,

Illinois, Abraham Lincoln, former Whig congressman, did not vote.[1] In four states of the future Confederacy fewer than half of the eligible voters went to the polls. In the eleven states of the future Confederacy the Democrats garnered 56 percent of the popular vote, 7 percent higher than in 1848. Pierce's strength lay in the South; the combined vote of Whigs and Free-Soilers in the North slightly exceeded Pierce's vote in the section. The Whig vote in some Lower South states shrank drastically compared to 1848, in Alabama dropping by one-half, in Georgia and Mississippi by one-third, and in Florida by one-quarter.

The electoral vote was lopsided, 254 to 42. Pierce had won all but four states—Kentucky and Tennessee in the Upper South, and Vermont and Massachusetts in the Upper North. The Free-Soil vote had shrunk to about one-half of the 1848 total. "I am by no means sure Massachusetts Whiggery will survive the shock the passage of the Fugitive Bill has given it," said Robert Winthrop, former Whig speaker. The Whig chieftain, Thurlow Weed, lamented, "There may be no political future for us." During the campaign the old party leaders, Clay and Webster, died. Their deaths marked the passing of a once great national party in a two-party system.

GROWTH OF ANTI-SLAVERY SENTIMENT. Anti-slavery sentiment mounted rapidly in the decade of the fifties. Many elements formed this feeling: political, as parties vied for votes and denounced "the Slave Power"; moral and economic, among others. Early in 1852 Harriet Beecher Stowe published in book form a novel that had run as a serial of the influential anti-slavery newspaper, the *National Era*. Much of the moral fervor arose from the fugitive slave law, and her book, *Uncle Tom's Cabin*, in a highly readable story-form, told a heart-wrenching drama of white brutality toward slaves and black courage and humanity. Within little more than a year over 1,200,000 copies had been sold; and crafted into a play it caught the hearts of thousands.

The unexampled popularity of Mrs. Stowe's book sprang partly from her sensational account of a fugitive slave chase, contributing to the widespread excitement about enforcement of

[1]I am indebted to my colleague Kenneth J. Winkle for this information.

the fugitive slave law. In her tale Eliza fled to freedom, crossing the Ohio River on the ice, carrying her boy Harry; and in Ohio she followed the "Underground Railway," evading the slave catchers who were in frantic pursuit. (*See Reading No. 13.*)

Fearful that the fugitive slave issue would distract attention from slavery itself, the abolitionist editor, William Lloyd Garrison, kept focusing on slavery. "Our warfare," he insisted, "is not against slave-hunting alone, but against the existence of slavery." Wendell Phillips, the leading abolitionist orator, rejected the notion that slavery could be destroyed by church resolutions and political parties. He called upon a professedly Christian nation to be converted to the motto of "IMMEDIATE, UNCONDITIONAL EMANCIPATION." (*See Reading No. 14.*)

Through his newspaper, *The North Star*, his platform orations, and his correspondence, Frederick Douglass spoke out against slavery, "the first and greatest evil in this country." Neither the Whigs nor the Democrats intended "to blot out the foul disgrace," he charged. The Free-Soilers, he wrote on the eve of the 1852 election, give evidence "of an unconquerable spirit, and a firm resolve." Meanwhile, he endeavored to unite the free black people of the United States in the common cause of insisting on their rights as Americans.

GROWTH OF PRO-SLAVERY SENTIMENT. Northern attacks on the South's "peculiar institution" were countered with heated defense of slavery by Southerners. Politicians like Calhoun who affirmed that slavery was a positive good had for years defended the institution. Intellectuals of varying backgrounds sprang to slavery's justification: college presidents, scientists, clergymen, poets, and journalists. Reviewing *Uncle Tom's Cabin*, Professor George F. Holmes of the University of Virginia linked it with other "dangerous and dirty little volumes" written by Northern agitators, and denounced Mrs. Stowe. (*See Reading No. 15.*)

In the same year in which *Uncle Tom's Cabin* appeared, a summary statement of the Southern belief that slavery was a positive good was published under the title, *The Pro-Slavery Argument*. Written by college professors and leading political figures, it presented a number of arguments: slavery had sanction in the Scriptures; slavery enhanced the South's prosperity;

blacks were biologically inferior and, therefore, should be slaves to a master race; slavery as in ancient Greece provided a foundation for a superior culture; and slavery educated and elevated a savage and pagan people.

Southern writers in their eagerness to vindicate slavery argued that slavery was the basis of free government in the South. It divided society into two classes, freemen and slaves, attaching all white men to free institutions. As Robert Toombs put it at this time, "Public liberty and domestic slavery were cradled together." Beyond all this, slavery erased class differences among whites, achieving an equality, one writer claimed, "as nearly as can be expected or desired in the world." Slavery was a safeguard against the dangerous and radical "isms," then sweeping the western world. A free society produced a large propertyless class, creating gross inequality among classes. A slave society gave every white an interest in laws protecting property rights. With every white man equal, with all property in the hands of whites, slavery created a conservative bulwark against those dogmas that would take property from the rich.

Clergymen quoted the Bible to justify slavery as well as to quell rebellious feelings among slaves themselves. A Baptist minister in Virginia, the Reverend Thornton Stringfellow, wrote a widely read pamphlet, "A Scriptural View of Slavery." He cited the Old Testament, with its numerous references to slave dealings in Israel, and the New Testament, with chapter and verse demonstrating that Jesus Christ recognized the institution of slavery. The words of the apostle Peter were apt: "Servants, be subject to your masters."

Edmund Ruffin pointed to "the patriarch Abraham, who owned so many domestic slaves that he could suddenly call out and lead 318 of them to bear arms, to repel and punish the invasion of foreign hostile tribes." Freedom for blacks in the North, where they were outcasts, and in Africa, where they were savages, the pro-slavery argument ran, was a curse.

"Why peril, then, the Negro's humble joys,
Why make him free, if freedom but destroys?"
asked the South Carolina poet William J. Grayson. Beyond these apologies for slavery drawn from the Bible, history, social theory, and a misguided humanitarianism, abided a belief common to that generation that blacks were biologically inferior.

GENERAL BELIEF IN BLACK INFERIORITY. Northern attitudes toward blacks, though not toward slavery, were startingly similar to those held in the South. Northerners shared a belief in black inferiority, and insofar as they could, kept their distance from free blacks. Only in New England, Connecticut excepted, were blacks allowed to vote; in New York they had to own a freehold estate worth $250. Blacks attended separate schools, and when Boston lawyer and soon-to-be United States Senator Charles Sumner challenged segregated education in the citadel of abolition, on behalf of the black girl Sarah Roberts, the Supreme Court of Massachusetts ruled against him—and her.

Northern white labor feared competition with black workers. White laborers refused to allow blacks to join their unions; they consigned blacks to menial jobs, saying they did not possess the mental capacity to be skilled workers. In the 1840s and 1850s, with the coming of large numbers of immigrants who often took unskilled and low-paying jobs, friction between the two groups erupted. Relations between the Irish, who themselves were victims of discrimination, and blacks were strained. The practice of hiring blacks as strikebreakers fomented violence. Although they were more critical of slavery than the Irish, German immigrants also succumbed to racial prejudice. A German-language newspaper in 1851 described racial equality as "unnatural," and branded blacks as "the apes of the white race," who belonged in Africa.

In these exploitative circumstances black ghettos grew up in the North's largest cities. Boston had its "Nigger Hill," New York its Five Points district, Philadelphia consigned its blacks to cellars and alleys, Cincinnati had a shantytown called "Little Africa." Health conditions were poor and rents were high. Few blacks escaped the cities to live in rural America, despite the abundance of land. "They will endure any amount of hardship and privation," lamented Frederick Douglass, "rather than separate and go into the Country."

Politicians of both major parties shrank from endorsing black equality. In Illinois, Stephen A. Douglas upheld the state law, typical in the Northwest, excluding further incoming of blacks. He declared he did not want to see his state become "an asylum for all the old and decrepit and broken-down negroes that may emigrate or be sent to it." David Wilmot called his proviso, barring slavery from territories acquired from Mexico, the "White Man's Proviso."

Abolitionists and Free-Soilers were not immune to racial prejudice. Many of them were uneasy in the presence of blacks. A companion of an abolitionist recorded this comment, "I can recall the time when in walking with a colored brother, the darker the night, the better Abolitionist was I." The anti-slavery newspaper, the *National Era*, charged that the New York Barnburners opposed extension of slavery "on the ground of an abhorrence of 'black slaves,' rather than of slavery itself." The Free-Soil movement was in fact more anti-slavery than abolitionist. It sought to check the Slave Power and sustain opportunity for free white labor.

The early years of the 1850s were seemingly tranquil, after the shock of crisis at the opening of the decade. Party issues that had previously drawn throngs to the voting places were forgotten, and parties themselves seemed weak and pallid. However, there was a widening divergence over the morality of slavery, accompanied by a growing degradation of blacks in American society.

NATIONAL ECONOMIC GROWTH. The creak of wagon wheels turning westward, the stroke of the pioneer's axe, the rasp of the plow in virgin soil, the whir of machinery, the locomotive's shrill whistle, the blast of the steamship's horn, the click of the telegraph—these were the sounds that denoted the economic boom of the fifties.

The prosperity that followed the Panic of 1837 evidenced unexampled economic growth. The nation both grew and changed. It experienced an explosion in population and an alteration in its ethnic make-up. It witnessed an internal migration as Americans moved into the Mississippi Valley and along the Pacific Coast. Its cities became centers of commerce and manufacturing, their populations comprised of a new plutocracy, a middle class base, propertyless workers, and newly arrived immigrants. It reveled in the doubling of the national wealth in a single decade. It welcomed steam power to do its work, producing its wares, transporting its goods on water and land, and hastening travelers on their way. It marveled over the electric telegraph that transformed journalism and business.

In the fifties the numbers living under the American flag

leaped upward by more than a third. Nearly twice as many people were added to the population in the decade as in the 1830s. The increase of 8,250,000 people brought the nation to about eight times the size of the republic at the time of the first census in 1790. Census takers enumerated 31,500,000 Americans.

The rate of growth was uneven in its geographic impact. The nation added new states in the fifties, exclusively in the North. Besides California, Minnesota and Oregon joined the Union.

In generalizing about "the South," historians have distorted popular understanding of racial proportions in the South that seceded. While the nation as a whole grew in population by 36 percent, the states of the future Confederacy grew by only 25 percent. The proportions between slave and white changed markedly in the South during the decade. Slaves decreased in proportion in the four slave states that remained loyal to the Union in 1861, but increased in seven of the eleven states that became the Confederacy, and stayed about the same in the other four states, except Virginia which saw a decline. In the future Confederacy by 1860 lived two-thirds as many blacks as whites, in the whole slaveholding South—the historians' "South"— only one-third as many blacks as whites.

THE ADVANCING NORTH. The upsurge of population, especially in the North, sprang from the arrival of large numbers of foreigners, as well as from natural increase. Impelled by the Irish potato shortage and the failure of the European revolutions of 1848, immigration rose sharply in the late 1840s, and in 1850, for the first time, exceeded one-third of a million. In the 1850s over 2,800,000 immigrants reached American shores, coming mainly from Ireland and the Germanies. Predominantly male they settled in the free states, adding to the industrial and military strength of the section. Southern cities attracted foreigners, who settled in substantial numbers in New Orleans, Mobile, Charleston, and Richmond. However, Upper North states extending from Massachusetts to Wisconsin, where in 1860 one-third of the people had been born abroad, absorbed most new arrivals. By that date the number of foreign-born in the United States was greater than the number of slaves. (*See Reading No. 16.*)

The area of the United States, so greatly expanded in the 1840s, gained another 29,640 square miles in 1853 with the Gadsden Purchase. What was more remarkable was the shift in residence of large numbers of Americans as they moved westward. One-quarter of the whole population increase occurred in only four states in the Mississippi valley: Illinois, Indiana, Iowa, and Missouri, none of them members of the future Confederacy. Though no state exceeded the prodigious growth of Illinois, in the lower Mississippi valley Alabama, Mississippi, and Louisiana grew vigorously.

The tendency of Americans to live in cities continued in its rapid mid-century advance. By 1860 nearly one in five persons lived in urban places of 2,500 or more. The Northeast boasted primacy in urbanization, with New York far in the lead, followed by Philadelphia and Brooklyn, at that time separate from New York City. Only one of the top ten lay in the future Confederacy, New Orleans, "the Crescent City," now ranking sixth. Inclusion of Cincinnati, St. Louis, and Chicago in the top ten demonstrated the rise of the West. Chicago had enjoyed phenomenal growth, in only a score of years bursting from 4,500 to 109,000 in population.

Although most Americans resided on the land and made their living by farming, growing numbers found employment in factories and mills, turning out textiles, boots and shoes, flour and meal, men's clothing, machinery, carriages and wagons, and leather wares. Others worked in the rising lumbering and mining industries. Seth Thomas clocks, Colt revolvers, and McCormick reapers were familiar household words. Isaac Singer's sewing machine displaced hand labor in clothing and shoe factories, but had not yet displaced the domestic seamstress. Value added by manufacturing jumped from $240 million in 1839 to $815 million twenty years later.

CLASS AND SECTION. The national wealth, i.e., total valuation of real estate and personal property, made a startling leap of more than 300 percent in the score of years ending in 1860. Development of the factory system made class differences more pronounced. A simpler society had known a landed and a commercial aristocracy. Now an industrial aristocracy appeared. The millionaire was less a rarity than earlier in the century. In the 1850s an estimated twenty millionaires lived in New York City, eighteen in Boston, and twenty-five in Philadelphia.

The status of skilled craftsmen changed according to their skill, thus weavers lost status with the coming of mechanical weaving, while metalworkers gained status with the new demand for their services. An industrial labor class was emerging in urban centers, men, women and children who were without their own tools or property and were dependent upon capitalists for their livelihood. The development of a diversified economy would throw advantages to the North in materials and skills vital in waging a modern war.

The sectional distribution of wealth greatly favored the free states. Control of ocean-going and coastal commerce centered in New York City. Banking and credit were concentrated in the Northeast; in 1860 southerners owed over $200 million to Northern merchants. The disparity between the two sections widened in the 1850s. In 1860 no Southern state contained real and personal property valued at one billion dollars; but Pennsylvania and Ohio each had property of that magnitude, and residents of New York City owned property worth nearly two billion dollars. The decade witnessed rapid growth of wealth in the North in general; two differing economies were coming into being.

The trend toward regional specialization, earlier noted, maintained it course. In general, manufacturing was concentrated in New England and the Middle Atlantic states. The Northeast led the nation in the making of textiles (cotton, wool, and silk), machinery, ships, clothing, furniture, vehicles, and stoves. At the same time agriculture continued to flourish in the Northeastern states. For example, in 1860 New York, though a financial, commercial, and industrial giant, had the largest number of farmers of any Northern state, and was the nation's foremost producer of fruit and hay. Pennsylvania owned the sinews of industrialization, iron and coal; it stood foremost in making iron products as well as machinery, and in mining soft coal.

Industrialization was spreading westward. Lumbering flourished in the Middle Atlantic states and the West, flour and meal manufacturing in the West, and men's clothing manufacturing extended from Boston to Cincinnati. The most spectacular increase in the West was in the making of agricultural implements: western production swelled in value more than fourfold in the 1850s.

Wheat-growing expanded westward; the Mississippi valley accounted for the country's phenomenal 72 percent rise in wheat production in the 1850s. By 1860 wheat, or as the English termed it corn, was a rival for the throne claimed by King Cotton. The West's superiority over the East is suggested by comparative figures of average farm production in New York, 44 bushels, and 226 in Wisconsin.

The South enjoyed an economic boom of great proportions in the 1850s. Cotton still reigned, nearly doubling in production in the decade, and tripling in the score of years since 1840. The price of upland cotton, which had reached a high point in 1850, fell off, then moved upward again. Sugar cane production remained steady, but planters relished a handsome rise in prices. Depressed by low prices tobacco cultivation dropped in the 1840s, but at the start of the 1850s a dramatic surge in prices, which continued high during the decade, encouraged tobacco planters. By the end of the decade production, with Virginia in the lead, was more than double the output of 1839. All the while, slaveowners took satisfaction in the rising value of their slaves.

King Cotton extended his empire west in the 1850s. Mississippi became the leading cotton state, its total alone surpassing the combined output of the three old, proud seaboard states of Georgia and the Carolinas. Alabama stood second; and the trans-Mississippi states of Louisiana, Texas, and Arkansas ranked third, fifth, and sixth in cotton production. Cotton accounted for nearly three-fifths of the value of United States exports on the eve of the Civil War. Flush times in agriculture nourished a spirit of optimism in the Lower South.

Just as industrialization produced an urban elite, cotton growing produced a planter elite. In the leading cotton states the average size of farms and plantations increased during the 1850s, running counter to the national trend toward smaller farms. Concentration in land ownership and cotton production marked the cotton states. The rich delta country in Mississippi, Louisiana, and Arkansas produced a plutocracy. Once described as the "largest cotton planter in the world," John Routh was rivaled by

Stephen Duncan, who owned eight plantations, and the Surget family of four brothers and two sisters who, in all, owned over 90,000 acres of cotton land in the three lush states.

MODERNIZATION. Though profoundly rural in outlook the South welcomed the industrialization that was sweeping the Western world. In the South the chief manufactures were extractive: lumbering and the processing of tobacco and flour. Efforts to establish cotton-cloth making in South Carolina proved abortive, but Virginians founded a sizable iron industry at Richmond. Capital invested in manufacturing increased in absolute figures, but not in proportion to the increase elsewhere in the nation. The future Confederate states in 1860 produced less than one-tenth of the value of the country's manufactured goods.

Regional specialization of the kind we have been witnessing had two faces. One reflected a differentiation of sections and appeared divisive in nature. The other reflected an interdependence of section and appeared unifying. In this second aspect the sections exchanged goods and services with one another. The same dualism is true of the developing transportation and communications systems. During the decade, the nation made huge strides toward creation of a continental market, as rails thrust their way across mountain and prairie, canals attained a peak of construction, and the new telegraph spanned the continent.

But inland waterways froze in winter and, moreover, could not be fashioned into a transportation network as readily as rail systems. Railroad rates dropped, the level of comfort rose, and time required for shipment grew shorter. Rail construction shot ahead in a greater than threefold increase in the decade. The celebrated Erie Canal bowed to the superiority of the rail lines connecting the port of New York with the Great Lakes and the West. As early as 1850 more miles of canals were being abandoned than being constructed.

The North benefited from this spread of railways more than did the South. By 1860 major lines connected the Atlantic ports of Boston, New York, Philadelphia, and Baltimore with the West. Chicago had become the world's largest railroad center. The new grid bound the Northeast and the Northwest together, and free soil politicians strove to separate the Northwest from its traditional allegiance with the South.

When the war came the North possessed about 22,000 miles of rails and the Confederate states only 9,000. The Southern grid was less well developed and unified than the Northern, but both Norfolk and Charleston had access to Memphis on the Mississippi River. A mighty effort to tie the Northwest and the Lower South by rail had begun in 1850 when Senator Stephen A. Douglas had persuaded Congress to subsidize a railroad intended to link Chicago and Mobile. Progress was slow, and not until 1861 was the line completed, too late to bind the sections together. Proposals for a transcontinental railroad fell afoul of a rivalry between South and North over which section would gain the benefit of such an ambitious enterprise.

The communications revolution moved even faster than the transformation of water and rail transportation. Not invented until 1844 the magnetic telegraph, beginning with a small subsidy from Congress, sped across the nation with an astonishing velocity. By 1860 the nation had no fewer than 50,000 miles of lines and the next year boasted the triumph of coast-to-coast communication by wire, in time to be useful, especially to the Union, in waging war.

CHAPTER 5

PARTY REALIGNMENT

Prosperity and the Compromise of 1850 sank the old political issues that had so excited partisans and defined parties. Contemporaries noted the subsidence of party warfare over the national bank issue, tariff, and internal improvements. "The acknowledged issues between the two parties are now of no . . . practical bearing," a Whig senator noted after the election of 1852. The territorial issue seemed settled for all time; Congress had arranged for the future of slavery in all the territories. The public mind was quiet with regard to slave expansion. Meanwhile, in local and state politics new issues of temperance and anti-foreignism were at work dissolving party loyalties.

THE KANSAS-NEBRASKA ACT. A bombshell burst over this quiet scene in early 1854 when Senator Stephen A. Douglas, chairman of the committee on territories, introduced a bill to organize the northern part of the Louisiana Purchase as the Nebraska Territory. Beginning innocently as a measure to establish territorial government and prepare the way for construction of a transcontinental railroad and settlement by pioneers, the bill took a sharp twist when with President Pierce's blessing, an amendment repealed the Missouri Compromise.

In effect for a third of a century, the Missouri Compromise—a product of national crisis—had divided the Purchase between slavery and freedom. Its existence was part of the reason the public mind had been at ease before Douglas's new bill. In place of the compromise line the bill substituted the principle of popular sovereignty, applied to the Mexican Cession in 1850. Overeager to organize the territory, Douglas had accepted the amendment, which seemed to assure Southern support of a measure that might lead to construction of a railroad benefiting the free states. (*See Reading No. 17.*)

In agreeing to the drastic shift in the national compact toward slavery in the Louisiana Territory, Douglas acknowledged risk. "By God, sir," he exclaimed to a colleague who pressed him to accept the amendment, "I will incorporate it in my bill, though I know it will raise a hell of a storm."

Douglas, one of the craftsmen of the Compromise of 1850, belonged to the new generation of American statesmen. Born in Vermont in 1813, he had migrated west to Illinois where he strode ahead in the legal profession with such success he was at the age of twenty-eight a member of the state Supreme Court. Short in stature—he stood at five feet four inches—he had a huge head and strong square shoulders that won him the nickname "the Little Giant." An ardent believer in Manifest Destiny, he strove for both continental and overseas expansion. His interest in promoting rail development and uniting sections had already borne fruit in the congressional land grant for the Illinois Central Railroad. He was simultaneously a speculator in urban real estate and a donor of land for the future University of Chicago.

The principle of popular sovereignty agreed with his faith in local self-government. Insensitive to the explosive moral issue of slavery, he was driven by ambition. At the age of thirty-nine he aspired to the Democratic Party's presidential nomination in 1852. Imbued with great energy, he was in early career described as a "Steam engine in britches."

More like a tornado than "a hell of a storm," a sense of outrage tore across the North. Politicians of both parties, press, and pulpit united to denounce ripping open the old wound, presumably closed by the "finality" of the Compromise of 1850. On the day after Douglas reported his amended bill, an impassioned document called "Appeal of the Independent Democrats" appeared over the signatures of Free-Soilers and Democrats, members of Douglas's party. (*See Reading No. 18.*)

They spoke of a betrayal of the national honor and a politicians' plot against freedom, appealed to immigrants and workers, and foresaw the spread of slavery into the area that became Kansas and Nebraska. Douglas had miscalculated in his zeal to open the West to settlement, his indifference to slavery, his belief that slavery could not flourish in the area, and his expectation that the storm would blow over. It would, in fact, continue blowing, intermittently, until the tempest of civil war.

Douglas's errors consisted of disturbing the national repose, of supposing slavery to be a local issue, and of accepting slavery as a permanent social arrangement. Angry debate broke out in Congress, not as eloquent or dramatic or as statesmanlike as the debate in 1850, but more divisive of sections and parties and more portentous for national unity.

The republic quivered in a shock that the old Jacksonian issues and the new temperance and nativist issues could not evoke. With the Democrats holding comfortable majorities in both houses, the Pierce administration pushed the bill, now providing for the organization of two territories, Nebraska and Kansas, through the Senate. Only two senators from the future Confederacy voted against the measure. Passage in the House, where free-state Democrats outnumbered slave-state Democrats, 91 to 67, was another matter. Seven weeks elapsed before a determined Douglas and his cohorts drove the bill to a narrow margin of victory of 113 to 100. A full half of the Northern Democrats voted against the bill; all slave-state congressmen but 9 voted supported it.

The Kansas-Nebraska Act wrought the greatest party realignment in United States history. It shattered party loyalties in the North, fostered a solid South, and rent the nation. The old Whig Party suffered a mortal blow; never again would it offer a presidential candidate. Northern and Southern Whigs were henceforth forever parted. Only one Southern Whig in the Senate (Bell of Tennessee) voted against the law. Of the 23 Southern Whigs in the House only 7 voted No—all but one (Hunt of Louisiana, later a brigadier in the Confederate service) were from the Upper South.

PARTY REALIGNMENT. The years after passage of the Kansas-Nebraska Act witnessed this convulsive party realignment. By 1860 the old party system was gone, replaced by what historians call the third-party system. The first two years saw the most startling aspects of this change as parties crumbled and many Democrats and Whigs sought new affiliations.

Many Northern Democrats found it impossible to swallow the notion that popular sovereignty superseded the Missouri Compromise. These Democrats abandoned the old party, dividing it on a sectional line and solidifying its Southern bloc. Many Northern Whigs took up repeal of the Missouri Compromise as the issue to defeat the Democrats. The imperative of defending slavery—with its presumed need to expand, stress on states' rights, and assurance of security for Negro slavery—drove some Southern Whigs into the Democratic Party. The Tennessee Whig John Bell, who had cast a lonely vote against the Kansas-Nebraska bill, observed it had "put an extinguisher upon the Whig party."

The old order changed but it did not immediately yield to the third-party system. A strange interlude occurred, profoundly important in shaping party loyalties and continuing in importance until the 1890s. An issue swiftly arose, produced not by racial slavery but by ethno-cultural tensions among white Americans.

Two European factors of the 1840s altered both the composition of American society and of political parties. A prolonged, severe potato shortage in Ireland and the failure of liberal revolutions on the continent impelled almost three and one-half million Europeans to make the westward crossing of the Atlantic. In the year before the Kansas-Nebraska Act, over 368,000 immigrants arrived; the next year arrivals peaked at 427,833.

The inpouring of foreigners alarmed many native Americans. The newcomers were mainly from Ireland and Germany and were unfamiliar with the values of Protestant, republican United States. Many were Roman Catholics and encountered historic fears of papal and priestly influence in politics and distrust of Catholic dogma.

The Democratic Party with its traditional appeal to the common man and individual liberty welcomed the foreign-born. Its success in attracting Roman Catholics and the solidarity of the Catholic vote alarmed native Protestants. Though unfamiliar with American government the new arrivals speedily sought voting privileges. Native Americans, observing a rise in crime, disease, and pauperism, were prone to pin the blame on foreigners. The cost of welfare, law enforcement, and prison facilities concerned taxpayers.

In local and state matters the foreign-born often pushed for parochial schools, contrary to a strong public-school movement; the right to consume alcoholic beverages, contrary to a growing temperance movement; and the particular right to drink on Sunday, contrary to an ardent Protestant belief in a puritanical keeping of the Sabbath.

Accompanying these ethno-cultural tensions were economic strains. The modernization of the American economy unsettled employment for countless workers and members of the middle class. Foreigners accepted work in factories and railroad building at low wages, displacing native-born laborers. Americans disadvantaged in this process countered by joining an anti-foreign, anti-Catholic movement, begun in the 1840s and now revived by the troubling events of the 1850s. The Whig Party was no solution for such persons, because it had attempted to secure the Catholic vote in 1852 and it numbered among its leaders William H. Seward, who as governor of New York had been friendly to Catholics.

Only weeks after enactment of the Kansas-Nebraska Act a political convention, attended by delegates from thirteen states, wrapping themselves in the raiment of patriotism, formed the American Party. Its platform called for protecting all the rights of American citizens, resisting the "insidious policy of the Church of Rome," entrusting public offices only to native-born Protestant citizens, and upholding the Union.

Deep in its bigotry, more anti-Catholic than anti-foreign, appearing at a crucial juncture in party realignment, the American Party contributed to the break-up of the old second party system. At first employing rituals and a pledge of secrecy—giving rise to the response by party members, "I know nothing," when questioned by outsiders, the Americans or Know Nothings in 1854 had a phenomenal appeal. Nearly two-thirds of the voters in Massachusetts cast their ballots for Know Nothing candidates. In Pennsylvania the proportion was two of every five voters and in New York one of every five. Though largely a Northern movement, because foreigners and Catholics were concentrated in the free states, Know Nothingism attracted former Whigs in the South who desired a union with the North and a means to oppose Democratic Party strength. The congressional elections in 1854 sent about seventy-five Know Nothings to the House of Representatives—a surprising turn of events in American politics.

EXPANSION ABROAD. In this same year the administration's pursuit of a foreign policy contributed to party deterioration and sectional division. President Pierce had picked up the expansionist policy that had led to the purchase of Louisiana, the occupation of Oregon, the annexation of Texas, and the Mexican Cession. He was motivated in part by the historic tendency to expand United States territory and civilization, and by the popularity earlier presidents had won through efforts to add to the national domain, as well as by a hope to distract popular attention from domestic troubles. He declared forthrightly in his inaugural address: "My administration will not be controlled by any timid forebodings of evil from expansion."

An early partial success came in Pierce's policy to add more territory from Mexico. He dispatched Christopher Gadsden of South Carolina to Mexico with instructions to buy the northern part of five Mexican states. Failing that he was to buy a strip wide enough to build a railroad to southern California. The Mexican leader Santa Anna, though not disposed to sell a substantial part of his country, agreed to sell a route for the transcontinental railroad for two million dollars.

When Gadsden's modest treaty reached the Senate early in 1854, a bloc of free-state senators, not wanting to see potential slave land acquired, defeated the proposal. Only by slicing off 9,000 square miles from the original area did it become possible to secure the necessary two-thirds vote to ratify the treaty. Twelve free-state senators held steadfast in their opposition, and the treaty gained approval through the combined vote of a solid core of twenty-one Southerners and twelve Northerners.

Manifest Destiny, which had carried the flag to the Pacific along a rim from the 49th parallel past San Diego, seemed in danger of becoming sectionalized. For many years some Americans had sought to acquire the slaveholding island of Cuba, only ninety miles from the south Florida coast. Polk had tried to buy it from Spain; and with the failure of government action private citizens, often with tacit government support, attempted to seize it. Filibustering expeditions sailed from United States shores.

In 1854 the American minister in Spain, with the secretary of state's knowledge, arranged to meet the United States ministers to Great Britain and France in Belgium at Ostend in October. In a memorandum that inflated Manifest Destiny to balloon-like proportions, the three Americans asserted that Cuba "belongs naturally to that great family of states of which the Union is the Providential Nursery." To acquire the island the United States "with conscious rectitude" should offer to buy it. If that failed and if Cuba presented a threat to the Union's "internal peace and existence," then "we shall be justified in wresting it from Spain if we possess the power." (*See Reading No. 19.*)

The diplomats' memorandum fell into the hands of the press, which published it as "the Ostend Manifesto." Critics denounced the administration policy of "shame and dishonor" and branded the ill-advised statement "a buccaneering document." A blunder on the part of the Pierce administration, second only to the Kansas-Nebraska Act in its injurious effect on his presidency, the Ostend Manifesto in 1856 incurred condemnation by the Republicans as a "highwayman's plea."

Pierce's diplomatic acts—the Gadsden Purchase, the support of filibusters, the secret effort to seize Cuba—had had the leadership of Southerners and seemed to look to adding more slave territory to the Union. The acts, especially those involving Cuba, not only weakened the national administration but also further divided the nation. Many Northerners distrusted the expansionist policies of the Southern-oriented Democrats, while many Southerners were moving toward the idea that expansion southward could best be accomplished by an independent South.

BIRTH OF THE REPUBLICAN PARTY. Amidst these circumstances of domestic and diplomatic blunder emerged a Northern party, directly inspired by the Kansas-Nebraska Act and destined to become a major party in a continuing two-party system and to win the presidency within a surprisingly short time. Its origins were in the grass roots of the Upper Northwest, without a single, great leader and without common agreement on specific policy. It first appeared in small-town and rural America, in a response to the Kansas-Nebraska Act that was immediate and virtually spontaneous. Reopening the slavery extension issue gave opponents of slavery a specific issue to attack. It brought together people of many persuasions, often for diverse reasons arrayed against the expansion of slavery.

Well before the notorious Kansas-Nebraska bill became law a coalition of anti-slavery Democrats, Whigs, and Free-Soilers met in Ripon, Wisconsin. These persons urged formation of a new political party based on opposition to the spread of slavery. They suggested taking the name Republican, borrowing from the defunct party of Thomas Jefferson and appealing to the popular idea of republican government.

To some Northerners the Kansas-Nebraska Act was a breach of faith. To others it was evidence of a slave power conspiracy, intent on dominating the government. Some persons feared the republic was in peril. Workers feared for their jobs, the opportunity to migrate to free soil in the West, and the future of free labor. Historians have often been misled by the cry for freedom in the 1850s. The cry was not for freedom for the slaves but freedom for whites who felt threatened by slavery.

The movement, at first, had not only no great leader but also no national organization, and no directing genius. Protest meetings were held, fusions of groups occurred, names of various kinds—People's Party, Opposition, anti-Nebraska, Republicans —were employed. The movement was conservative; probably most participants declined to accept the demand—no more slave states. Respect for states' rights remained strong and the anti-slavery issue for many voters was the narrow one of repealing the obnoxious law, thus restoring the status quo before 1854.

In Illinois the contest saw a little-known Whig, Abraham Lincoln, return to politics. The former one-term congressman felt roused by the new law, he declared, "as he had never been before."

Speaking in Peoria, in answer to Senator Douglas, who had defended his bill, Lincoln condemned the law, called for its repeal, and disavowed a belief in a slave power conspiracy. In measured words he acknowledged the constitutional rights of Southerners, opposed slavery in once free territories, and supported a fair fugitive slave law. He appealed for the "spirit of mutual concession" in order to save the Union. (*See Reading No. 20.*)

The fall elections were a turning point in party realignment. The formation of a one-party South became more possible, as the ailing Whig party quietly succumbed. The Democrats in the slave states kept all but four of sixty-seven slave-state seats. In the North the Know Nothings scored the remarkable success earlier noted. The Democrats retained only twenty-five of ninety-one free-state members. Whigs incurred disastrous defections from New England through the Middle West, as anti-

Nebraska men became the single largest element in the next Congress.

Slavery was simultaneously shattering the old party system, sectionalizing parties, weakening the old alliance between the South and the West, and forming a growing Northern host antagonistic to the spread of slavery. The future of the Union darkened as a result of the autumnal balloting, but at the same time shone with a glimmer of light—new on the American scene—for freedom.

SECTIONAL REACTIONS. Party reaction to the Kansas-Nebraska law was but one reflex. Passage of the law inspired six states to enact personal liberty laws in 1854 and 1855. Intended to prevent free blacks from enslavement, they extended rights of counsel, *habeas corpus*, and trial by jury to apprehended blacks. They denied use of jails to incarcerate the accused and made seizure of free blacks a crime.

Massachusetts enacted one of the most stringent personal liberty laws. It expressed the popular revulsion to the case of the fugitive Anthony Burns, who amidst mob violence in which a federal marshal was killed, was returned to slavery under heavy guard. Passed over the governor's veto, the law assured the writ of *habeas corpus*, prohibited officeholders from issuing warrants under federal fugitive slave legislation, prohibited the state militia from assisting in any seizure of an alleged fugitive, and withheld use of Massachusetts jails to detain anyone accused under federal fugitive slave laws. (*See Reading No. 21.*)

The theatrical scene staged by the abolitionist, William Lloyd Garrison, surpassed this extreme assertion of states' rights in defiance of federal law. At a protest meeting in Massachusetts, Garrison read from the Bible and compared the Declaration of Independence with the judge's decision to return Anthony Burns to slavery. Then, lighting a candle he burned a copy of the United States Constitution, condemning it as a "covenant with death."

These actions in the North bode ill for the future of the Union. They interposed states' rights against national legislation—the very doctrine Northerners accused Southern states of holding; they demonstrated bad faith in upholding the solemn agreement of 1850, whose test Southerners had made the enforcement of the fugitive slave law; and they revealed a strain of idealistic violence in Northern thought.

Southerners were disturbed by such Northern reactions to the Kansas-Nebraska Act. In an open letter to Northerners the *New Orleans Bulletin* demanded, "Why wait for a formal rupture and separation from you? You have not done so. Our compact is broken by you," it accused. Southern resentment over Northern obstruction of the return of fugitives continued to fester through the secession crisis of 1860–1861, bursting forth in secession ordinances.

THE KANSAS QUESTION. Meanwhile, territorial Kansas was presenting a travesty of popular sovereignty. Pierce named as governor a pliable Pennsylvania politician, Andrew H. Reeder. Under his lax supervision the election of a territorial delegate to Washington took place at the end of the year. The situation invited trouble. Just east of the Missouri River, dividing Missouri and Kansas, lay the most heavily slave-populated counties of Missouri. Nearly one-quarter of the people in six western counties were black. The slave population of the entire state grew by 50 percent during the forties. Clearly, the creation of a free state across the river threatened the stability of the slave system in Missouri.

Heaping fuel on this tinderbox was the federal government's unpreparedness to open Kansas territory to white settlement. Washington officials and their agents had failed to agree upon land policy or to settle Indian claims. When the territory was opened for settlement, a rush to claim land led to violent disputes. Partisans struggled with one another, as much over coveted land sites as over slavery. Jayhawkers, who later provided a nickname for all Kansans, were anti-slavery guerrilla fighters; and bushwhackers became a term for Confederate guerrilla fighters.

Pro-slavery forces quickly won control of Kansas territory. Violence, fraud, and participation by some 1,700 armed marauders from western Missouri flawed the delegate election. Election of a pro-slavery delegate followed and then of a territorial legislature in early 1855. This time thrice the number of Missourians, some 5,000, took part in the voting. The resulting legislature passed laws that not only sanctioned slavery, but also decreed severe punishment for anti-slavery agitators, including death for persons convicted of raising a rebellion of blacks, and authorized requiring officials to swear to uphold the fugitive slave law.

The "Kansas question" had erupted on the political scene. For four years it would dominate political discussion, further shaping party alignment, dividing the nation, and weakening faith in the government at Washington. The eastern press—its influence widened and accelerated by the high-speed printing press and the telegraph—took up the Kansas question. Anti-slavery papers branded the fraudulent Missouri voters as the "Border Ruffians" and the fraudulent pro-slavery legislature as the "bogus legislature."

The territorial governor, threatened by gunmen, recognized the illegitimate election of the legislature. This body ignored his plea for moderation when it met to establish slavery on Kansas soil. When he went to Washington to solicit help in setting aside the frauds, the Pierce administration, deeply indebted to its Southern supporters, declined to heed his pleas.

At the same time that the weakness of the central government lay exposed, Georgia's Toombs advocated a slaveholding South united against the North. "The true policy of the South," he declared, "is to unite; lay aside all party divisions. Whigs, Democrats and Know Nothings should come together and combine for the common safety." The governor of South Carolina held a more extreme outlook, announcing he preferred civil war to agitation of the slavery question.

PARTIES IN FLUX. As the year 1855 advanced, progress in party realignment was evident. The Know Nothings, though still an important force, suffered a rift between the Northern and Southern members at their national convention. In the Lower South while the Know Nothings were waning the Democrats were gaining. The great Georgia Whigs, Toombs and Stephens, embraced the Democrats. In the North a Republican party was organized in the nation's largest state, New York, where Seward after being reelected United States senator, joined the Republicans. In Illinois Abraham Lincoln exclaimed in bewilderment, "I think I am a Whig but others say there are no Whigs and that I am an Abolitionist. I now do no more than oppose the extension of slavery." Throughout the nation many voters and leaders like Lincoln at this time were unwilling to change party allegiance. Attached to their old parties, inured to distrust the opposition, they continued to vote as they and their fathers had. "The outlook as to the formation of a triumphant anti-slavery party was not so promising towards the close of the year 1855 as it had seemed in the spring of the preceding year," lamented the Indiana abolitionist, George W. Julian.

THE FIRST REPUBLICAN VICTORY. When the Thirty-fourth Congress assembled December 3, 1855, the fragmentation of parties was painfully evident. No party commanded a majority in the House, where there existed a rough classification —in these times of changing and imprecise party labels—108 Republicans, 83 Democrats, and 43 Know Nothings or Americans. Without a majority no party could elect a speaker, and without a speaker the House could not organize to conduct the nation's business.

For a second time since 1848 a speakership crisis—symptomatic of the two-party system's deterioration—paralyzed the American political process. For eight weeks the House was unable to agree upon a speaker. Members fruitlessly balloted 132 times on candidates. Only when they agreed to decide by a plurality instead of a majority did they name Nathaniel P. Banks of Massachusetts. A former Know Nothing, now a Republican, he was hailed as the symbol of the first Republican victory in national politics. Julian judged this success to be "largely the fruit of the 'Border Ruffians' attempts to make Kansas a slave state."

Some Northerners regarded Banks's election as a victory over slavery and the Slave Power, and others looked on it as a victory of a developing sectional anti-slavery party. One observer discerned the issue, "the Election of Banks will contribute to consolidate the union of our friends. It is possible that his Election is indispensable for union."

In the years 1854 and 1855 the United States—while its economy was booming, its population increasing, its pride in exemplifying successful republicanism glowing—was fumbling in its policies of domestic and foreign expansion. Slavery had handicapped efforts to administer the western territories and to acquire new ones. Political parties, which had been the cement of union, were crumbling under the pressures of slavery expansionists. Cracks were visible along a fault line dividing free and slave states. The year 1856 would bring a presidential election. With disarray in Washington, flux in parties, violence in Kansas, and public opprobrium over foreign policy, what turn might events take in 1856?

CHAPTER 6

POLITICIANS AND JUDGES

The momentous year of 1856 witnessed bitter rivalry for land and office in Kansas, violence in the territory and the United States Senate, and futile wrangling by the nation's legislators over the future of Kansas and the Union. Party realignment culminated in formation of a new major, sectional party committed to the containment of slavery. Slavery, long avoided by political leaders as a party question, now sprang forth as a national issue with alarming implications for the unity of the republic. A presidential election swiftly followed by a Supreme Court decision further divided the nation.

THE STRUGGLE FOR KANSAS. Kansas became the focus of national politics. What of the old issues, Seward asked, "The tariff, National Bank, internal improvements, and the controversies of the Whigs and Democrats? No, they are past and gone. What then, of Kansas . . . the extension of slavery in the territories of the United States? Ah yes, that is the theme . . . and nothing else."

Would Kansas be free or slave? The territory was the arena of sectional rivalry. Lying in the same latitudes as slaveholding Virginia, Maryland, Kentucky, and Missouri, it offered the prospect of adding yet another slave state to the minority section. The South's security, future, and honor were at stake. The struggle for Kansas challenged Southern Democrats to demonstrate that slavery was safe in their party's hands. If slavery itself could not be planted in Kansas, at least the principle that Southerners had the constitutional right to take slaves into the national territories needed vindication. A South united—but still within the Union—was required to assert Southern principles.

Confronting this Southern outlook was apprehension of further growth of what Northerners, perhaps with a touch of paranoia, termed the Slave Power. Continuing Southern domination of the Union meant expansion of slavery—increasingly regarded as immoral sullying the republic's honor—thwarting the economic future of free labor and industry, and loss of place and power by Northern politicians hard put to know where voters' loyalties lay. In the last months of 1855 the contest for Kansas heated up. Free-state settlers gathered their forces to oppose the pro-slavery territorial government. They branded it illegal and at Topeka drafted a constitution prohibiting slavery. Sensitive to racial antipathies they drew up an ordinance prohibiting the entry of blacks. Sympathetic free-state voters approved the constitution and the exclusion ordinance. A month later under this new constitution voters chose a free-state governor and legislature. Kansas now had two governments, both of dubious legality, but one having the sanction of Washington, the other plainly a rump movement.

Meanwhile, the pro-slavery forces became more firmly entrenched. The governor, who had opposed the pro-slavery legislature and also had unwisely speculated in land, was removed and replaced by a pro-slavery appointee. Pro-slavery forces reelected their pro-slavery delegate to Congress; and free-state forces quickly countered by naming the deposed governor as their delegate to Congress.

Armed conflict portended. Arms came into the territory from Northern sources. Free-staters appointed a temperamental politician from Indiana, James H. Lane, commander of free-state military forces. In mid-November 1855 pro-slavery men organized a Law and Order Party. Later in the month, violence flared near Lawrence along the Wakarusa River in the so-called "Wakarusa War." Again, "Border Ruffians" from Missouri, numbering this time about 1,500, ventured into the frontier area; hearing that the free-state town of Lawrence was well defended they refrained from attacking it. The "war"—actually not much more than some shootings and brawls, common on the frontier —ended after President Pierce authorized use of force. Exaggerated newspaper accounts inflamed national emotions at the very time the Congress, elected in the aftermath of the Kansas-Nebraska Act, was convening in Washington.

CONGRESS DEBATES KANSAS. The Thirty-fourth Congress, split into factions, faced the problem of dealing with two governments in strife-torn Kansas. While the House was endlessly balloting for a speaker, Pierce in a special message denounced the formation of the Topeka government as an act of rebellion and virtually recognized the pro-slavery legislature. Shortly thereafter, in a proclamation warning both the free-state forces and "Border Ruffians" to disperse, he made it clear he supported the pro-slavery government.

Undeterred by presidential opposition the Topeka legislature asked Congress for statehood and presumptuously elected its United States senators—Reeder, the governor removed by Pierce, and Lane, commander of the free-state militia. Statehood for Kansas—and if so, slave or free?—that was the question posed to Congress.

On the Democratic side of the Senate, Stephen A. Douglas, still chairman of the committee on territories and aspirant for his party's presidential nomination in a few months, introduced a lawyerlike enabling act for Kansas that provided for election of a constitutional convention and creation of a state government, but only when the territory held a sufficient number of persons (93,000) to warrant a representative in the House. Like Pierce, he denounced the rump free-state government; and he went on to censure as a lawless body the New England Emigrant Aid Company, formed to assist emigration of free-state settlers. (*See Reading No. 22.*)

The statehood issue sharpened when Seward presented a bill, unrealistic in practice but useful for partisan purposes, calling for immediate admission of Kansas as a free state under the Topeka constitution. In a statesmanlike move Toombs amended Douglas's bill to require a free and open election of delegates to the constitutional convention. "Border Ruffians" and interlopers would be excluded from the state-making process. The Democratic Senate gave its approval by a nearly three to one vote. The House under Republican leadership never considered the measure, which if passed might have quieted the Kansas issue. The developing strength of partisanship manifested itself when the House voted 99–97 to admit Kansas under the Topeka constitution.

While Kansas territory was in turmoil and Congress in ferment, the politicians' quest for a party formation that could win the presidency in the fall moved forward. The process of party realignment posed three questions. What would the Know Nothings do? What was the outlook for the unorganized anti-Nebraska groups, existing in variously named factions? Where would the Democrats, suffering from the ineffectual Pierce and the notoriety of some of its extremist leaders, turn for a candidate?

THE KNOW NOTHINGS SPLIT. The Know Nothings had demonstrated their strength the previous year when perhaps 121 members of the House had enjoyed Know Nothing backing. Speaker Banks, chosen after this result, was a Know Nothing Republican. The incoming of foreigners continued, nursing anti-foreign and anti-Catholic sentiment. The party had split at a national council in 1855 when a number of free-state delegates walked out over a Southern demand to call existing legislation the final settlement of the slavery issue.

The break became final in February 1856 at the party's national convention. A number of Northern delegates bolted the convention after a Southern majority defeated a resolution to repeal the Kansas-Nebraska Act. The slavery issue had split the nativists. The South Americans, as they came to be called, stayed in session and named ex-president Millard Fillmore, who had approved the Compromise of 1850 and was popular in the South, as their presidential candidate.

What was left for the North Americans, a minority in their once-national body but perhaps not in the North, was to attract anti-Nebraska voters. They seized an opportunity by scheduling their own convention on the eve of a convention just called by the newly-formed Republican Party. If thereby the North Americans could preempt the nomination of an anti-slavery candidate, a new major party—the American Party—would confront the Democrats in the presidential contest.

The idea of uniting illiberal anti-foreign and liberal anti-slavery sentiment in a single party was not as preposterous as it might sound. The newly-organizing Republicans numbered many nativists, Protestants, and temperance men opposed to those they sneered at as rum-swilling Irish Catholics and beer-guzzling Germans. Republican and American members shared a penchant for paranoia, the first fearing a Slave Power Conspiracy, the other a Papal Plot.

"BLEEDING KANSAS." Before the conventions met, violence that took a startling turn broke out in Kansas. The arming of free-state forces had proceeded with rifles—sent from the East and sanctioned by the popular Brooklyn preacher, Henry Ward Beecher, brother of Harriet Beecher Stowe—called "Beecher's Bibles." In late May a pro-slavery force made up of Kansans including the Kickapoo Rangers, "Border Ruffians," and expeditionary forces led by Colonel Jefferson Buford of Alabama attacked the free-state town of Lawrence. The invaders wreaked destruction, burning the Free-State Hotel, said to be fortified, destroying the presses of the two anti-slavery newspapers, and even pillaging private homes. Though only two lives were lost, sensational press accounts turned "the Sack of Lawrence" into inflammatory copy. (*See Reading No. 23.*)

Three days later John Brown, with excessive anti-slavery zeal, sought out certain pro-slavery settlers in the area. Leading a band of seven, including four of his sons and a son-in-law, he brutally murdered five persons, butchering their bodies. This atrocity at Pottawatomie Creek became known as the Pottawatomie Massacre and further inflamed feeling in Kansas and Washington.

The day before the Sack of Lawrence, Senator Charles Sumner, a former Free-Soiler, self-consciously scholarly, and vain, had delivered a blazing oration in the Senate. In a speech entitled "The Crime Against Kansas," he had not only attacked slavery but also in offensive language an elderly senator from South Carolina. The senator's nephew, a member of the House of Representatives, in a fury repaired to the Senate chamber, and finding Sumner sitting at his desk severely beat him with a cane. The assault made Sumner a martyr among some Northerners and made the nephew a hero among some Southerners. Coming in this crucial month while Congress was debating the future of Kansas and politicians were shaping parties and platforms, the caning of Sumner heightened tensions and made calm deliberation difficult.

THE DEMOCRATS. The quest for party unity and a winning candidate accelerated in June. The Democrats, members of the only truly national party, met first. The Kansas-Nebraska Act and its tumultuous aftermath dominated delegates' thinking. Sectional strain within the party appeared when Southerners balloted first for Pierce and then for Douglas, hailing their roles in the Kansas controversy, while Northerners balloted against leaders so prominently associated with the divisive issue. Not until the seventeenth ballot could Southerners and Northerners agree upon a candidate with the requisite qualifications—a Northern man with Southern principles who had not been associated with the Kansas-Nebraska Act. The man who fitted this formula was a perennial aspirant for the nomination, sixty-four year old James Buchanan of Pennsylvania, who had been in London as United States minister while the Act had been passed.

After upholding the Fugitive Slave Act, the Democrats in their platform affirmed the principle of popular sovereignty in the territories—to be exercised by actual residents whenever the number of inhabitants justified it—to form a constitution with or without slavery. To this, in a direct thrust at the Republicans and abolitionists, they added their advocacy of congressional non-interference with slavery, whether in the territories, states, or the District of Columbia.

In affirming popular sovereignty the Democrats had fastened upon the sole formula that could bind the party together. Southern Democrats found satisfaction in repudiation of the Wilmot Proviso doctrine, now the heart of Republicanism, while Northern Democrats could assure constituents that popular sovereignty would contain slavery.

THE REPUBLICANS. Republicans, gathering from many diverse anti-slavery sources, met a fortnight later. The North Americans, five days earlier, had nominated Banks for president, hoping to force the Republicans to endorse their anti-slavery, nativist candidate. But Republicans could not risk antagonizing immigrant voters. Moreover, they had a secret understanding with Banks: he would withdraw in favor of the Republican nominee.

Nor could the Republicans risk nominating a candidate prominently connected with the Kansas controversy, not Chase or Seward. Party leaders were conscious of the need to divert votes, at least in the Border states, from the Northern ex-Whig, Millard Fillmore, nominee of the South Americans.

In a remarkable show of party unity the heterogeneous Republicans nominated a candidate on the first ballot. He was John Charles Frémont, famed as an explorer of the West, a former

Democrat who as United States senator from California had fallen out with Pierce. At forty-three he was twenty-two years younger than the "Old Public Functionary," Buchanan. A romantic adventurer with a claim to military glory for his role in the conquest of California, he was married to Jessie, the spirited daughter of Thomas Hart Benton. Not linked to the nation's troubles, he was a fresh face, a welcome change from the professional politicians and machine politics. Though he possessed all these virtues, he was politically inexperienced, naive, and impetuous—poorly endowed for presidential office. His views on urgent public questions were unknown. The slavery issue, as it had for years, prompted politicians to seek success through evasiveness and mediocrity.

The North Americans, with Banks's prompt withdrawal, discovered that the tables had been turned upon them. They now found it expedient to endorse Frémont, but stubbornly clung to their vice-presidential nominee until in the late summer Frémont persuaded him to withdraw.

If the Republicans had sought neutrality in their nominee, they were more forthright in facing slavery than any previous major party had been. In a studiously deliberate platform, they aimed to narrow the canvass to the expansion of slavery issue. They used the Fifth Amendment to the Constitution—which banned Congress from depriving any person of life, liberty, or property without due process of law—to deny authority to Congress or a territorial legislature to legalize slavery. Popular sovereignty, they were saying, is unconstitutional.

Advancing from this ground—in language that would have been impossible before 1854—they proclaimed: "It is both the right and the imperative duty of Congress to prohibit" slavery in the territories. Republicans arraigned the Pierce administration for a catalog of frauds and violent deeds in Kansas, and demanded immediate admission under the present free constitution.

The platform touched lightly on other issues, denouncing the Ostend Manifesto and calling for a transcontinental railroad through a central route and for improvement of rivers and harbors. The final plank, inviting affiliation of men of all parties, ended with ambiguous language capable of being interpreted as nativist or anti-nativist.

Though the Republican Party is sometimes considered as an agent of Northern capitalism, the 1856 platform concentrated on expansion of slavery in the territories—saying nothing about not only fugitive slaves or slavery in the District of Columbia, but also banks, tariffs, and homesteads. Its economic thrust was minimal. In invoking a secular right under the Constitution to prohibit slavery in the territories, it suggested a moral dimension in politics by also claiming a duty to prohibit it and by condemning slavery as well as polygamy as "relics of barbarism." (*See Reading No. 24.*)

CAMPAIGN ISSUES. When the Whigs failed to hold a national convention and a remnant endorsed the South American candidate, Fillmore, the contest became sectional and three-cornered: Democratic, Republican, and American. Each party made crafty appeals for votes in a campaign dominated by the Kansas issue but containing other important elements.

"Bleeding Kansas" continued to heap fuel on the political fires of the 1856 campaign. Guerrilla war raged in Kansas territory, forming a violent backdrop to the presidential campaign. Before the election a new governor with firm and fair hand, John W. Geary, employed federal forces and personal persuasion to bring about a truce.

Religious and racial prejudice, to a greater degree than historians have traditionally recognized, also marked the canvass. The American Party sustained popular fears of foreigners and Catholics with some success, hurling the allegation that Frémont was a Catholic. The Republicans, having absorbed most of the North Americans, countered with an anti-Catholic tract, and in state politics exploited nativist issues.

Racism was conspicuous in campaign rhetoric. Democrats and Republicans exploited fears of black equality. Democrats were perhaps more blatant, accusing Republicans of being "nigger lovers," who would free the slaves, allow free blacks to stream into the North, take white men's jobs, and marry white women. Republicans sought to give assurance that theirs was a white man's party, that they had no intention to free the slaves, and meant to maintain white supremacy. "NO NEGRO EQUALITY IN THE NORTH," proclaimed a banner at a Republican rally in Illinois.

Republican orators strove to make it clear that party cries of Free Speech, Free Men, Free Soil, and Frémont meant freedom of opportunity, in general, for white people and free soil in Kansas for white settlers. The slaveholding South they portrayed as the Slave Power, holding the nation in its grip, restraining the economic progress of a free economy.

If Northerners discerned a threat by the South to their liberty, Southerners saw a threat by the North to theirs. The Republican Party was the first substantial anti-slavery party. Its appeal was clearly sectional—to Northerners. Its existence compelled Southerners to vote against it—or consider withdrawing from the Union.

Disunion talk was in the air. Various Southern leaders declared they favored secession; the governor of Virginia called a meeting of Southern governors to deliberate the course the South should follow. To Buchanan the overriding question was "the grand and appalling issue of Union or Disunion." The fear of secession was of incalculable weight in determining the outcome of the canvass, many persons casting their votes for Buchanan in order to avoid disunion.

A HOUSE DIVIDING. No uniform election day existed in the mid-nineteenth century, and two states crucial to carrying the North—Pennsylvania and Indiana—voted in October. Pennsylvania, in particular, was important; its twenty-seven electoral votes were second highest, exceeded only by New York's thirty-five. Normally Democratic, the home state of James Buchanan, by dint of habit and local pride it would vote for its native son. The Democrats outspent the Republicans, as quantities of money were lavished on the state to sway voters. Pennsylvania, as well as Indiana, went Democratic, darkening the outlook for Frémont.

The excitement of the contest drew voters to the ballot box in proportions not seen since 1844. Four of every five eligible voters took part in naming the next president. Results revealed fears of disunion and secession were not unwarranted. Frémont's vote was entirely sectional; he gained votes in only four slave states, three of which did not secede—a grand total of 1,194 supporters. The contest had resolved into two battles: one be-

tween Buchanan and Frémont in the free states, the other between Buchanan and Fillmore in the slave states.

The customary citation of electoral votes does not reveal the
sharpness of the sectional split: 178 for Buchanan, 114 for Frémont, and 8 for Fillmore. Frémont garnered 45 percent of the
free state vote—a plurality, Buchanan only 41, and Fillmore but
13. In the slave states Buchanan won a commanding 56 percent,
Frémont a minuscule .0005 percent, and Fillmore a very substantial 44 percent. Buchanan swept all the slave states except
Maryland, won by Fillmore.

In those states that formed the Confederacy the Democratic
Party grew in strength. While the total national vote rose by 22
percent, the Democratic vote in these eleven states leaped upward by 40 percent. In 1852 Tennessee had been the only one of
these states not to vote Democratic. In 1856 Virginia was the
only one to give Frémont any votes—291 of about 150,000 votes
cast. The section seemed moving toward a Solid South.

What did the future hold? Buchanan was a minority president,
winning only 45 percent of the national vote. In Congress the
Democrats would have a number of seats equal to the opposition
in the House, and they had lost four seats in the Senate. The
three-sided contest ended with the death of the American
Party—the second party, following the Whigs, killed by slavery.
Party realignment was working toward a new two-party system.
A new party had absorbed much of the Whig and American
vote. But the party, unlike the case in the second-party system,
was sectional, holding a lead in the free states and only a trace of
support in the slave states. The Democratic Party had lost its
dominance in the free states and now rested on a Southern base.

The durability of the new party alignment remained to be
tested by the continuing stresses of slavery and sectionalism.
The anti-slavery party, organized in February and nearly victo-
rious in November lifted the hopes of anti-slavery Americans
and excited the fears of pro-slavery Americans.

The poet Whittier wrote:

> "If months have well-nigh won the field,
> What may not four years do?"

PRESIDENT BUCHANAN. James Buchanan, fifteenth
president of the United States, nearly sixty-six years of age,

unlike Pierce, Fillmore, and Taylor, was a seasoned politician. He had served in both houses of Congress, was Polk's secretary of state, made a bid for his party's presidential nomination in 1848, had been Pierce's minister to Great Britain, in which capacity he had helped write the Ostend Manifesto. His narrow construction of the Constitution and his indebtedness to the slaveholding South for his nomination and election limited his bounds as president. He reposed his faith in rigid adherence to law, in local government, in party loyalty, and in sparing use of executive power. As president he would suffer in historical reputation as the nation would in domestic tranquility because of his purblind view of his authority.

He began his high office with an indiscretion that damaged him politically. Just before he took the oath of office, the spectators saw him talking with Chief Justice Roger B. Taney, who would administer the oath. A few minutes later in his inaugural address he declared that the disruptive issue of slavery in the territories was "a judicial question which legitimately belongs to the Supreme Court of the United States, before whom it is now pending, and will, it is understood, be speedily and finally settled." Two days later the chief justice and the high court handed down a decision that, instead of settling the troublesome constitutional question, played into the hands of the Republicans and helped to split the president's party.

DRED SCOTT'S CASE. The court case with such important results involved a lowly slave, Dred Scott, who had been taken by his owner from slaveholding Missouri to the free state of Illinois and the northern part of the Louisiana Territory, made free soil by the Missouri Compromise of 1820. After returning to Missouri, with the help of others he filed suit for his freedom, claiming his residence on free soil had made him free.

Dred Scott's case crept through the court system until in early 1856 it reached Taney's Supreme Court. Behind Scott's claim to freedom under the Missouri Compromise lurked not merely dry legal matters but also the explosive political issue of the power of Congress to prohibit slavery in the territories. Dividing party and nation since David Wilmot's proviso back in 1846, it was the issue that president-makers had sought to dodge for a decade.

When Scott's appeal for freedom appeared on the docket, the thorny matters presented to the justices caused them to postpone a decision until the end of the year. By that time the presidential election—centering on the territorial question—would conveniently be over.

The justices held a re-hearing in December but did not have a consultation among themselves until three weeks before Buchanan's swearing-in. In the interval between the re-hearing and his inauguration, Buchanan, eager to have a judicial disposition of the vexing question, unethically entered into correspondence with two justices. From this he learned the court would make a broad ruling which perhaps would be supported by six of nine justices.

THE DRED SCOTT DECISION. The Supreme Court in 1857 was of a character to sustain the suspicion nursed by some Northerners that the government was in the clutches of the Slave Power. Five of the justices including the chief justice—a majority—were Southerners. Three were currently slaveowners; two others—Taney and John A. Campbell—had freed their slaves. On the other hand, one of the judges, the Northerner John McLean, was hopeful of receiving the anti-slavery party's nomination for the presidency.

Taney read the opinion usually cited as the Dred Scott decision. He ruled on three major questions. First, was Scott a citizen? Taney declared he was not a citizen and, therefore, not entitled to sue in a court of the United States. He arrived at the conclusion by a train of thought offensive to many Northerners. At the time the Constitution was written, he said, blacks were "considered as a subordinate and inferior class of beings [who] . . . had no rights or privileges but such as who held the power and the government might choose to grant them." Blacks were not included, and are not included under the word "citizens" in the Constitution, he flatly stated.

Secondly, had Scott been made free by his residence in Illinois and the Louisiana Territory? Taney asserted temporary residence on free soil had not given him freedom. "He is still a slave." The law of the slave state of Missouri governed his status.

Finally, Taney took up the explosive question whether Congress had the constitutional authority to prohibit slavery in the territory. He cited the Fifth Amendment, which prohibits Congress from depriving persons of their property without due process of law. Slaves were property, he intoned, and Congress was barred from depriving persons of their slave property. The Missouri Compromise "is therefore void."

In ruling that blacks were not citizens and Congress could not banish slavery from the territories, Taney had hurled a bombshell. Six other justices assisted in this detonation, writing similar opinions. But, in fact, some Northern states considered blacks to be citizens, having the right to vote. The matter of federal citizenship was murky; not until the Fourteenth Amendment was ratified in 1868 was a clear definition of citizenship made. (*See Reading No. 25.*)

Taney's conclusion that Congress could not banish slavery from the territories put the Republicans in the position of advocating an unconsitutional measure and raised the question whether a territory, created by Congress, could banish slavery from the territories.

NORTHERN REACTIONS. Two Northern justices dissented from their brethren. Their very strong intention to speak out had probably prompted the court to go beyond the simple question of Scott's personal status and grasp the prickly issue of the power of Congress over slavery in the territories. The dissenters ruled, in contrast to Taney, not only that free blacks were citizens of the United States but more pointedly—in this partisan context—Congress had authority to regulate slavery in the territories. They pointed to the provision that Congress had the power to "make all needful Rules and Regulations respecting the Territory." Republicans and abolitionists gleefully seized upon the dissenters' opinions for their partisan and humanitarian ends.

The majority opinion was more important for its political impact than for its constitutional doctrine. Rather than settling the question of who had authority over slavery in the territories, it provoked a new storm of controversy. Critics levelled their charges against the sectional and partisan nature of the decision. They pointed out that it was not one decision but nine; every justice wrote a separate opinion. The majority had been formed by five Southerners and one Northerner. Three Northerners did not concur in important aspects of the ruling; and two were in vigorous dissent.

The high court had only once before overturned an act of Congress (*Marbury v. Madison*, long ago in 1803 and on a minor matter). Lincoln and others charged that in going beyond the question of Scott's status the justices had exceeded their jurisdiction.

Taney, himself, came under attack. A Southerner, former slaveholder, racist, Democrat, Roman Catholic, and seventy-nine years of age, he was vulnerable to scurrilous criticism. The anti-slavery press raged about "a Jesuitical decision," filled with "gross historical falsehood." Seward, the leading Republican, describing "the whisperings carried on between the President and the Chief Justice" at the inaugural ceremony, accused the two of forming a conspiracy against American liberty. Frederick Douglass declared, "Judge Taney can do many things, but . . . . He cannot change the essential nature of things—making evil good, and good evil." (*See Reading No. 26.*)

CHAPTER 7

BUCHANAN, LINCOLN, AND DOUGLAS

All the institutions of government now seemed to have sided with slavery and its defenders. Congress had overthrown the long-standing Missouri Compromise of 1820 and had opened the territories to slavery. The chief executive had permitted a pro-slavery government to be installed by fraud and force in Kansas. The third arm of government, the Supreme Court—once described by Alexander Hamilton as "the least dangerous branch" —had snatched away from the nation's lawmakers the authority to enact the kind of compromise that had kept peace and unity, if uneasily, since the beginning of the republic.

BUCHANAN BELEAGUERED. Buchanan's woes assailed him from another quarter. Congress, following the Democratic dogma of low tariff, had reduced the tariff in the spring of 1857. Months later, in August, a financial panic set in. The Panic of 1857 was partly inspired by an unsettled world economy and partly by speculation in the United States in railroads and lands, assisted by banks. The American economy sagged as imports fell, and in consequence, government income from tariff receipts dwindled. Banks suspended specie payments. In these straits the administration borrowed money—placing the nation in debt—to operate the government. Buchanan in his annual message pinned the blame on the banks.

Republicans responded in partisan terms, charging the government with extravagance and financial mismanagement. They pointed to a need for a higher tariff to meet government expenses and to protect American workers' jobs. Northeastern Republicans, representing a developing industrial region, called for upward revision of the tariff. All the while, especially during these hard times, Northerners were chafing under the continuing defeat by Southern Democrats and the pro-Southern president of economic measures regarded as important to the Northern economy. Besides tariff protection these measures included land grants for railroad construction, a homestead law, and river and harbor improvements.

The panic eased before long and banks resumed specie payments. The political and sectional consequences, however, were significant. The South had been largely exempt from the panic's effects. Cotton prices continued high. The plain lesson to some Southerners was the superiority of their economy over that of the Northern. "Cotton is king," crowed South Carolina's fire-brand senator James H. Hammond. (*See Reading No. 27.*) The lesson to some Republican politicians was the partisan need to advocate tariff revision and homestead legislation in the next presidential contest.

A SLAVE CONSTITUTION FOR KANSAS. Kansas continued to sever the nation, not merely setting Republican against Democrat but splitting the Democrats—the only national party. Congress in 1856, it will be recalled, had reached a stalemate, the Democrats seeking an enabling act to elect a constitutional convention for Kansas, the Republicans demanding immediate admission under the free-state constitution.

Meanwhile, the territory lay under the control of the pro-slavery territorial legislature at Lecompton. Early in 1857 over the governor's veto it called a constitutional convention and made no provision to submit the constitution to popular vote. Failing to get support from the outgoing President Pierce, the frustrated governor resigned on the day Pierce left office.

The Kansas controversy now was in the hands of Buchanan, a political veteran ambitious to have an honored niche in history. Believing that the troublesome issue of slavery could be resolved if legitimate residents had a truly free choice, he appointed an experienced politician as the territorial governor. He was Robert J. Walker, the skillful architect of the successful Democratic platform in 1844. Aware of Pierce's vacillation, no fool in public life, Walker sought to nail down Buchanan's backing of his governorship. He gave out a public letter saying he understood the president and cabinet desired a fair vote by actual residents on a constitution and their social institutions.

In Kansas Governor Walker reckoned that free-state settlers outnumbered pro-slavery settlers by more than two to one. The prospect of Kansas becoming a free state seemed promising. He was, however, unable to persuade free-state settlers, disgruntled and distrustful of the pro-slavery element, to take part in the June election of delegates to the constitutional convention that would not submit its product to a popular vote.

Pro-slavery voters named their choices for a convention and met at Lecompton in the fall. The constitution guaranteed owners of the approximately 200 slaves in the territory their property rights, prohibited any amendment for seven years, and on the burning issue of introducing more slaves into the territory, the framers permitted only the choice in voting for "the constitution with slavery" or "the constitution without slavery." Either way, Kansans must vote for a constitution making secure the slaves already in the territory.

Shortly before this mockery of the democratic process, election of a new territorial legislature, under Walker's supervision, took place. He threw out thousands of fraudulent votes, leaving free-state elements in the majority.

Hearing that Buchanan had changed his mind about submitting the constitution to the *bona fide* resident settlers and might support the Lecompton monstrosity, Walker hastened to Washington. His worst fears were fulfilled: Buchanan embraced Lecompton, and sent a message to Congress defending it. A week later Walker, for some time attacked in the South by the press, politicians, and legislatures, resigned.

In making his catastrophic decision Buchanan was surely aware he owed his office to Southern support. Now South Carolina, Georgia, Alabama, and Mississippi were muttering secession. His party controlled the Senate, though the outraged Douglas sprang into opposition; and Democrats outnumbered Republicans in the House. Patronage and appeals to party loyalty might push Lecompton through. And once Kansas became a state the matter would be forgotten. He seemed impervious to the possibility he might split the Democratic Party.

While Buchanan was taking the fateful step, events in Kansas were working against his policy. Voting on Lecompton attracted few free-state men, who abstained from voting, and many fraudulent voters, as later examinations showed. Meanwhile, the free-state forces persuaded the acting governor to advance the day for convening the newly elected free-state legislature. It called for a fresh vote on Lecompton, allowing a clear choice for and against Lecompton. Unfettered, Kansas decisively rejected Lecompton

with 10,226 negative votes, against only 13 for the constitution
with slavery and 24 for the constitution without slavery.

BUCHANAN SPLITS HIS PARTY. The voice for freedom
was loud and clear, but Buchanan, already having removed the
acting governor from office, ignored it and stubbornly clung to
his course. The way now lay open for a disastrous confrontation
between president and party. On February 2 Buchanan called on
Congress and his party to approve Lecompton. The next day
Douglas, angry and ambitious, raised his standard of party
revolt. The advocate of popular sovereignty saw his principle of
local self-government being trampled upon. The senator from
Illinois also saw his chance of being reelected later this year and
nominated for president two years later in jeopardy. Public
opinion in Illinois and elsewhere in the North decried the
Lecompton constitution. Principle aside, if he wanted to survive
in politics, he must fight the president's policy.

The struggle in the Senate was in part between Buchanan and
Douglas, two Democrats bitterly fighting one another. It also
split off from the administration a broad front of opponents led
by Douglas and supported by eastern Republicans. Talk of
forming a new Northern party to oppose the administration and
Southern disunionists revealed the fluidity of party lines.

Buchanan had been correct in his anticipation he could ram
Lecompton through the Senate. Skillfully wielding the power of
the patronage, he triumphed over Douglas by a vote of 33 to 25.
But what would the House do? Buchanan planned to use whip
and spur, and as he said, drive the unamended Lecompton bill
"naked . . . through the House."

To his dismay a bloc of anti-Lecompton Democrats formed
against him and accepted an amendment to resubmit Lecompton
to Kansas voters in a fair and supervised election. Administration Democrats capitulated and the House passed the revised
measure by a vote of 120 to 112.

Now the question was, what would the Senate do? Resubmis-
sion was distasteful to Southerners, as compromise was to many
House members, and only after resistance from triumphant
House members was a conference agreed upon. An obscure
Indiana Democrat, William H. English, produced the key to the
deadlock. Representing an anti-Lecompton district, but a friend

to the Buchanan administration, he devised a scheme that cleverly provided, not for resubmission of the constitution, but of a related question of a land grant to Kansas.

In admitting new states, Congress customarily gave a grant of public land. The Lecompton framers in their audacity asked for six times the usual grant. Seizing upon this, English proposed that the land grant be reduced to normal proportions and the land grant question be submitted to Kansans. Tied to this referendum was the stipulation that if the voters accepted the reduced grant, Kansas would be admitted under Lecompton. If they rejected it, Kansas would not be eligible for statehood until its population had reached the figure required for representation in Congress.

This political contortion signified that Kansas was entitled to statehood, though its population did not warrant a representative in the House, if the voters accepted a pro-slavery constitution and a normal land grant. It was not entitled to statehood if the voters rejected the pro-slavery constitution and a normal land grant. In this light the proposal was a travesty of popular sovereignty. Senator Jacob Collamer of Vermont said, "There were people enough to hold slaves, but not enough to enjoy freedom." The English bill was an example of the desperate logic being applied to American politics in the 1850s. It also represented a successful stroke of compromise in a legislative tangle.

The English bill settled the Kansas troubles. The Senate approved it 31 to 22 with Douglas in opposition, and the House with 9 anti-Lecompton Democrats reversing themselves approved 112 to 103, and Buchanan signed it—all acting on the same day. Three months later, Kansans, voting for a third time on Lecompton, repudiated the land grant and the pro-slavery constitution by a more than 6 to 1 margin. Kansas would be admitted in 1861 as a free state under a constitution that, reflecting prevalent white racism, did not give blacks the right to vote.

Buchanan claimed victory. Kansas had not been admitted in 1858 as a free state. But the price of this strange victory was high. Lecompton was widely unpopular in the North. He had split his party, forfeiting supporters in the North. He was at odds with Douglas, the leading Northern Democrat. He had been unable to drive Lecompton "naked" through Congress. Kansas had not been admitted as a slave state. Southern Democrats had failed in their effort to gain another slave state. They had uncovered an enemy in their house—the Northern Democrat Douglas. If he should win reelection he must be shorn of power. If popular sovereignty was to succeed in the territories, the federal government, rather than not intervening, must protect slavery in the territories until statehood.

But would Douglas be returned to the Senate? Illinois Republicans, unlike some eastern Republicans, discerned a difference between non-extension and popular sovereignty, and were unwilling to endorse Douglas in spite of his opposition to Buchanan. They wanted to preserve the Republican Party, and gird themselves to defeat his bid for reelection.

LINCOLN VERSUS DOUGLAS, " 'A house divided against itself cannot stand,' " quoted the Republican nominee for United States senator while the Lecompton controversy was raging in Congress. "I believe this Government cannot endure permanently half slave and half free."

Abraham Lincoln in this gloomy scriptual prophecy struck the keynote of events in 1858–1859. The Dred Scott decision and Lecompton, with their dire implications for the nation's harmony, overhung public discourse. The senatorial contest in Illinois commanded uncommon attention throughout the country. The elections of 1858 would form a referendum on the Buchanan administration. They also held the key to organization of the next Congress and finally they might provide a clue to president-making in 1860. By 1858 Douglas was virtually a fixture in Congress. First elected in 1843 he swiftly strode to leadership, becoming chairman of the Senate committee on territories. He had helped frame the Compromise of 1850 with its new doctrine of popular sovereignty, and had secured repeal of the Missouri Compromise. But when popular sovereignty under weak presidential leadership had broken down he had challenged the president, alienating many Southern Democrats and attracting many eastern Republicans. Douglas, himself, was on trial in 1858 and in a sense so, too, was the unity of the Democratic Party.

By 1858 Lincoln—four years older than Douglas—had served but a single term in the House of Representatives, and thereafter for a time had lost interest in politics. Once back in politics he was driven by a thirst for success; when he failed to win the United States senatorship nomination in 1855, he wrote: "The agony is over at last." He threw himself into the Republican cause with such force and effectiveness, making a fighting speech in May 1856, he received 110 votes for the party's vice presidential nomination.

Illinois Democrats drove another wedge in their splitting party, when the Democratic state convention endorsed Douglas for reelection as United States senator. Buchanan and party regulars labored for Douglas's defeat. Victory might give him leadership of the party in the North and alienate Southerners— the foundation of the party's structure.

Illinois Republicans, on the other hand, strove to prevent a party rift that would occur if eastern Republicans had their way and supported Douglas in his feud with Buchanan. Illinois Republicans nominated a candidate who discerned the difference between popular sovereignty and congressional prohibition of slavery in the territories. In accepting his party's nomination, Lincoln gave his "house divided" speech, carefully stating, "I do not expect the Union to be dissolved."

Having won his party's nomination, Lincoln craftily challenged Douglas to a series of debates. Less well-known than Douglas he had much to gain in public recognition. Douglas accepted, and the candidates agreed to engage in seven "joint debates" at various places in the large heterogeneous state that extended from the Great Lakes to the Ohio River. Douglas held national renown, the "Little Giant," a nickname appropriate to his short height (just over five feet) and great energy. Broadshouldered and round-faced, a good orator, he exerted a personal magnetism. His long experience in politics made him one of the ablest debaters in the nation. Self-confident and ready of mind, he was a formidable opponent, accustomed to winning in public discourse.

Lincoln, at six feet four inches tall towering over Douglas, was a striking figure. Gaunt and ungainly, long of arm and leg, he had hollow cheeks, deep-set, sad gray eyes, wore rustic clothes, and in a high-pitched voice spoke in the accents of a mid-Western farmer. Though less experienced in debate than his opponent, he was a seasoned stump speaker, who expressed himself with wit and logic and clarity—revealing a mind that had carefully thought out what he wanted to say.

The Lincoln-Douglas debates, as famous and consequential as any in American history, were full of pageantry and excitement. They drew large numbers of people, who came in wagons, buggies, railroad cars, boats, and on foot. Torchlight processions the night before debates, daytime parades, banners, booming cannons, brass bands, speakers' stands decorated with bunting —all attested to the enthusiasm of a people who set an admirable record of voter participation in mid-nineteenth century America.

ISSUES OF THE DEBATES. So much attention has been devoted to the color and circumstances of the great forensic match that there is a danger the substance of their discourse may be neglected. The substance, however, is important, both for what was not said and what was said. The old issues that divided parties—tariff, banking, internal improvements, public land policy—were not the subject of debate. Ever since 1844 these issues had not figured largely in political discourse.

Slavery was the overriding issue, but not slavery in the states or even in the District of Columbia. The contestants gave scant attention to the issue of fugitive slaves. They reduced the slavery issue to expansion in the territories and the racial implications of American Negro slavery.

Some historians, e.g. J. G. Randall, have minimized the differences between the two debaters. But real differences existed and they were significant. The issues they addressed embraced the Union, the Dred Scott decision, Kansas, race, slavery, and the Declaration of Independence—all as these related to Negro slavery.

Though both men were passionately committed to maintenance of the Union, they differed markedly in how to accomplish the result. Lincoln, seeing slavery as the only thing that endangered the Union, believed the danger would persist until the public mind rested in the conviction that slavery had been put in the course of ultimate extinction. Only the national government could do this. Douglas in contrast put his faith in local government—the source of American liberty, believing agitation of slavery might disrupt the Union; while local action—popular sovereignty—on what he believed a local issue would resolve the matter. Local option, as on the liquor question, should prevail; the Union could survive only by tolerating diversity of local institutions. Douglas asserted Republican policy would destroy the Union, and exploited Lincoln's statement that a house divided against itself could not stand.

Lincoln retorted that popular sovereignty had failed in Kansas. He wanted congressional prohibition instead of popular sovereignty. He sought to mollify fears aroused by his "house divided" speech by giving assurance that the Republicans would respect the federal Constitution's guarantees of slavery in the states, would enforce the fugitive slave law, and, Douglas pressed him on this, admit new slave states if the inhabitants wrote a pro-slavery constitution.

THE NEGRO AND SLAVERY. As with slavery and its relation to the Union, the two men disagreed significantly in their view of the Negro. Douglas expressed the almost universal white prejudice against blacks, and accused Republicans of seeking full equality, culminating in intermarriage. He denied that the Declaration of Independence embraced blacks in its sweeping assertion that all men are created equal. He charged Lincoln with adapting his racial views to the varying constituencies in anti-slavery northern Illinois, moderate central Illinois, and pro-slavery southern Illinois, saying Lincoln was "jet black" in the north, a "decent mulatto" in the center, and "almost white" in the south.

Lincoln claimed he was consistent in his views about blacks. With a measure of courage he branded slavery as immoral and insisted the Declaration of Independence incorporated the Negro, a man and not an animal, in its equalitarian and libertarian creed. He professed a hatred of slavery because it denied humanity to Negroes; and he argued that because slavery violated equality it must not be allowed to spread but must be put in the course of ultimate extinction.

Ultimate extinction, ending the only thing that threatened the Union, itself threatened the integrity of the Union, which as Lincoln's later conduct would show he valued for its republican principles above emancipation. To resolve this conflict he would not move against slavery in the states and he would enforce the fugitive slave law.

Lincoln's dilemma, posed by idealistic doctrine and racial prejudice, revealed the depth of white racism in America. How would ultimate extinction be achieved? He answered rather vaguely and lamely that it would occur gradually over a period of "a hundred years at least." What then? What shall be done with the free Negro? He was compelled to acknowledge, "If all earthly power were given me, *I should not know what to do*."

Lincoln explained why the race problem seemed incapable of solution. A "physical difference" would forever forbid the two races living together on terms of social and political equality. He frankly favored the "superior position assigned to the white race"; and he would not accord to blacks the rights to vote, hold office, serve on juries, be citizens of Illinois, or intermarry with whites.

Thus far, what he had been saying was conventional white racism appealing to most voters, especially Irish-Americans, meeting Douglas on common ground. The territories should be legally organized so "that white men may find a home," he said, describing one motive behind the Republican stand on non-extension of slavery. He qualified his remarks, saying that blacks possessed rights defined in the Declaration of Independence: they were entitled to freedom and the right to eat the bread they earn. Colonization was his preferred solution to the racial problem. "What I would most desire would be the separation of the white and black races."

The Dred Scott decision figured importantly in the debates. Lincoln brought out the apparent incompatibility between the decision and popular sovereignty. At Freeport Lincoln asked his rival how the people of a territory, under popular sovereignty, could outlaw slavery in the face of the court's ruling that Congress had no power to do it. Douglas replied that slavery could not exist without police regulations. If the territorial legislature failed to provide friendly regulations, slavery could not exist. Douglas's answer, called the Freeport doctrine, was not new in the dialogue between the two men, but it did underscore the inconsistency between the Dred Scott decision and popular sovereignty. It further emphasized the difference between Douglas and the Southern Democrats, who believed the Dred Scott ruling provided security for territorial slavery.

A MORAL ISSUE. What was equally notable was the contrasting attitudes held by the two political leaders toward the morality of slavery. Douglas seemed indifferent to the matter; he regarded slavery as a local issue, best left to states and territories. As early as 1854 Lincoln described Douglas as a man who had "no very vivid impression that the Negro is a human."

In stark contrast was Lincoln's eloquent statement, made in the final debate, "The real issue of this controversy—the one pressing upon every mind—is the sentiment on the part of one class that looks upon the institution of slavery *as a wrong*, and of another class that *does not* look upon it as a wrong . . . . The Republican party . . . look upon it as being a moral, social and political wrong . . . and one of the methods of treating it as a wrong is to *make provision that it shall grow no larger* . . . . (*See Reading No. 28.*)

The curious outcome of this contest was that the Republicans won a plurality of the popular vote, but failed to win a majority in the state legislature. That body returned Douglas to the United States Senate.

The Lincoln-Douglas debates had served several purposes. They had given Lincoln, the prairie lawyer and one-term congressman, an enhanced national reputation. They had pointed up the differences, not perceived by some eastern Republicans, between the Republican creed and popular sovereignty. They had also pointed up the differences between Douglas Democrats and Southern and administration Democrats. They spelled the defeat of Buchanan and the strengthening of Douglas as leader of the Northern faction of his party. Picturesque as they were, revealing flaws in both men, they gave Lincoln a forum from which to denounce the immorality of slavery. Looking back over events of a decade, we note that few aspirants for high office in 1848 could have dared so boldly to declare the injustice of slavery and the necessity of ending it.

ELECTIONS OF 1858. Voters in the congressional elections in 1858 returned a verdict on Lecompton and demonstrated to what lengths party realignment had advanced. Lecompton was not the sole issue; though overall, the free-soil issue including the threat of the Slave Power to Northern interests, shaped voters' thinking. Mindful of the economic recession as well as the failure to carry certain regions in 1856, the surviving strength of Know Nothingism, and the discontent of anti-administration Democrats, Republicans adapted their appeal to local conditions. In New England, Pennsylvania, and New Jersey, they stressed the tariff. Massachusetts, where the Know Nothings were strong, was a special case. Here the Know Nothing-Republican governor, none other than N. P. Banks, added to economic issues a call for amending the state constitution to prohibit naturalized citizens from voting until two years after naturalization. In New Jersey and Pennsylvania, Republicans fused with Know Nothings to form People's parties. On the other hand, "In Maine," W. P. Fessenden wrote, "the opposition [to the Democrats] has no other distinctive appellation than 'The Republican Party.' " In Indiana Republicans went so far as to endorse Douglas's popular sovereignty doctrine. Homestead legislation was offered voters in western states.

Republican strategy sought to broaden the party's base. The means used were flexibility to individual state needs, fusion with Know Nothings and anti-Lecompton Democrats, and the state party organizations swinging to left and right as local interest indicated. Seward, for one, thought some party leaders were going too far in making concessions to interests other than slavery. Speaking in October in upstate New York, he made an extremist speech that shocked some fellow Republicans and sent shivers down the spines of some Southerners.

Seward exploited Northern fears of the Slave Power. "The Democratic party must be permanently dislodged from the government," he asserted, because it "is identical with the Slave Power." The phrase that further linked Seward, remembered for his "higher law" doctrine of 1850, with radicalism was "irrepressible conflict." Slavery and republicanism were antagonistic principles. An "irrepressible conflict between opposing and enduring forces," existed he proclaimed, "and it means that the United States must and will, sooner or later, become either entirely a slave-holding nation, or entirely a free-labor nation."

Election returns showed the rapidly increasing strength of the Republican Party, the repudiation of Buchanan, and the ominously changing structure of the Democratic Party. Republicans and their allies had carried every Northern state but Illinois and Indiana, where, however, they made notable gains. In populous New York they won twenty-nine of the state's thirty-three congressional seats. Buchanan's home state, pivotal Pennsylvania, swung against him; and Simon Cameron, a key figure in the state, rejoiced, "Poor old Mr. Buchanan had no friends left in Pennsylvania and will soon return there disgraced."

The Democrats lost eighteen Northern seats and control of the House. During the campaign the editor of the Jackson *Mississippian and State Gazette* had said, "One after another, the links which have bound the North and South together, have been severed . . . [but] the Democratic Party looms gradually up, its nationality intact, and waves the olive branch over the troubled waters of politics." The election returns in actuality revealed that the party's "nationality" had been dealt a severe blow. In the Thirty-fifth Congress there had been fifty-three free-state Democrats paired with seventy-five slave-state members; in the next Congress there would be only thirty-two free-state Democrats, including twelve anti-Lecompton Democrats, paired with sixty-nine slave-state members.

The Democratic Party—the only national party—had lost its sectional equilibrium in the elections. Moreover, although they retained control of the Senate, the Democrats faced the fact that since the previous Congress two new free states, Minnesota and Oregon, had entered the Union. Republican leadership in Congress was gathering might. In the Senate, Seward of New York, Wade of Ohio, Lyman Trumbull of Illinois, W. P. Fessenden of Maine, Zachariah Chandler of Michigan, and Henry Wilson of Massachusetts joined in attacking the administration and advancing the Republican cause. In the House, John Sherman of Ohio, Schuyler Colfax of Indiana, and Elihu Washburne of Illinois played similar key roles.

The election of 1858 brought the Republicans closer to victory in 1860. The Republican coalition was forming, as Know Nothings and anti-administration Democrats were drawn to it, and key states like Pennsylvania and Indiana were losing faith in the administration party.

CHAPTER 8

THE CRITICAL ELECTION

Striking events in 1859 and 1860 further split the Democratic Party and the nation. Slavery issues erupted: a startling move to reopen the African slave trade; another pro-slavery ruling by the Supreme Court; another fanatical act by John Brown; another congressional deadlock and sectional cleavage over electing a speaker; frustration of the Republican program for the economic future; and an extremist demand from the Lower South—amidst secession threats—for federal protection of slavery in the territories. All the while the bitter feud between the two Democratic leaders, Buchanan and Douglas, raged. The Republicans harvested gains from their rivals' quarrels and divisions, the administration's obstruction of a revived Whiggish program, exposure of corruption in the Buchanan administration, and continuing evidence of Southern militancy. A growing legion of Southerners was preparing to take its stand, to live and die for Dixieland.

SLAVERY PROBLEMS. The United States had long distinguished between the trans-Atlantic slave trade and domestic slavery. Prohibiting the first with little opposition in 1808, it regarded slavery with a certain complacency until mid-century. By that time a belief widened in the North that slavery was a threat to the republican ideal, the free labor philosophy, and the Judaeo-Christian morality.

A movement to reopen the African slave trade therefore shocked many Americans, Southerners included. The move began in South Carolina, when in 1856 Governor James H. Adams advocated reopening the trade. Though Adams and his supporters encountered heavy opposition at home, the proposal gained stature when the Southern Commercial Convention, meeting in Vicksburg, reversed its earlier stand, and in May 1859 advocated repeal of all laws prohibiting the trade. The convention's act was the crest of the movement. No Southern legislature, including South Carolina's, endorsed reopening. But Republicans exploited the issue.

101

The fugitive slave controversy worsened as Northerners continued to defy the federal law. Northern opposition took the shape not only of mob rescues of black fugitives but also of exercise of states' rights against the national statute. Feeling no embarrassment over Northern use of a presumably Southern doctrine, anti-slavery forces encouraged state nullification.

In Wisconsin an abolitionist named Sherman Booth, who had assisted in rescuing a fugitive slave, was arrested and convicted in the United States District Court of violating the Fugitive Slave Act. The Wisconsin Supreme Court ordered him freed and coolly declared the federal law unconstitutional. Here was a bold act of state nullification, springing not from South Carolina, but from the Upper North state of Wisconsin! Federal and state authority had collided.

The hapless federal marshal, Stephen Ableman, who had in vain arrested Booth, appealed to the United States Supreme Court. Northern resort to states' rights doctrine found no comfort in the high court of Chief Justice Taney. The author of the Dred Scott decision in a unanimous ruling in 1859 rejected the claim of a state court to interfere in federal cases. Casually, in a concluding statement, he remarked that the fugitive slave law was constitutional.

No less defiant than South Carolina in 1833, the Wisconsin legislature retorted that the federal government was not the final judge of the powers delegated to it. Invoking Calhoun's theory that the Union was a compact of the states, the lawmakers of the state that had given birth to the Republican Party proclaimed, each state "has an equal right to judge for itself" both of infractions and manner of redress.

The decision deepened party and sectional divisions. Douglas Democrats in their 1860 platform condemned state laws "subversive of the Constitution," and Southern states in 1860–1861 in part justified secession by crying that Northern states had already broken the constitutional compact.

HARPERS FERRY. Far more disruptive was the crime committed by John Brown at Harpers Ferry, Virginia. His violent deed demonstrated how far slavery had pushed the pre-Civil War generation from calm, rational thought. His plan had the backing of some of the North's leading abolitionists. At best it was a hare-brained scheme to seize a federal arsenal with a tiny band of twenty-one men and from that base free a large number of slaves.

He was successful in taking the arsenal. But after two days, during which the slaves in the neighborhood did not rise, Brown and his men, now reduced to seven, were taken prisoner by United States Marines led by Col. R. E. Lee. Brown, in very short order, was brought to trial in a Virginia court, indicted on triple charges of treason against the state of Virginia, criminal conspiracy to incite slave insurrection, and murder. The court convicted him on all charges and sentenced him to be hanged only one month later on December 3, 1859.

The emotional impact of Brown's deed and death was dismaying. Among many Northerners the man who gave his life to free the slaves won eulogies and martyrdom. In the South, Brown incurred condemnation as an inciter of insurrection and murder. To Southerners the North's outpouring of praise was a portent of the meaning of a Republican victory—sanction of private wars against the South, bloody risings of slaves, and race war.

What was of crucial importance was the strong push Harpers Ferry gave the South toward a sense of alienation from the North and of unity as a section. The Richmond *Enquirer* noted, "The Harpers Ferry invasion has advanced the cause of disunion more than any other event that has happened since the formation of the government." Fear swept the South only months before a fateful presidential election, reaching all the way from Harpers Ferry to remote Texas.

To be sure, some Northerners kept calm heads, none wiser perhaps than Abraham Lincoln, who observed that although Brown "agreed with us in thinking slavery wrong, that cannot excuse violence, bloodshed and treason." John Brown was not a Republican, Lincoln declared; and the party platform months later denounced the lawless invasion of any state "as among the gravest of crimes."

DEMOCRATS QUARREL. Three days after John Brown swung from his Virginia gallows, the Thirty-sixth Congress, elected in 1858, convened. Southern Senate Democrats, who controlled the chamber, turned on Douglas, who had increased his unpopularity in the Lower South by publishing a sensational article in *Harper's Magazine*. By this time he had announced he was a candidate for the Democratic presidential nomination on the stand of popular sovereignty. He now rejected the Southern argument, bolstered by the Dred Scott decision, that a territorial legislature could not exercise over slavery a power not possessed by Congress. The true dividing line between national and territorial authority, he claimed, lay in powers which Congress may confer but cannot exercise. Slavery was such a power, prohibited to Congress but available to a territorial legislature.

Douglas's attempt to preserve popular sovereignty widened the gulf within his party. Georgia's belligerent senator, Alfred Iverson, menacingly declared that if the Southerners were unable to defeat Douglas's notion at the national convention, they would "break up the Convention and take proper and effective steps to unite the whole South upon Southern rights principles and Southern rights candidates in the Presidential election of 1860."

Within a week after the Senate convened Southern and administration Democrats stripped Douglas of his long-held chairmanship of the Committee on Territories. The Lower South's ringing rejoinder to Douglas's notion came from Jefferson Davis, senator from Mississippi, who sponsored resolutions stating that neither Congress (as the Republicans argued) nor territorial legislatures (as Douglas argued) could outlaw slavery in the territories. Brushing aside states' rights doctrine, Davis demanded federal protection, if needed, of slavery in the territories. The theme of an angry debate, Davis's resolutions—the program of Southern extremists—won approval by the Democratic caucus on May 24, in Douglas's absence.

THE THIRD SPEAKERSHIP CRISIS. While the Senate was the scene of intra-party strife, the House became an armed arena over choosing a speaker. The congressional elections had failed to form a majority. The Republicans hoped to name John Sherman as speaker, who then would appoint the committees and give Republicans control over the chamber.

Sherman's candidacy fell afoul of his casual endorsement of a Republican campaign document, an abridgement of an incendiary assault on slavery written by a Southern white man, Hinton R. Helper. Drawing on census returns, Helper demonstrated that the North was rapidly surpassing the South in population, culture, and wealth. He shouted his explanation in a single boldly printed word—SLAVERY!—"wrong both in principle and in practice." Helper made a melodramatic appeal to the non-slaveholders of the South to join in overthrowing the slaveholding oligarchy.

With the possibility that Sherman might be elected speaker, Southern anger flared. Furious Southerners burned copies of Helper's book, treated owners of copies as public enemies, and hounded from the state a North Carolina clergyman who circulated copies. Sherman came within three votes of victory, and what was not known until long after, the nation came close to bloodshed in the event of Sherman's victory. The governor of South Carolina said, "I am prepared to wade in blood," and was willing to "have a regiment in or near Washington in the shortest possible time." Hostilities may have begun in the hall of Congress, instead of Fort Sumter, if the Republican sponsor of Helper's aptly named *The Impending Crisis* had been elected speaker.

In the end an inoffensive, conservative, newly-hatched Republican, William Pennington of New Jersey, won by the precise number of votes necessary for election. The whole affair exposed the weakness of the party system, its inability to form a majority, and the strength of Southern intransigence.

NORTH-SOUTH FRICTION. Sectional antagonism also thwarted Republican efforts to enact a series of measures looking to the modernization of the nation. These sought to foster a free-labor economy and society, marked by vocational training of farmers and artisans, ownership of homesteads by white heads of families, promotion of manufacturing, linking the Pacific coast by rail to the East, and improving rivers and harbors.

In Southern eyes such steps would increase the population of the free states by luring immigrants to western lands; subsidize Yankee factory owners; erect tariff barriers in the world market where the South bought and sold; and encourage an internal commerce beneficial to Northerners.

Brandishing his veto power Buchanan struck down a land grant college bill, a homestead bill, and an internal improvements bill to assist the Great Lakes area. The Democratic Senate blocked a bill to raise the tariff, even though the existing tariff failed to meet the government's financial needs. Two of these measures played into the hands of Republicans eager to broaden their Northern coalition. In their platform, drafted after the failure of the homestead and tariff bills, they demanded a homestead law and urged a tariff policy for industrial development.

The Republicans gained from most of the events of 1859 and early 1860. Meanwhile, Southerners drew together, apprehensive about the forthcoming election. On balance, the nation was the loser, with gains in sectional Republican unity on the one hand, and in Southern unity on the other. These months raised alarming signs of the disintegration of the Democratic Party and the national fabric on the eve of a presidential contest.

The year 1860 was the most fateful year in American history since 1776. In the latter year, united colonies declared their independence from Great Britain. Nearly a century later the Lower South voted its rejection of the majority sentiment of the nation, invoked the revolutionary tradition, and put itself on the course of independence.

SECESSION THREATS. Threats of secession should a "Black Republican" be elected president rumbled through the Lower South early in 1860. State legislatures affirmed the right to secede, appropriated money for arms, and arranged to call secession conventions. The moderate Vicksburg *Whig*, in alarm, charged that the Mississippi Democratic Party was full of "fire eaters" seeking to destroy the Union.

The threat to the South was not only from a Republican victory. It sprang also from the Northern branch of the Democratic Party. In the Lower South, party conventions instructed their delegations to insist upon a slave code platform; and the Alabama convention ordered its delegates to withdraw if such a platform was not adopted. In the Upper South, the Richmond *Examiner* asked, "Shall Democratic minorities in Republican States be allowed to shape the policy of the Democratic Party with regard to the institutions of slavery which exist only in Democratic states?" To some Southerners the enemy was as much in the Democratic Party as in the Republican.

Fear gripped the South. Governor Ellis of North Carolina charged, "The abolition of slavery here at home is the design of our opponents." The Richmond *Enquirer* perceived Lincoln as "an illiterate partisan . . . possessed only of his inveterate hatred of slavery and his openly avowed predilection of negro equality."

LINCOLN'S MODERATION. During these early weeks of the campaign year, Abraham Lincoln, speaking in New York before an audience of eastern Republicans, gave an address that impelled him along the path toward nomination. To prepare his remarks he read debates in the constitutional convention and in Congress, and old newspapers. The western lawyer, aware of his rural origin and lack of formal education, wore a new broadcloth suit and carefully delivered a logical, persuasive speech.

Lincoln's investigation of the Founding Fathers drove him to the conclusion—in refutation of both the Dred Scott opinion and Stephen Douglas—that most of them believed the federal government could control slavery in the territories. The Republican Party, he went on, was not radical or revolutionary, but conservative, seeking to maintain old policies, whereas the South had rejected the old policies.

The South and North disagreed on slavery. "Their thinking it [slavery] right, and our thinking it wrong is the precise fact upon which depends the whole controversy." Inspiring a long ovation, Lincoln declared, "LET US HAVE FAITH THAT RIGHT MAKES MIGHT AND IN THAT FAITH LET US, TO THE END, DARE TO DO OUR DUTY AS WE UNDERSTAND IT." This address at the Cooper Union made a profound impression. The next morning four New York newspapers printed it. In his home state the Chicago *Tribune* published it as a campaign pamphlet.

DEMOCRATIC SPLIT. In an apprehensive atmosphere the national nominating conventions took up their tasks early in the year. The Democrats, hoping to heal the rift in the party, had selected Charleston, South Carolina, the very heart if not the soul of secession, as their meeting site. Their blunder soon became plain, when anti-Northern men in great numbers congregated in the city.

As party chieftains faced the election prospects, they recollected that the Republicans had nearly won in 1856. Victories in

Pennsylvania, Indiana, and Illinois had given the Democrats the presidency. Confident they could carry most of the South, the Democrats needed Pennsylvania or Indiana and Illinois. Many persons believed adoption of a slave-code plank in the platform would cost the party the presidency. Douglas's adherents sought to avert adoption; Lower South forces, as we have seen, insisted upon adoption.

An unfortunate decision to write the platform first, then nominate a candidate made a fight inevitable. The platform committee comprised one member from each state; and a combination of Southern and Buchanan Democrats gave the anti-Douglas faction a majority. So constituted the platform committee made two reports—a majority report framed by the seventeen anti-Douglas delegates that called for a federal slave code and a minority report from sixteen Douglas delegates that upheld the 1856 platform on popular sovereignty. The pro-Douglas report stressed that the party would abide by the decision of the Supreme Court on legal questions concerning party differences.

Stripped of constitutional verbiage, the issue for many delegates was whether slavery would be permitted to expand and flourish or be checked and perhaps ultimately ended as a divisive national problem. A mixture of motives animated some anti-Douglas delegates: to defeat Douglas, to split the party, to throw the election into the House of Representatives, and to break up the Union. The whole proceeding occurred in an indescribably emotional atmosphere. Perfervid rhetoric poured from the lips of the fire-eater Yancey, author of the slave code platform, militantly asserting the merits of black slavery. "You would make a great seething cauldron of passion and crime if you were able to consummate your measures," he recriminated Douglas delegates. In equally belligerent tones Ohio's Senator George E. Pugh flatly repudiated the idea that Northern Democrats would mildly put their hands over their mouths. "Gentlemen of the South," he cried, "you mistake us. We will not do it."

One week after the convention opened it voted to adopt the pro-Douglas report, 165 to 138, by a sectional vote. Obeying instructions the Alabama delegates stalked out. The same day the delegations from Mississippi, Louisiana, South Carolina, Florida, and Texas followed. The next day most of the Georgians left, followed by Arkansas delegates. The last national party had broken in two.

The remaining delegates, forming a majority, now endeavored to name a candidate. Thwarted by the party's rule requiring a two-thirds majority of *all* delegates, the convention adjourned, to reconvene June 18 in more friendly Baltimore. The break proved beyond repair. When the Baltimore convention approved a report to seat newly named Douglas delegates, a second walkout occurred, this time led by states of the Upper South, Virginia first, followed by North Carolina, Tennessee, a sprinkling of Border slave state delegates, and Arkansas. The pattern of secession—first the Lower South, then the Upper South, and uncertainty in the border—was foreshadowed in the summer's disruption of the Democratic Party. The Baltimore convention proceeded to nominate Douglas and adopt a popular sovereignty platform. (*See Reading No. 29.*) The bolters met the next day and nominated Buchanan's vice president John C. Breckinridge for president and adopted a demand for a federal slave code. The movement toward secession had gained in velocity. (*See Reading No. 30.*)

CONSTITUTIONAL UNIONISTS. While these momentous events were taking place, two other party conventions were being held. Old Whig and Know Nothing holdouts, most numerous in the borderland between slavery and freedom, came together in the Constitutional Union convention at Baltimore in early May. Though they had no clearly recognized leader, on the second ballot they nominated John Bell of Tennessee, a persistent Whig who had opposed both the Kansas-Nebraska Act and the Lecompton measure. The party of compromise and national unity, it adopted a brief platform advocating *"The Constitution of the Country, the Union of the States, and the Enforcement of the Laws."* (*See Reading No. 31.*)

REPUBLICANS DRAW TOGETHER. If the site of the initial Democratic convention was ill chosen, the place of the Republican gathering was well selected. The choice of Chicago recognized the rising influence of the West, as well as the pivotal importance of Illinois. Moreover, it favored the nomination of

Abraham Lincoln, who as events demonstrated, could be a winning candidate. Enthusiastic Republicans filled the convention hall called the Wigwam and spilled over into the city streets as the party sought to frame a platform.

Slavery was, of course, the major issue. After recognizing the right of each state to maintain slavery, the platform denounced "the infamous Lecompton constitution" and "the dangerous political heresy" that the Constitution carries slavery into the territories. Invoking the Fifth Amendment's guarantee that no person shall be deprived of *liberty* without due process of law—in striking contrast to Taney's emphasis that no person shall be deprived of *property* without due process of law—the Republicans denied the right of either Congress or a territorial legislature to legalize slavery in a territory.

The Republican platform condemned disunionism, John Brown's raid, and reopening of the slave trade. It refrained from the moral indictment of slavery found in the 1856 platform and only after a floor fight once again quoted the Declaration of Independence's stirring pronouncements about human equality and liberty.

If more moderate than in 1856, the platform broadened its appeal, urging a protective tariff and river and harbor improvements, and demanding passage of the homestead bill. On the sensitive nativist issue the platform favored "full and efficient protection to the rights" of both native and naturalized citizens. The 1860 platform was, in part, aimed to woo voters in doubtful states, Pennsylvanians with tariff protection and Indiana and Illinois with homesteads. (*See Reading No. 32.*)

When it came to nominating a candidate, Seward stood above all others. For a decade he had provided leadership in the anti-slavery cause, but to some he seemed an extremist because of his "higher law" and "irrepressible conflict" speeches. Further, his friendliness while governor of New York to Roman Catholics made politicians wary about his acceptability to nativists.

Though no other Republicans enjoyed his stature, Seward was unable to command a majority in the convention. His strength lay in the Upper North; suspicion and mistrust dogged him in the Lower North. As Lincoln put it, Seward "is the very best candidate we could have for the North of Illinois, and the very *worst* for the South of it." On the third ballot the backing of a number of minor candidates broke, shifting to Lincoln, who became the victor. "Fire the salute! Abe Lincoln is nominated," cried an official while the Wigwam exploded in cheers.

A FOURFOLD CHOICE. Four candidates thus presented a choice to voters. Breckinridge, candidate of the Lower South; Douglas, candidate of Northern Democrats; Bell, candidate of the Border; and Lincoln, candidate of the Northern Republican Party. They stood for distinct differences in policy: Breckinridge for the protection and expansion of slavery, Bell by implication for compromise and maintaining a dividing line between slavery and freedom; Douglas for popular sovereignty and final determination by the Supreme Court; and Lincoln for federal law to abolish slavery in the territories.

On questions other than slavery, the Republicans offered a program for the modernization of the nation, espousing positive action by the national government in behalf of industry, commerce, transport, farmers, and free laborers. As for the immigrant vote, the Republicans sought to present themselves as friends of foreigners, pointing to the platform plank upholding the rights of immigrants and their advocacy of a homestead law making non-citizen immigrants eligible for land. They had passed over the candidacy of Edward Bates, an ex-Know Nothing, and they created a campaign bureau, headed by a German Forty-Eighter, Carl Schurz, to win immigrants to the Republican cause. In practice the Republican appeal was mainly to Protestants, recognizing almost a "given" that immigrant Catholics would vote Democratic.

The campaign assumed a special character. Young men turned out in large numbers, campaigning for their favorite candidates. Partisan organizations such as the Wide Awakes carried torches for Lincoln; "Little Giants" paraded for Douglas, and "National Democratic Volunteers" for Breckinridge; and Bell adherents carried bells in the political pageant. Exploiting the corruption in the Buchanan administration, Republicans portrayed Lincoln as "Honest Old Abe," and maintaining the demagoguery of the 1840 log-cabin campaign described him as the rail-splitter candidate. Lincoln, himself, was silent, confiding to a correspondent, by "The united voice of all discreet friends, I am neither [to] write or speak a word for the public."

Orators and others spoke for him and other candidates. Lincoln's silence, in an hour of gigantic misunderstanding between North and South, has raised the question whether he was wise in failing to give assurances he had no intention to move against slavery in the states. But it is doubtful that he would have been heeded, any more than Douglas was heeded in the South. For unlike Lincoln, Douglas took the stump, traveling from New England to Iowa, then boldly moving into the Lower South, reaching the Gulf Coast just before the election. If it is true that Lincoln and the Republicans underestimated the danger of disunion, Douglas faced it head-on. North Carolinians heard Douglas promise that if secession took place, he would do all in his power to maintain the supremacy of the laws. When Lincoln's prospects brightened, thereby deepening fears in the South, Douglas told his audience, I "appeal to you on behalf of the Union."

Contemporaries saw a diversity of issues in the canvass. The editor of the *Springfield Republican* believed the issue to be majority rule, while others in the North believed in a Southern conspiracy to break up the Union. To some the future of republican government, threatened by the Slave Power, was at stake, and to still others a free labor society and economy. Racism figured in Northern—as well as Southern—minds as the editor of the *New York Herald* on election day wrote, playing on the prejudices of white workingmen, "If Lincoln is elected today, you will have to compete with the labor of four million emancipated Negroes."

Southerners saw Northern domination of the government: legislation favoring industry and, in general, Northern economic interests; slave insurrections abetted by Northerners; and emancipation of slaves valued as property worth four billion dollars and at the same time as inferior human beings unworthy of freedom. "The issue before the country is the extinction of slavery," exclaimed the Charleston *Mercury*. "Has a man's own brother . . . a right to invade the sacred precincts of his fireside, to wage war upon him and his family, and deprive him of his property?" asked the *Mercury*.

THE ELECTION'S OUTCOME. The high stakes of the election drove voters to the polls in record proportions. The election of 1860 saw slightly more than four out of every five eligible voters exercise the privilege. Some 650,000 more voters than in 1856 took part in the most exciting—and disturbing—presidential election to that time. (It must always be kept in mind citizens in South Carolina did not vote for president, and the legislature chose the members of the electoral college.)

The outcome, prefigured by the summer's Democratic Party split, made painfully plain that the house had divided. In examining the political revolution of 1860 we must go beyond reporting the number of votes in the electoral college. They gave Lincoln 180 votes, Douglas 12, Breckinridge 72, and Bell 39. How unrevealing these votes are: Douglas, who ranked fourth in electoral votes, ranked second in the popular vote.

Voters had drawn a line between freedom and slavery. Lincoln carried *every* free state, with the small exception of New Jersey's seven electoral votes, three of which Douglas won. Equally striking in this multi-party contest, Lincoln gained clear majorities in all but three of the free states: New Jersey, California, and Oregon. Arrestingly, although the election was nationwide, Lincoln's name was not on the ballot in the states south of Virginia, Kentucky, and Missouri. His meagre share of ballots in those three states was respectively: 1.15 percent, .93 percent, and 10.29 percent, giving him .014 percent of his national total. (*See map.*)

THE SOUTH AND THE ELECTION. In examining voting patterns in the South it must be noted the choice of an anti-slavery candidate was eliminated. Southern voters chose among (1) a federal slave code, (2) popular sovereignty, and (3) the Constitutional Union platform, indicating no changes such as suggested by Breckinridge Democrats and Republicans and implying a compromise line through the territories. All three choices made possible the expansion of slavery.

The South's rejection of containment of slavery—whether by the Lincoln or Douglas formula—further emerges from examining the Douglas vote. In the eleven states soon to form the Confederacy he polled less than 9 percent of the vote, in the Lower South only 7 percent. In none of the eleven states did he win more than 15 percent of the vote. The North's preference for the Lincoln formula is clear: though Douglas won over four-

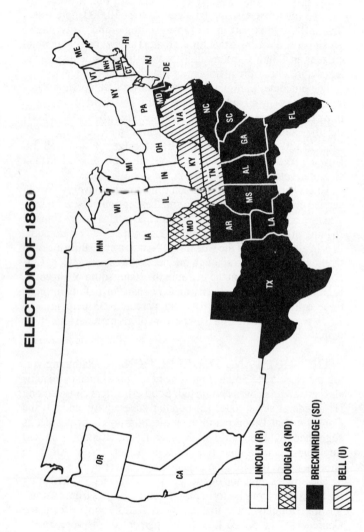

ELECTION OF 1860

LINCOLN (R)
DOUGLAS (ND)
BRECKINRIDGE (SD)
BELL (U)

fifths of his vote in the free states, he carried only the three electoral votes in New Jersey. Of all thirty-three states in the Union he won only one state, Missouri, prevailing over Bell by a hair (.26 of a percentage point). Within the North his strength was regional; it lay in the Northwest. Together the two Northern candidates, Douglas and Lincoln, polled about 70 percent of the national vote.

Breckinridge's vote was also sectional, though less emphatically so than the Lincoln and Douglas results. Breckinridge carried eleven of the fifteen slave states, losing Missouri to Douglas and the Upper South states of Virginia, Kentucky and Tennessee to Bell. His strength resided in the Lower South, the first seven states to secede and form the Confederacy, where he gained clear majorities in Mississippi, Alabama, Florida, Texas (and doubtless would have in South Carolina); he gained 49 percent of the vote in Georgia, and 45 percent in Louisiana. In the Upper South he scored a majority in Arkansas, polled half of the North Carolina vote, 44 percent of the Tennessee vote, and lost Virginia by .19 percent to Bell. (*See Table 3.*)

Breckinridge's success in the South was less than Lincoln's in the North. He failed to gain clear majorities in six Confederate states, won only 45 percent of the popular vote in the fifteen slave states, and gained nearly one-third of his total vote in free states (with a thumping 178,871 votes in Pennsylvania). Moreover, Southern participation in voting, despite the gravity of the election, fell below the national average. Though participation in the Confederate region rose over the 1856 level, only two states, Mississippi and Georgia, sent voters to the polls in higher proportions than the national average.

Bell, with the smallest number of popular votes, carried three states—all of them slave and in the Upper and Border South. In none of the three did he win a majority: in Virginia his margin, as earlier said, was .19 percent, in Kentucky a healthy 8.7 percent, and in his home state of Tennessee a bare 2 percent. In each case Breckinridge was his nearest rival. His strength, in general, lay in the slaveholding South, where except for the states he carried, he ran second to Breckinridge. He won two of every five votes in the future Confederacy—a remarkable achievement for a temporary, conservative, neutral party.

Table 3
Statistics for Lower South, Upper South & Border States

State	Date Seceded	Total Population	% Slave	% Pres. Vote:	
		Lower South			
S.C.	Dec. 20, 1860	703,708	57.2	Breckinridge	
Miss.	Jan. 9, 1861	791,305	55.2	Breckinridge	59%
				Bell	36%
				Douglas	4.75%
Fla.	Jan. 10, 1861	140,424	44	Breckinridge	59%
				Bell	38%
				Douglas	3%
Ala.	Jan. 11, 1861	964,201	45.1	Breckinridge	54%
				Bell	38%
				Douglas	3%
Ga.	Jan. 19, 1861	1,057,286	43.7	Breckinridge	54%
				Bell	31%
				Douglas	15%
La.	Jan. 26, 1861	708,002	46.9	Breckinridge	49%
				Bell	31%
				Douglas	15%
Tex.	Feb. 1, 1861	604,215	30.2	Breckinridge	75%
				Bell	25%
		4,969,141			
		Upper South			
Va.	Apr. 17, 1861	1,220,154	30.7	Breckinridge	44.46%
				Bell	44.65%
				Douglas	9.74%
				Lincoln	1.15%
Ark.	May 6, 1861	435,000	25.5	Breckinridge	53%
				Bell	37%
				Douglas	10%
Tenn.	May 7, 1861	1,110,000	24.8	Breckinridge	45%
				Bell	47%
				Douglas	8%
N.C.	May 20, 1861	993,000	33.4	Breckinridge	50%
				Bell	47%
				Douglas	3%
		3,758,154			
		Border States			
Del.		112,216	1.6	Breckinridge	45.62%
				Bell	24.03%
				Douglas	6.39%
				Lincoln	23.71%

Table 3 *Continued*

State	Date Seceded	Total Population	% Slave	% Pres. Vote:	
Md.		687,049	12.7	Breckinridge	45.6%
				Bell	24.03%
				Douglas	6.39%
				Lincoln	23.71%
Ky.		1,156,684	19.5	Breckinridge	36.3%
				Bell	45%
				Douglas	17.5%
				Lincoln	.93%
Mo.		1,182,012	9.7	Breckinridge	18.92%
				Bell	35.27%
				Douglas	35.53%
				Lincoln	10.29%
		3,137,961			

Historical Statistics of the United States, passim.

The combined opposition to Breckinridge left him only one in seven of the national votes. Though Breckinridge's strength was concentrated in the Lower South, he fared relatively poorly in the cities and, surprisingly, among large slaveholders, who appeared to cling to their Whiggish persuasion.

The election, it has been said, had in a sense been two elections, one in the free states between Douglas and Lincoln, the other in the slave states between Breckinridge and Bell. In this view the election returns showed that the house had divided, all free state electoral votes, with the New Jersey exception, going to Lincoln, all slave state electoral votes going against him. We may modify this interpretation by observing that in the future Confederacy another election was being held between Breckinridge and Bell. Breckinridge carried all the future Confederacy except two states, which he lost by thin margins. Within these eleven states he polled 51 percent of the popular vote, Bell receiving 40 percent.

For the first time in America's history a sectional party had captured the presidency—an astounding triumph for a party only four years old. The winning coalition had made three important additions to its body of voters by November 1860. First, it had adherents from non-Catholic immigrants, who had been Democrats. Second, it had attracted a large number of young, native-born voters. And third, it had lured former Know Nothings or Americans into the Republican fold. In 1856 Fillmore received 13.4 percent of the free-state vote, in 1860, Bell, only 2.6 percent. The shift in the Know Nothing vote may have been crucial. Moreover, the higher turnout in the North undoubtedly helped the Republicans.

The national rupture apprehended by Calhoun in 1850 had occurred. The churches were already divided. The Democratic Party split in the nominating process, and fatefully broke apart in the election. The last national party now was no more, a victim of sectional antagonism.

The anti-slavery vote had swelled from a mere 62,000 in 1844 to 1,866,000 in 1860 (counting only the Lincoln vote). *(See Table 4.)* Charles Francis Adams, son and grandson of presidents, the day after election rejoiced: "There is now scarcely a shadow of a doubt that the great revolution has actually taken place, and that the country has once and for all thrown off the domination of the Slaveholders." On the same day the governor of Georgia dispatched a special message to the legislature requesting military

Table 4
Popular Vote, 1844–1860*

	Antislavery	Whig/Other	Democratic	Percentage Voter Participation
1844	62,000 L +	1,300,000 W	1,338,000	78.9
1848	291,000 F-S	1,361,000 W	1,222,000	72.7
1852	156,000 F-S	1,385,000 W	1,601,000	69.6
1856	1,340,000 R	872,000 A	1,833,000	78.9
1860	1,866,000 R[†]	593,000 U	1,383,000 ND 848,000 SD	81.2

*Source: *Historical Statistics of the United States,* II, 1080, 1072
Party Names: L = Liberty; F-S = Free-Soil; R = Republican; W = Whig; A = American; U = Constitutional Union; ND = Northern Democrat; SD = Southern Democrat
[†]Counting only Lincoln vote

preparedness. " 'The argument is exhausted,' " he charged, "and we now 'stand by our arms.' "

The old party system, once boasting two major parties, each strong both in the North and South, had been shattered. Four parties, each regional in appeal, had replaced the old Union-binding, peace-keeping two-party system. Majority rule, if in one sense vindicated by Lincoln's victory in the electoral college, produced a minority president, supported by only two of every five voters in the nation.

Yet, a remarkable feature loomed in the process. Viewed against the background of bloodshed in Kansas, armed legislators in Washington, intemperate rhetoric, a brutal attack on a United States senator, a fanatic's invasion of slavekeeping Virginia—in short, years of inflamed emotion—it was noteworthy that the election had been conducted without violence and the democratic process had been peacefully observed. Though secessionists frequently uttered threats to act, formulated plans for armed resistance, and voiced a call for a Southern convention, no candidate had run on a secessionist platform.

What would be the response from the hypersensitive, defeated minority? Concentrated in one region of the nation, apprehensive about the victor's intentions, bound together by the presence of large numbers of black slaves and plantations, a pro-slavery conviction, and party unity, the Lower South looked to the protection of its vital interests in the crisis of November 1860.

CHAPTER 9

THE FAILURE OF COMPROMISE

Lincoln's election sounded a shrill alarm throughout the South. The victor was the first president elected by a purely sectional vote. He was the first anti-slavery president. He had united the free North, dramatically demonstrating the minority position of the slave South. The census of 1860, taken in the summer, and the prospective reapportionment of representation in the House drove home the point—the South was a minority. In the reapportionment the eleven states that formed the Confederacy would lose five seats.

THE PATTERN OF SECESSION. The cleavage of the future Confederacy from the Union further appears from the fact that every governor but one (Houston of Texas) and virtually every senator and representative in Congress from the first seven states to secede had gone on record as favoring secession in the event of a Republican victory.

By 1860, the Southern states shared a history of grievances against the North ranging from territorial restriction of slavery in fact and in intent; surging anti-slavery agitation; broad sanction of John Brown's violence; an economic posture threatening Southern interests; formation of a sectional party hostile to the South's peculiar institution; and repeated Northern defiance of the Constitution in deed, as in the personal liberty laws, and in word, as in Seward's "higher law" doctrine and the Republican Party's denunciation of the Supreme Court's "new dogma" of the Dred Scott decision. By 1860, Southerners warmly embraced the view that states, having made the Constitution, retained the right to secede peaceably from the constitutional compact.

The dilemma of the Lower South in the winter of 1860–61 was not whether to submit or to secede, but immediate secession by individual states or cooperative action by sister states, with a few of the "cooperationists" favoring waiting until the Republican administration had committed an act of "aggression" against the South. Those advocating immediate action had more vigorous

121

leadership and a clearer objective than the cooperationists. The fire-eaters advocating immediate, unilateral secession included Robert Barnwell Rhett, the South Carolina agitator; William Lowndes Yancey, the Alabama architect of the federal slave code platform; and Edmund Ruffin, the Virginia torchbearer.

The process of secession began with immediatists taking the lead. Of the fifteen slave states, seven seceded immediately, that is, before the Republican president was inaugurated; four seceded after the new president called out troops against the seven; and four remained loyal to the Union. Both the pattern and the timing of secession bear a strong correlation to the percentage of slaves in each state and to the percentage of Breckinridge support.

In general, states with the greatest proportion of slaves in their population and the highest Breckinridge votes were the earliest to secede. South Carolina, having a black majority and solid support for Breckinridge, was the vanguard state. State after state acted in a descending order of proportions of blacks and Breckinridge strength. In all seven states, Texas excepted, blacks formed over 40 percent of the population and Breckinridge, with two exceptions, garnered a majority. Breckinridge enjoyed 56 percent of the popular vote in the seven states. (*See Table 3*.)

South Carolina's rush to secession had been preceded by three decades of restlessness in the Union. Here, the question was not whether South Carolina would secede but with what speed. The state's timetable accelerated with news from Georgia that this neighboring state was considering secession. Had the secession crisis occurred a few years earlier, before rail and more particularly wire linked the Southern states, South Carolina's secession would have occurred later and the entire tempo of secession would have slowed and possibly differed in other particulars.

SOUTH CAROLINA TAKES THE LEAD. South Carolina, on hearing news that Georgia was moving toward secession, shortened her time for deliberation and called for a convention a month earlier than first planned. It was fortunate for the immediatists because secession sentiment was waning. South Carolina's decision to strike quickly influenced decisions to act throughout the South. In just over three weeks after Lincoln's election all the Lower South but Texas had made arrangements for calling state conventions. Momentum built up, and when South Carolina, on December 20, announced her secession, the state's decision encouraged other states to act with haste.

"The Union is Dissolved," rejoiced Rhett's *Charleston Mercury*, after South Carolina's convention adopted its ordinance of secession. A Declaration of Causes justified South Carolina's secession. For twenty-five years Northerners had denounced slavery as sinful, permitted establishment of anti-slavery societies, and encouraged slaves to flee and revolt. "A geographical line has been drawn across the Union, and all the States north of that line have united in the election of a man to the high office of President of the United States whose opinions and purposes are hostile to slavery."

South Carolina feared a future Union in which the South would be excluded from the territories, the courts would be dominated by the North, and a war would be waged against slavery. For self-protection from the North's erroneous political and religious beliefs, South Carolina dissolved its connection with the Union and announced her independence. (*See Reading No. 33.*)

THE LOWER SOUTH SECEDES. South Carolina's Declaration spoke for many Southerners. Some Mississippians added to the advantages of secession the prospect of expanding slavery southward into Mexico and the Caribbean. Spurred by an "Address of Certain Southern Members of Congress to Our Constituents," bearing thirty signatures, that "The argument is exhausted," the work of secession sped forward.

The election of delegates to state conventions resulted in a narrow victory for the immediatists. The Georgia legislature was the scene of a notable struggle between Toombs and Stephens. Seeing that the North was growing rich through favorable legislation, Toombs exhorted Georgia to secede without delay. "Strike while it is yet time," he cried. In reply, Stephens pointed out that the Republicans did not control the House and Senate. "The President is no emperor, no dictator," he observed. Here the forces seemed balanced, but in the end Georgia decisively voted for immediate secession.

In only forty-two days, seven states withdrew from the Union.

Speed was of the essence, as South Carolinians knew. The future Confederate secretary of the treasury, a South Carolinian, wrote, "Our great point is to move the other Southern States before there is any recoil." Cooperationists failed to gain approval of plans for concerted action with other states, and of a requirement to submit ordinances of secession to popular ratification, Texas excepted. After these failures the sentiment for cooperation subsided. In the six states that acted following South Carolina's unanimous secession, 695 delegates voted for immediate secession, 175 against. Over one-half of the opposition votes were cast in Georgia, where nearly one-third of the delegates favored cooperation.

Seven states seceded, subtracting nearly 5,000,000 people free and slave, from the whole population of 31,400,000. Eight slave states in the Upper South and along the Border now remained in the Union. Actions in a number of these states failed to achieve immediate secession. Virginia and Arkansas provided for conventions and elected majorities of anti-secessionists; Tennessee and North Carolina voted not to have conventions.

Closer geographically to the free states these eight states had economic ties binding them to the North, had given Bell strong support, and owned fewer slaves in proportion to their population (the highest percentage, one in three, was in North Carolina). Moderate in outlook, many persons in these states hoped for compromise and conciliation.

By the time Congress convened on December 3, the Lower South was far advanced toward secession. Five states had summoned state conventions and a sixth had called its legislature into special session to summon a convention. The rush to secede continued unabated while Congress considered compromise. As state after state withdrew from the Union the ability of Congress to function as a national, deliberative body shrank.

CONGRESS AND THE CRISIS. The lame-duck session of the Thirty-sixth Congress, elected in 1858, heard the annual message of the beleaguered President Buchanan with special interest. Confronted by the greatest crisis the nation had experienced, surrounded by pro-Southern advisers, sworn to uphold the Constitution, having only a few weeks left in office, he understood the gravity of what was happening.

The president's message contained a mixture of naïveté and evasion. The crisis had come, he said, because of the long-continued interference of Northerners with slavery, leading to the formation of hostile geographical parties. In his view, not slavery but opposition to slavery had produced the crisis. The South's remedy, however, was unconstitutional. "Secession is neither more nor less than revolution." Could he (in the Jackson tradition) or the Congress coerce a state into submission? He believed no such power had been delegated to him or to Congress. Personally unable to act, he proposed that Congress call a constitutional convention for the purpose of recognizing slavery in the states, protecting it in the territories, and affirming the right to recover fugitive slaves. The legislature not the executive, he believed, should act, and its action should underpin the position of the Lower South on slavery. (*See Reading No. 34.*)

The Congress upon whom Buchanan lodged responsibility for compromise legislation held a majority from his party. But the Democratic Party, having split, could not act as a cohesive national force. South Carolina had no representation in the Congress and the other six states of the Lower South, claiming twelve senators and thirty representatives, were not interested in compromise. Their interest in being in Washington was twofold: to prevent Republican control of the House and to urge separation of the nation on their Upper South colleagues. Secession by their states during the session undermined their efforts.

The Douglas wing claimed to have 37 seats in the House. Douglas by now was not only a vigorous foe of secession but also an ardent believer in conciliation. The Republicans counted 99 seats in the House; they needed 120 to elect a speaker and control the chamber in the next session, and if the Democrats could hold together they could prevent Republican control.

Like the president, this Congress had a lame-duck status; it would expire March 4. Many of its members had been repudiated at the polls and did not represent their constituents' will. On the whole, American political institutions were functioning poorly in their hour of peril.

The crisis of 1860 differed from the one of 1850 in important ways. A sectional anti-slavery party had now elected a chief executive with an unwavering commitment to contain slavery. Before Congress began to consider compromise, Lincoln sent

word to Republican members of Congress, "Entertain no proposition for a compromise in regard to the *extension* of slavery."
Fillmore had been willing to approve any compromise worked
out by Congress. Lincoln believed Congress could work out only
the Missouri line or popular sovereignty. "Let either be done, &
immediately filibustering and extending slavery recommences.
On that point hold firm, as with a chain of steel," he said.

Lincoln's opposition to compromise and his responsibility for
its failure require further analysis. He was fearful not only that
congressional solutions would lead to further agitation to expand
slavery, but also that his party's victory would be thrown away; if
compromise occurred "all our labor is lost, and sooner or later
must be done over." Moreover, a crisis had been reached in an
inevitable conflict. "The tug has to come & better now than
later." On one Southern grievance he was willing to be conciliatory. Northern state opposition to the fugitive slave law ought to
cease. The law, itself, ought to be enforced, but free blacks
should be protected against kidnapping, private citizens ought
not to be required to help in executing it, and resisters should be
punished.

In further contrast to 1850, the Lower South was now not
merely threatening secession it was actively in the process of
carrying it out. A decade of partisan and sectional friction had
passed, etching hatred and misunderstanding in the hearts of
Northerners and Southerners. Both sides gravely miscalculated.
Lincoln as late as mid-February 1861 told a Pittsburgh audience,
"*there is no crisis*, excepting such a one as may be gotten up at
any time be designing politicians . . . just as other clouds have
cleared away in due time, so will this . . . ." In the South a
saying ran, "A lady's thimble will hold all the blood that will be
shed."

COMPROMISE PROPOSALS. Unwillingness by Republicans and Breckinridge Democrats to yield on the territorial
question, ten years of sectional stress, miscalculation on both
sides, all this made compromise in 1860 a formidable undertak-
ing. The Senate was the scene of the main effort to forge a
compromise. John Jordan Crittenden of Kentucky, heir to the
peacemaking mantle of Henry Clay, led the attempt to find an
acceptable middle ground. His plan centered on extension of the

1820 compromise line through remaining territory, leaving future states formed both north and south of the line to decide on slavery. The federal government would compensate slaveholders for slaves whose return had been obstructed. Crittenden proposed that his plan become part of the Constitution; and no future amendment would be allowed to authorize Congress to abolish slavery. (*See Reading No. 35.*)

On December 22, two days after South Carolina seceded and the day when *The New York Times* announced Lincoln's unyielding opposition to slavery expansion in the territories, a Senate committee, in Seward's absence, divided six to six on approving Crittenden's compromise. Toombs immediately fired off a widely disseminated communication to the "People of Georgia," asserting the Republican members had rejected the Compromise, the hope of constitutional guarantees was gone, and exhorting secession before Lincoln's inauguration.

When Seward returned to the committee deliberations, he voted against the compromise. Acting on a negative report, the Senate rejected the compromise, twenty-five Republicans saying *nay*, twenty-three Democrats yea, and six Southern Democrats who did not want compromise abstaining. By this time, January 16, four states had seceded, withdrawing eight votes in the Senate. Though the Republicans who cast the majority vote against the compromise bore the onus of causing defeat—no Republican ever voted for the Crittenden plan—if the abstainers and seceders had joined in voting for the compromise, it would have enjoyed a majority of twelve votes. Extremes had jelled: Republicans who adhered to Lincoln's views and Southern Democrats who advocated secession.

Compromise fared no better in the House, organized under a Republican speaker. Obstructed by Republican members and balloting without the participation of Lower South Democrats, the House committee could not agree on a comprehensive plan. It made a set of reports to the House, the most striking of which recommended a constitutional amendment guaranteeing forever slavery in the states. Approved by Republican committee members, the proposed amendment won House approval by an overwhelming vote of 133 to 65. It passed the Senate—two days before Lincoln's inauguration—by a decisive vote of 24 to 12.

Outside the halls of Congress efforts at compromise also failed. A caucus of seven Republican governors in December agreed to recommend repeal of their state personal liberty laws. In the following months several states took steps to repeal or modify their obnoxious laws. Their action had no perceptible effect in arresting the secession movement.

A second effort arose from Virginia under the leadership of a former president of the United States, John Tyler. Once a powerful voice for nationalism, boasting the names of Washington, Madison, Marshall, and Jefferson, Virginia found its call for a national peace conference heeded by only twenty-one states. The seven states of the Lower South had by the date of the conference, February 4, already seceded and had agreed to attend on that same day a convention at Montgomery, to form a new confederacy. Three states from the Upper North and the two distant Pacific states did not send delegates. The delegates to this unrepresentative conference could do no better than agree on a plan similar to the already defeated Crittenden Compromise.

In all these attempts at conciliation a common difficulty persisted: failure to achieve full national participation and unbudging opposition from Republicans and Lower South Democrats alike. If the Lower South had taken part in the attempts or if Republican members had voted for conciliation, a compromise could have been agreed upon.

The roots of opposition ran deep. The party and sectional split had been long in the making. In addition to the political, constitutional, cultural, and economic forces of division, contemporaries discerned racial and moral factors at work. The veteran Virginia statesman, who participated in the Virginia-sponsored convention, William Cabell Rives, rejected the view that slavery was the cause of secession. "In fact it is not a question of slavery at all. It is a question of race."

Frederick Douglass, the slave who became an abolitionist, believed racial slavery was the mortal disease afflicting the nation. It had demoralized the South, blinding it to "the eternal laws of liberty, goodness, justice, and progress." Voicing a moral revulsion rapidly spreading through the North, he said, "Slavery is the disease, and its abolition in every part of the land is essential to the future quiet and security of the country."

During these efforts at compromise President Buchanan stiffened his policy. His administration was notable for the influence the cabinet held over the chief executive. As in the Kansas crisis, Southerners shaped presidential policy. The secession crisis disclosed that some cabinet members were sympathetic with secession. A series of resignations enabled Buchanan to reorganize and strengthen his cabinet, placing staunch Unionists in key positions.

In a special message to Congress, January 8, Buchanan reaffirmed his belief that he had no right to recognize the independence of a seceded state, and Congress alone had the power to meet the crisis. "On them, and on them alone, rests the responsibility." He urged Congress to accept the proposed compromise dividing the territories between freedom and slavery, a line that "ought to receive universal approbation." His policy, he said, was not to increase excitement, and he pointed to how prudently he had dealt with the crisis developing at Fort Sumter in South Carolina.

The federal government had a garrison at Charleston under the Kentuckian, Major Robert Anderson. Stationed on the mainland at the time South Carolina was about its business of seceding, it lay exposed to capture. After South Carolina seceded the garrison was vulnerable, and given discretion by the War Department, Anderson transferred his troops to the island where Fort Sumter stood guard in the harbor. Northerners cheered the move while South Carolinians condemned it and seized the evacuated mainland fort.

Fort Sumter became the symbol of the clash between federal authority and state rights. Buchanan rejected a demand by South Carolina for withdrawal of all federal troops from Charleston. If Anderson had acted wisely in abandoning an indefensible mainland fort, he had placed his men in a fort dependent for supplies either from the mainland or from the sea. By the end of December, Buchanan now backed by a Unionist cabinet, determined to support Anderson from the sea. He authorized dispatching a relief ship with supplies and men to reenforce Fort Sumter. Apprehensive about antagonizing South Carolina, he avoided dispatching a warship and chartered an unarmed merchant vessel, the *Star of the West*. When it approached Charleston Harbor, January 9, South Carolina, alerted to its coming by Buchanan's secretary of the interior, a Mississippian, and others, opened fire. The *Star of the West* turned around and sailed for New York.

South Carolina had attacked a federally-chartered vessel. Buchanan had justification to retaliate, defending federal authority and the Stars and Stripes. He chose not to do so. A call to arms might have precipitated civil war, encouraged the rapidly building secessionist movement, and destroyed hopes of compromise. Buchanan left the problem of Fort Sumter to his successor, who three months later would sound a call to arms over the fall of a symbol of federal authority—the beleaguered garrison at Fort Sumter.

CHAPTER 10

THE HOUSE DIVIDES

Abraham Lincoln, fifty-two years of age when he took the oath of office, was among the least impressive figures in appearance and experience that the nation had ever had as president. An English journalist who visited him in the Executive Mansion described the chief executive as "a tall, lank, lean man, considerably over six feet in height, with stooping shoulders, long pendulous arms, terminating in hands of extraordinary dimensions, which, however, were far exceeded in proportion by his feet." The journalist noted "flapping and wide projecting ears . . . the mouth is absolutely prodigious; the lips straggling and extending almost from one line of black beard to the other . . . the nose itself—a prominent organ—stands out from the face with an inquiring, anxious air . . . ."

LINCOLN TAKES COMMAND. Unlike most earlier presidents, this strange-looking man had very little formal education or experience in national public life. Although self-taught, he was at home in the Bible and Shakespeare, and his prodigious reading of newspapers had sharpened his understanding of politics. Schooled in the Illinois legislature, he had briefly held a post in national affairs as a single-term member of the House of Representatives. A Henry Clay Whig, he believed in a strong national government that encouraged economic development. In the exciting years since passage of the Kansas-Nebraska Act, he had been driven by a love for the Union and a hatred for slavery.

Lincoln now was not only the head of the nation but also of a new party that had never possessed the presidency. From the moment of election he was beset by one of the vexations and opportunities of public office arising from the party system. Many persons had labored to bring the Republican Party to power; they and others now sought their rewards in the spoils of office. Patiently, almost endlessly, he heard their appeals and dispensed patronage the best he could in the interest of party harmony.

131

Filling his cabinet proved to be especially trying. State after state demanded a place in the president's council. With consummate skill Lincoln named a coalition cabinet, embracing four disparate rivals for the presidential nomination. He balanced factions and sections in a cabinet comprising four ex-Democrats and four (counting himself) ex-Whigs, easterners and westerners, radicals and conservatives, and even included two members from the slave states. His completed cabinet augured well for the president's future political success and the North's unity in crisis.

He accepted suggestions from Seward, once the foremost Republican and now designated secretary of state, in drafting his inaugural address. But the policy enunciated was his own, and he sought, after his long silence during the campaign, to make plain his views on slavery, the Constitution, and the newly formed Confederacy. He hoped to conciliate slaveholding states, reassure slaveholders, sustain Northerners, and by logical and emotional appeal, restore national unity.

As for slavery, in his address Lincoln quoted from one of his speeches and from his party's platform to reaffirm that he had no intention or lawful right to interfere with slavery in those states where it existed. Going far beyond this, the man who would become known as "the Great Emancipator," announced he had no objection to the proposed constitutional amendment stating that the federal government shall never interfere with slavery in the states. He noted the constitutional provision for return of fugitive slaves, a sore point for a decade, and gave assurance that he would enforce a fugitive slave law, which he thought should be revised.

Tracing the origin of the Union past the Constitution to the Articles of Association of 1774, he argued that the Union was perpetual, incapable of being broken unless by agreement of all parties. The central idea of secession was "the essence of anarchy," and once put into operation could be repeated without end. As chief magistrate he had a solemn duty to see that the Union "will constitutionally defend and maintain itself." Faced with a formidable attempt to disrupt the Union, he would hold places belonging to the government, collect duties and imposts, and refrain from appointing "obnoxious strangers" to federal offices in hostile communities. Mail delivery would continue everywhere, "unless repelled." In short, he would uphold national authority and at the same time avoid irritating and provoking Southerners. He sanctioned the idea, endorsed by both Buchanan and Seward, of calling a convention to amend the Constitution.

Realistically he pointed out, "Physically speaking we cannot separate." North and South, though politically separate, "remain face to face, and intercourse, either amicable or hostile, must continue between them. Is it possible, then, to make that intercourse more advantageous or more satisfactory *after* separation than before?" The old questions would remain, he observed.

Lincoln moved on to urge acceptance of popular government. "Why should there not be a patient confidence in the ultimate justice of the people? Is there any better or equal hope in the world," he inquired rhetorically. He gave assurance that war would come only at the instance of the secessionists. "In your hands, my dissatisfied fellow-countrymen, and not in mine, is the momentous issue of civil war. The government will not assail you."

He closed with an eloquent appeal, drafted by Seward, to American nationalism. "Though passion may have strained, it must not break our bonds of affection. The mystic chords of memory, stretching from every battle-field and patriot grave to every living heart and hearthstone all over this broad land, will yet swell the chorus of the Union when again touched, as surely they will be, by the better angels of our nature." (*See Reading No. 36.*)

Southerners' response to the inaugural was mixed. To some he seemed guilty of double talk. He would hold government property in the South, but there would be "no bloodshed or violence." He would maintain the Union, but there would be no invasion. He was going both to conciliate and coerce. The hostile Richmond *Dispatch* charged that, "The Demon of Coercion stands unmasked. The sword is drawn and the scabbard thrown away."

The cooler-headed editor of the anti-secessionist *Raleigh Standard* said, "we are willing to forbear—to watch and wait." He pointed out, "If the seven cotton States had remained in the Union, both branches of Congress would have been against Mr. Lincoln by large majorities, and the Senate could have dictated all his important appointments. But they abandoned the Union—abandoned it selfishly and for no sufficient cause . . . . *It is not a war message.*"

To some extent Lincoln had failed in his aim: to say he would preserve the Union by the policies he described, peacefully if possible, refraining from provocation, but accepting war if necessary.

FORT SUMTER CRISIS. The large issues of union or disunion, peace or war, came into focus over the crisis at Fort Sumter. The federal fort in Charleston harbor, virtually encircled by hostile guns, had become the symbol of national authority—the United States flag defiantly flying in the same breeze that spread the Confederate banner.

The day after his inauguration, Lincoln received a letter from the fort's commander Major Robert Anderson, reading only a "large and well appointed force" could relieve his garrison. He had supplies for just six weeks. Even more disturbing was a note from General Winfield Scott. The venerable Scott was not only general-in-chief of the United States Army, he was an institution —deemed the wisest military man in America. Older than the Constitution, he had served in the War of 1812 as well as the Mexican War; he had been the Whig nominee for the presidency in 1852; and he had long served as adviser to presidents. Scott advised, "I now see no alternative but a surrender in some weeks."

During the first week of his administration, Lincoln ordered Scott to "exercise all possible vigilance for the maintenance of all the places within the military department of the United States"; refused to approve Scott's draft ordering Anderson to evacuate Sumter; ordered strengthening Fort Pickens at Pensacola, Florida; and listened to a plan proposed by an ex-navy officer to reenforce the fort.

At a cabinet meeting on March 15, Lincoln polled members on the question of provisioning Sumter. Of the seven advisers only the postmaster general gave an unqualified yes. The secretary of state, Seward, and the secretary of the Navy, Gideon Welles, key counselors, flatly rejected the idea. On this day Seward, believing himself to be the "premier" of the administration, told a Confederate commissioner that Fort Sumter would be evacuated in a few days. Not long later a Lincoln confidante, who had been sent to Charleston to sound out the situation, told the governor of South Carolina that Fort Sumter would soon be evacuated. Lincoln had authorized neither of these statements; but when they proved false, they gave Lincoln the look of duplicity. Scott on March 28 advised the president to evacuate both Sumter and Pickens.

Increasingly resolved to hold the forts, Lincoln the next day summoned his cabinet to advise him. The attorney general stated the issue: the time had come for Fort Sumter "to be either evacuated or relieved." Seward alone squarely opposed provisioning Fort Sumter. Four members decisively sustained the president's clear desire to maintain the forts. Northern opinion had been hardening, demanding that the government do something.

It was a fateful decision. Lincoln, later that day, ordered the War and Navy departments to prepare an expedition to sail within a week.

In rejecting the advice of his general-in-chief and secretary of state, Lincoln was steadily assuming his rightful role as commander-in-chief and president. On April 1, Seward challenged the president's leadership, presenting him with a plan to evacuate Sumter and reenforce Pickens, saying this would change the issue from slavery to union or disunion. Another part of the plan astoundingly suggested making a demand on both Spain and France to explain their designs on the Caribbean and Mexico, and if their replies were not satisfactory, to ask Congress to declare war against them. A foreign war, he believed, would bring the seceded states back into the Union. Finally, Seward indirectly proposed that Lincoln delegate to him the responsibility for "energetic prosecution" of policy, in other words that he take over as head of state.

Lincoln coolly responded to this presumptuous proposal. He questioned the logic of Seward's statement about changing the issue from slavery to union, and firmly said that whatever must be done, he must do it. Seward soon came to respect the president's judgment and leadership. Seward's plan was in some degree a measure of Northern frustration. The editor of *The New York Times*, who was in close touch with Seward, penned an exasperated editorial, "Wanted—A Policy!"

THE FALL OF FORT SUMTER. Lincoln moved forward his policy of demonstrating national authority without provoking war. He ordered an expeditionary force consisting of three warships, one gunboat, three tugs, and a chartered steamer with 200 troops and provisions for one year to proceed to Fort Sumter. Cautiously, he sent a courier to Charleston with a message for the governor of South Carolina and the Confederate general in charge.

"I am directed by the President of the United States," read the message, "to notify you to expect an attempt will be made to supply Fort Sumter with provisions only; and that, if such attempt be not resisted, no effort to throw in men, arms, or ammunition will be made, without further notice, or in case of an attack upon the fort." Anderson was advised by letter that relief was coming.

Jefferson Davis, president of the seven states of the Lower South that had formed the Confederate States of America, greeted Lincoln's moderate message with deep distrust. Seward and others had spread a belief that Fort Sumter would be evacuated. Lincoln's message seemed not only a repudiation of these assurances, but a disguised and guileful threat of military reenforcements.

Davis and his cabinet determined that Fort Sumter must be captured before the relief expedition arrived. Davis dispatched an order to the Confederate general at Charleston, P. G. T. Beauregard: demand evacuation of Sumter; if refused, "reduce it." Presented with the demand, Major Anderson responded, if you do not batter the fort to pieces, "we shall be starved out in a few days." Beauregard relayed the message to Davis, who replied, if Anderson would state when he would evacuate, Beauregard was to avoid bloodshed.

Asked when he would evacuate in a confrontation at 3:15 a.m. on Friday, April 12, Anderson told Confederate representatives that he would evacuate on April 15, unless he received supplies or orders to the contrary. This was not satisfactory to the Confederates. An hour and a quarter later, before dawn, the Confederate bombardment began. Old Edmund Ruffin, a volunteer with the Palmetto Guard of Charleston, was allowed to fire the first shot.

Union and Confederate forces exchanged fire—almost five thousand artillery rounds in a ratio of about one Union shot for every four Confederate—for thirty hours. His barracks on fire, his ammunition virtually gone, Anderson on Sunday afternoon hoisted the white flag and gave up the fight.

"I accepted terms of evacuation offered by General Beauregard," Anderson reported, "and marched out of the fort . . . with colors flying and drums beating, bringing away company and private property, and saluting my flag with fifty guns."

A NORTHERN RISING. The Slave Power had fired on the old flag and it had been hauled down! The response of the North, for years respectful and fearful of Southern sensitivities and divided over policy toward the South and slavery, was extraordinary. For the moment, party differences seemed forgotten.

The secessionists had changed the issue from the expansion of slavery to the preservation of the Union and the integrity of the republican principle. Fort Sumter had united the North as it had never been united before. "Democrat as well as Republican, Conservative and Radical, instinctively feel that the guns fired at Sumter were aimed at the heart of the American republic," declared the *New York Tribune*. "It is hard to lose Sumter; it is a consolation to know that in losing it we have gained a united people . . . . Live the Republic."

Men and women proclaimed their patriotism. Phoebe Cary, Northern poetess, wrote in her "Voice of the Northern Women":

We are daughters of men who were heroes;
  We can smile as we bid you depart;
But never a coward or traitor
  Shall have room for a place in our heart.

(*See Reading No. 37.*)

Douglas, after some hesitation, remembering his adversarial relations with Lincoln and mindful that Lincoln had replaced some of his friends with Republicans, repaired to the Executive Mansion Sunday night. The meeting of the senator and president was cordial. Lincoln read the draft of a proclamation he intended to issue the next morning. It called to duty 75,000 militia to suppress rebellion. Douglas advised the number be raised to 200,000, and striding to a map designated strategic points he thought needed strengthening. The next morning he released a dispatch to the press, which Northerners could read alongside Lincoln's proclamation. Saying he "was unalterably opposed to the administration on all its political issues, he was prepared to sustain the President in the exercise of all his constitutional functions to preserve the Union . . . . A firm policy and prompt action was necessary."

Douglas soon undertook a speaking tour. "Every man must be for the United States or against it," he declared. "There can be no neutrals in this war, *only patriots*—or *traitors*." Ill and worn he died in the summer, depriving the nation and his party of leadership that would have been valuable during the long war.

In summoning this militia Lincoln drew a double-edged sword. In the North, youths rushed to join the colors in such numbers that recruiting officers, unable to provide enough arms and uniforms, sent many of them home. "The call was made," Lincoln told the Congress, "and the response of the country was most gratifying; surpassing, in unanimity and spirit, the most sanguine expectation."

THE UPPER SOUTH SECEDES. In the aftermath of Lincoln's call for militia, secessionists prevailed in four more slave states, adding strength to the Confederacy, and brought about a serious division of sentiment in the four Border slave states. "It is an odious task to force a government on an unwilling people," cried the editor of the *Louisville Democrat*, as it pointed to the Declaration of Independence and praised resistance as a patriotic virtue. "How easy it is to inflame the South against this conduct of coercion!" he exclaimed. Not the victory of an anti-slavery Northerner, but his resort to force effected the secession of the Upper South.

Throughout the secession crisis beginning in early November and continuing to mid-April, eight slave states had remained loyal to the Union. Four of these, comprising the Upper South, seceded in little more than a month after Lincoln's call to arms. The other four, the Border states, stayed loyal, thanks in part to federal military presence, suspension of the writ of *habeas corpus*, vigorous Unionists, and the enlightened understanding of Lincoln.

Though class differences among whites appeared in political action during the secession crisis, in the end common whites did not seriously challenge social inequality or slavery.

Race and party were keys to understanding the pattern of secession. In the Lower South nearly half the population was black (47 percent); in the Upper South nearly one-third (32 percent); in the Border states only one-seventh (14 percent), with over half the slaves concentrated in the crucial state of Kentucky. In the Lower South, Breckinridge polled 56 percent of the popular vote (South Carolina always excepted); in the Upper South he polled 59 percent (probably in actuality a lower percentage than in the Lower South because South Carolina's lack of a popular vote skews the returns); and in the Border states 32 percent.

In each of the four states of the Upper South, blacks accounted for at least one-quarter of the population. In each was a strong Whig tradition. In each, though it remained loyal until Lincoln appealed to arms, existed a tension between union and disunion. In each state the legislature called for an election to a secessionist convention; but the vote recorded in those elections often meant against secession unless the federal government attempted coercion. Both Virginia and Tennessee formally announced they would resist coercion.

Virginia led the Upper South in seceding after the Fort Sumter crisis. The scene of intermittent racial tensions for three decades, beginning with Nat Turner's insurrection and continuing through John Brown's invasion, it had conducted itself with restraint, rejecting South Carolina's exhortation to call a Southern convention early in 1860 and calling a peace conference early in 1861. By a wafer-thin margin Bell had carried the state in 1860.

Virginia had, however, the largest black population of any state, nearly half a million, amounting to three of every ten residents; and it had split its vote between Bell and Breckinridge in nearly equal numbers. Five days before it called for a peace convention, it called for an election for a convention to consider secession. In the election moderation prevailed, voters who insisted that a secession ordinance be submitted to popular ratification triumphed by more than two to one and delegates favoring immediate secession won only one-third of the places. The convention, meeting in mid-February, marked time hoping for compromise. It also sobered observers in other states.

Though Lincoln's election alone had not been a sufficient spur to secession, at about the same time that the legislators called for a peace convention, they also voted almost without dissent to resist any attempted coercion. The prestige of the Old Dominion throughout the South was great. Southerners looked to Virginia as the exemplar of Southern life and culture. She now stood as the domino whose fall would topple the other states of the Upper South and perhaps of the Border.

As tension heightened about the fate of Fort Sumter, Roger Pryor, an impatient Virginia secessionist, hastened to Charleston. In a stirring address on April 10 he predicted, *"The very moment blood is shed, old Virginia will make common cause with her sisters of the South."* Pryor proved correct. Two days after Lincoln's proclamation, Virginia voted to secede by a vote of 88 to 55. A little over a month later voters ratified the ordinance of secession by a three to one majority.

Arkansas was next to cut the cord of union. It had given 53 percent of its vote to Bell and it counted one slave in every four residents. In mid-January its legislature called for an election to a secession convention. Arkansans voted in favor of a convention and elected a Unionist majority, which in early March defeated secession. Reconvened on May 6, with only five dissenters, the convention took the state out of the Union.

Tennessee followed the next day. The home of presidents Andrew Jackson and James K. Polk, the Unionist candidate John Bell, and the anti-secessionist senator Andrew Johnson, Tennessee had given a plurality of its vote (47 percent) to Bell, and like Arkansas, numbered one slave in every four residents. Its 1,110,000 population made it the second largest state to withdraw. Its legislature had announced Tennessee would resist invasion and called for election of a secession convention. Acting on two issues, voters rejected a convention and expressed a three to one preference for Unionist against secessionist delegates, had there been a convention. On May 7 the legislature, bypassing the convention, adopted a Declaration of Independence, later approved by the voters.

North Carolina, the eleventh and last state to secede, had given half of its vote to Breckinridge and 47 percent to Bell. Blacks formed one-third of its nearly one million population. Long disdainful of South Carolina's "insufferable arrogance and conceited self-importance," North Carolinians rejected the notion of following its sister state's extreme example. Voters on a secession convention in late February not only opposed holding a convention, but also expressed a preference for Unionist delegates, should there have been one. Voters may have been misled by a telegram from the Virginia-sponsored peace convention that a compromise would be endorsed by Congress. In mid-May a convention heard Senator George Badger denounce "absolute subjection and abject slavery" and unanimously voted to secede.

The four Upper South states promptly joined the Confederate States of America. They increased the strength of the Confederacy by 3,758,000 forming 43 percent of the new nation's total of 8,727,000 persons, white and black.

ELEMENTS UNITING THE CONFEDERACY. The eleven states that struck for independence as a new slaveholding nation in 1861 had a common history stretching back at least as far as 1844. They possessed elements of economic unity in their production of staple crops by unfree black labor, most effectively organized in plantations, and defended by the Democratic Party. They believed the economic future of the states was tied to the expansion of their system, necessitating the extension of slavery.

The extensionist issue had been joined in 1844 with the Southern demand for Texas and the development of Northern resistance to the expansion of slavery into the territories. Major parties at first sought to evade the issue, but it became unavoidable. The politics of evasion went bankrupt. A Northern demand that slavery not be allowed to expand began to dissolve the two-party system that held the nation together. This demand ignored the national pact reaching back to 1787, that the territories be divided between North and South by a line drawn by Congress.

An effort to de-nationalize the issue, removing it as a cause of party divisiveness, won approval for newly acquired territories in the sectional crisis of 1850. But in the effort in 1854 to undo the national pact for the Louisiana Territory, the two-party system shattered. What many political leaders had long feared now developed: a sectional, anti-expansionist party sprang into being and arrayed itself against the Slave Power. With a speed frightening to Southerners, the Northern party nearly captured the presidency on its first try.

Southerners increasingly turned to the Democratic Party to defend their peculiar institution. The four and a half year contest for Kansas, both in the territory and in Washington, inflamed sectional sensitivities. Politicians declaimed and presidents blundered, unable to cope with the phenomenon of black slavery. Northern hostility to the institution of slavery deepened in the 1850s as men perceived the institution to be a threat to economic progress, the republican ideal, and Judaeo-Christian morality. Northern attitudes, shaped by apprehension of disunion, respect for state and property rights, and by a general belief in the racial inferiority of blacks, usually drew back from abolition. It may seem a remarkable fact of American history that no major abolitionist party ever emerged. The explanation is simple: an abolition party could not have succeeded. Political anti-slavery in the United States took the special form of containing the expansion of slavery.

To Southerners, containment meant ultimate extinction, subjecting the South to domination by the North, loss of property and prosperity, moral obloquy, and racial chaos. In the eleven Confederate states, rejection of the Republican Party was complete. The Lower South demanded federal protection of slavery in the territories.

The election of 1860 turned on the territorial issue and its implications. Victory of the Republican Party—sectional and anti-extensionist—impelled the Lower South to secede. The Upper South adopted a defensive posture, intent on guarding states' rights and slavery, but hopeful of a compromise that would restore the old balance between slavery and freedom in the territories.

Compromise failed; the Lower South, organized as the Confederate States of America, fired on the federal fort that symbolically threatened the Confederacy's validity; and the Republican president called out the militia. The call did what the election victory and the shooting at Fort Sumter could not do; it drove the Upper South to secede and join the Confederacy.

The union of these eleven states had been foreshadowed for more than a decade and a half. Possessing in common plantation agriculture, a high proportion of black slaves, and a tendency to look to the Democratic Party for the protection of Southern rights, honor, and racial slavery, they joined together in 1861 to attain their goals through independence.

Their new government was founded, the vice president Alexander H. Stephens said, "upon the great truth that the negro is not equal to the white man; that slavery, subordination to the superior race, is his natural and moral condition." (*See Reading No. 38.*) Their president, Jefferson Davis, responded to Lincoln's call for arms with a special message to his Congress, saying, "All we ask is to be let alone." (*See Reading No. 39.*)

These deeply rooted assertions on behalf of black slavery and Southern independence met defeat only after four years of bloody civil war.

PART II

READINGS

READING NO. 1

LIBERTY PARTY RESOLUTIONS, 1843[1]

*A pioneer in political anti-slavery the Liberty Party in 1843
adopted resolutions that summed up the nature of its opposition
to slavery.*

γ   γ   γ

LIBERTY PARTY NATIONAL CONVENTION, 1843.

The Liberty Party National Convention met at Buffalo, on the
30th of August. Leicester King, of Ohio, presided, and James
G. Birney, of Michigan, was unanimously nominated for President, with Thomas Morris, of Ohio, for Vice-President. Among
the resolves adopted were the following:

Resolved, That human brotherhood is a cardinal principle of
true Democracy, as well as of pure Christianity, which spurns all
inconsistent limitations; and neither the political party which
repudiates it, nor the political system which is not based upon it,
can be truly Democratic or permanent.

Resolved, That the Liberty Party, placing itself upon this
broad principle, will demand the absolute and unqualified divorce of the General Government from slavery, and also the
restoration of equality of rights, among men, in every State
where the party exists, or may exist.

Resolved, That the Liberty Party has not been organized for
any temporary purpose by interested politicians, but has arisen
from among the people in consequence of a conviction, hourly
gaining ground, that no other party in the country represents the
true principles of American liberty, or the true spirit of the
Constitution of the United States. . . .

Resolved, That it was understood in the times of the Declaration and the Constitution, that the existence of slavery in some of
the States, was in derogation of the principles of American
Liberty, and a deep stain upon the character of the country, and

---

[1]Horace Greeley and John F. Cleveland, compilers, *A Political Textbook for 1860*
(New York, 1860), 13–14.

the implied faith of the States and the Nation was pledged, that slavery should never be extended beyond its then existing limits, but should be gradually, and yet, at no distant day, wholly abolished by State authority. . . .

Resolved, That the provision of the Constitution of the United States, which confers extraordinary political powers on the owners of slaves, and thereby constituting the two hundred and fifty thousand slaveholders in the Slave States a privileged aristocracy; and the provision for the reclamation of fugitive slaves from service, are Anti-Republican in their character, dangerous to the liberties of the people, and ought to be abrogated. . . .

Resolved, That the peculiar patronage and support hitherto extended to Slavery and Slaveholding, by the General Government, ought to be immediately withdrawn, and the example and influence of National authority ought to be arrayed on the side of Liberty and Free Labor. . . .

Resolved, That freedom of speech, and of the press, and the right of petition and the right of trial by jury, are sacred and inviolable; and that all rules, regulations and laws, in derogation of either are oppressive, unconstitutional, and not to be endured by free people.

Resolved, That we regard voting in an eminent degree, as a moral and religious duty, which, when exercised, should be by voting for those who will do all in their power for Immediate Emancipation.

Resolved, That this Convention recommend to the friends of Liberty in all those Free States where any inequality of rights and privileges exists on account of color, to employ their utmost energies to remove all such remnants and effects of the Slave system. . . .

READING NO. 2

SOUTHERN SECTIONALISM AND THE TARIFF, GEORGE MCDUFFIE

Attacking the tariff system, Senator George McDuffie of South Carolina in 1844 described the United States as divided into manufacturing, farming, and planting sections, and warned the protective system was driving the planting South to "a point beyond which oppression would not be endured."

γ   γ   γ

He adverted to the decline of commerce, and traced its causes to the tariff system. He showed that, at one of the earliest conventions of this government at Annapolis, there was the greatest solicitude evinced for preserving and encouraging our foreign commerce, which showed that such was the design of the framers of the constitution. He showed that if this Union were divided into three confederations, the North and Northeast as one, the Southwest as another, and the southern States as another, the manufacturing States could not adhere to the protective system one year. They would have no revenue, and would be driven to direct taxation; whereas the southern confederation would become the importing States, receiving, in exchange, foreign manufactures for their rice, cotton, tobacco, and sugar —that the southwestern confederation would be exchangers with the southern confederation of their products for the products of Europe; for they never would be so foolish as to buy, of the New England confederation, its manufactures at 40 per cent higher in price than need be paid for the same goods in the southern confederation. The South would very soon export one hundred millions, and receive back one hundred and twenty in imports; on which a duty of 10 percent would yield twelve millions of revenue for the government of the confederation. The northern confederation would not, at the same time, either

---

[2]*Congressional Globe*, 28th Cong., 1st sess., 201

export or import 15,000,000, and could hardly realize 3,000,000 of revenue. In ten years there would be such a difference, that a person absent so long, returning, would be struck with the change in the condition of these sections of country. The West he would see grown up into a great and flourishing empire. The South, the seat of commerce and the arts, the great cities of Boston and New York, rebuilt in Charleston and New Orleans, and more flourishing than in their original, uncongenial climates. But in New England he would find the prosperity, comforts, wealth, &c., resulting from partial legislation, algone *sic*; houses falling to ruin, cities deserted, furniture selling by auction, and all the indications of indigence prevailing. On asking how came all this? he could be answered, not by any act of injustice or oppression; but by repealing unjust or oppressive laws; by letting industry seek its own level, and pursue its own advantages in its own way, without dependence on bounties or government for its support.

After a series of striking and eloquent illustrations of this nature, (here very briefly and imperfectly sketched,) Mr. McD. concluded by admonishing the friends of the protective system that there was a point beyond which oppression would not be endured, even by the most enslaved community in the world.

READING NO. 3

FREDERICK DOUGLASS,
A FUGITIVE SLAVE'S STORY[3]

Frederick Douglass, the escaped slave who became an aboli-tionist, in his autobiography told of taking up his work as an abolitionist and why he wrote an autobiography.

γ   γ   γ

Among the first duties assigned me, on entering the ranks, was to travel, in company with Mr. George Foster, to secure subscribers to the "Anti-slavery Standard" and the "Liberator." With him I traveled and lectured through the eastern counties of Massachusetts. Much interest was awakened—large meetings assembled. Many came, no doubt, from curiosity to hear what a negro could say in his own cause. I was generally introduced as a *"chattel"*—a *"thing"*—a piece of southern *"property"*—the chairman assuring the audience that *it* could speak. Fugitive slaves, at that time, were not so plentiful as now; and as a fugitive slave lecturer, I had the advantage of being a *"brand new fact"*—the first one out. Up to that time, a colored man was deemed a fool who confessed himself a runaway slave, not only because of the danger to which he exposed himself of being retaken, but because it was a confession of a very *low* origin! Some of my colored friends in New Bedford thought very badly of my wisdom for thus exposing and degrading myself. The only precaution I took, at the beginning, to prevent Master Thomas from knowing where I was, and what I was about, was the withholding of my former name, my master's name, and the name of the state and county from which I came. During the first three or four months, my speeches were almost exclusively made up of narrations of my own personal experience as a slave. "Let us have the facts," said the people. So also said Friend

---

[3]Frederick Douglass, *Life and Times of Frederick Douglass*, (Hartford, 1881), 159–162.

George Foster, who always wished to pin me down to my simple narrative. "Give us the facts," said Collins, "we will take care of the philosophy." Just here arose some embarrassment. It was impossible for me to repeat the same old story month after month, and to keep up my interest in it. It was new to the people, it is true, but it was an old story to me; and to go through with it night after night, was a task altogether too mechanical for my nature. "Tell your story, Frederick," would whisper my then revered friend, William Lloyd Garrison, as I stepped upon the platform. I could not always obey, for I was now reading and thinking. New views of the subject were presented to my mind. It did not entirely satisfy me to *narrate* wrongs; I *felt* like *denouncing* them. I could not always curb my moral indignation for the perpetrators of slaveholding villainy, long enough for a circumstantial statement of the facts which I felt almost everybody must know. Besides, I was growing, and needed room. "People won't believe you ever was a slave, Frederick, if you keep on this way," said Friend Foster. "Be yourself," said Collins, "and tell your story." It was said to me, "Better have a *little* of the plantation manner of speech than not; 'tis not best that you seem too learned." These excellent friends were actuated by the best of motives, and were not altogether wrong in their advice; and still I must speak just the word that seemed to *me* the word to be spoken *by* me.

At last the apprehended trouble came. People doubted if I ever had been a slave. They said I did not talk like a slave, look like a slave, nor act like a slave, and that they believed I had never been south of Mason and Dixon's line. "He don't tell us where he came from—what his master's name was—how he got away— nor the story of his experience. Besides, he is educated, and is, in this, a contradiction of all the facts we have concerning the ignorance of the slaves." Thus, I was in a pretty fair way to be denounced as an imposter. The committee of the Massachusetts anti-slavery society knew all the facts in my case, and agreed with me in the prudence of keeping them private. They, therefore, never doubted my being a genuine fugitive; but going down the aisles of the churches in which I spoke, and hearing the free spoken Yankees saying, repeatedly, "*He's never been a slave, I'll warrant ye,*" I resolved to dispel all doubt, at no distant day, by such a revelation of facts as could not be made by any other than a genuine fugitive.

In a little less than four years, therefore, after becoming a public lecturer, I was induced to write out the leading facts connected with my experience in slavery, giving names of persons, places and dates—thus putting it in the power of any who doubted, to ascertain the truth or falsehood of my story of being a fugitive slave. This statement soon became known in Maryland, and I had reason to believe that an effort would be made to recapture me.

READING NO. 4

JOHN C. CALHOUN,
SLAVERY IS A POSITIVE GOOD[4]

Responding to the numerous abolitionist petitions sent to Congress, John C. Calhoun, South Carolina senator, summed up the pro-slavery argument, emphasizing slavery's benefits to both white and black in the South.

γ　　　　　γ　　　　　γ

I hold that in the present state of civilization, where two races of different origin, and distinguished by color, and other physical differences, as well as intellectual, are brought together, the relation now existing in the slaveholding States between the two, is, instead of an evil, a good—a positive good. I feel myself called upon to speak freely upon the subject where the honor and interests of those I represent are involved. I hold then, that there never has yet existed a wealthy and civilized society in which one portion of the community did not, in point of fact, live on the labor of the other. Broad and general as is this assertion, it is fully borne out by history. This is not the proper occasion, but if it were, it would not be difficult to trace the various devices by which the wealth of all civilized communities has been so unequally divided, and to show by what means so small a share has been allotted to those by whose labor it was produced, and so large a share given to the non-producing classes. The devices are almost innumerable, from the brute force and gross superstition of ancient times, to the subtle and artful fiscal contrivances of modern. I might well challenge a comparison between them and the more direct, simple, and patriarchal mode by which the labor of the African race is, among us, commanded by the European. I may say with truth, that in few countries so much is left to the share of the laborer, and so little exacted from him, or where there is more kind attention paid to him in sickness or infirmities

[4]R. K. Cralle, ed., *The Works of John C. Calhoun*, II (New York, 1854), 629ff.

of age. Compare his condition with the tenants of the poor houses in the more civilized portions of Europe—look at the sick, and the old and infirm slave, on one hand, in the midst of his family and friends, under the kind superintending care of his master and mistress, and compare it with the forlorn and wretched condition of the pauper in the poor house. But I will not dwell on this aspect of the question; I turn to the political; and here I fearlessly assert that the existing relation between the two races in the South, against which these blind fanatics are waging war, forms the most solid and durable foundation on which to rear free and stable political institutions. It is useless to disguise the fact. There is and always has been in an advanced stage of wealth and civilization, a conflict between labor and capital. The condition of society in the South exempts us from the disorders and dangers resulting from this conflict; and which explains why it is that the political condition of the slaveholding States has been so much more stable and quiet than that of the North. The advantages of the former, in this respect, will become more and more manifest if left undisturbed by interference from without, as the country advances in wealth and numbers. We have, in fact, but just entered that condition of society where the strength and durability of our political institutions are to be tested; and I venture nothing in predicting that the experience of the next generation will fully test how vastly more favorable our condition of society is to that of other sections for free and stable institutions, provided we are not disturbed by the interference of others, or shall have sufficient intelligence and spirit to resist promptly and successfully such interference. It rests with ourselves to meet and repel them. I look not for aid to this Government, or to the other States; not but there are kind feelings towards us on the part of the great body of the non-slaveholding States; but as kind as their feelings may be, we may rest assured that no political party in these States will risk their ascendency for our safety. If we do not defend ourselves none will defend us; if we yield we will be more and more pressed as we recede; and if we submit we will be trampled under foot. Be assured that emancipation itself would not satisfy these fanatics:—that gained, the next step would be to raise the negroes to a social and political equality with the whites; and that being effected, we would soon find the present condition of the two races reversed.

They and their northern allies would be the masters, and we the slaves; the condition of the white race in the British West India Islands, bad as it is, would be happiness to ours. There the mother country is interested in sustaining the supremacy of the European race. It is true that the authority of the former master is destroyed, but the African will there still be a slave, not to individuals but to the community,—forced to labor, not by the authority of the overseer, but by the bayonet of the soldiery and the rod of the civil magistrate.

READING NO. 5

HENRY CLAY, LETTER TO THE
NATIONAL INTELLIGENCER, 1844[5]

The Whig Party nominee for the presidency, Henry Clay in late 1844 softened his earlier opposition to the annexation of Texas.

γ   γ   γ

In announcing my determination to permit no other letters to be drawn from me on public affairs, I think it right to avail myself of the occasion to correct the erroneous interpretation of one or two of those which I had previously written. In April last I addressed to you, from Raleigh, a letter in respect to the proposed treaty annexing Texas to the United States, and I have since addressed two letters to Alabama upon the same subject. Most unwarranted allegations have been made that those letters are inconsistent with each other, and, to make it out, particular phrases or expressions have been torn from their context, and a meaning attributed to me which I never entertained.

I wish now distinctly to say that there is not a feeling, a sentiment, or an opinion expressed in my Raleigh letter to which I do not adhere. I am decidedly opposed to the immediate annexation of Texas to the United States. I think it would be dishonorable, might involve them in war, would be dangerous to the integrity and harmony of the Union, and, if all these objections were removed, could not be effected, according to any information I possess, upon just and admissible conditions.

It was not my intention, in either of the two letters which I addressed to Alabama, to express any contrary opinion. Representations had been made to me that I was considered as inflexibly opposed to the annexation of Texas under any circumstances; and that my opposition was so extreme that I would not waive it, even if there were a general consent to the measure by all thestates of the Union. I replied, in my first letter to Alabama,

[5]Henry Clay, *Letter to the National Intelligencer*, September 23, 1844, *Niles' National Register*, October 5, 1844.

that personally I had no objection to annexation. I thought that my meaning was sufficiently obvious, that I had no personal, private or individual motives for opposing, as I have none for espousing the measure, my judgment being altogether influenced by general and political considerations, which have ever been the guide of my public conduct.

In my second letter to Alabama, assuming that the annexation of Texas might be accomplished without national dishonor, without war, with the general consent of the states of the Union, and upon fair and reasonable terms, I stated that I should be glad to see it. I did not suppose that it was possible I could be misunderstood. I imagined every body would comprehend me as intending that, whatever might be my particular views and opinions, I should be happy to see what the whole nation might concur in desiring under the conditions stated. Nothing was further from my purpose than to intimate any change of opinion as long as any considerable and respectable portion of the confederacy should continue to stand out in opposition to the annexation of Texas.

In all three of my letters upon the subject of Texas, I stated that annexation was inadmissible except upon fair and reasonable terms, if every other objection were removed. In a speech which I addressed to the senate of the United States more than three years ago, I avowed my opposition, for the reasons there stated, to the assumption, by the general government, of the debts of the several states. It was hardly, therefore, to be presumed that I could be in favor of assuming the unascertained debt of a foreign state, with which we have no fraternal ties, and whose bad faith or violation of its engagements can bring no reproaches upon us.

Having thus, gentlemen, made the apology which I intend, for my omission to answer any letters of inquiry upon public affairs which I have received; announced my purpose to decline henceforward transmitting answers for publication to any such letters that I may hereafter receive; and vindicated some of those which I have forwarded against the erroneous constructions to which they have been exposed, I have accomplished the purpose of this note, and remain, respectfully, your obedient servant,

H. Clay

Messrs. Gales & Shaton.

READING NO. 6

JAMES K. POLK,
WAR MESSAGE TO CONGRESS[6]

In a special message President James K. Polk described the circumstances that caused him to ask Congress to recognize a state of war between Mexico and the United States.

γ　　　　　γ　　　　　γ

Texas, by the final action of our Congress, had become an integral part of our Union. The Congress of Texas, by its act of December 19, 1836, had declared the Rio del Norte to be the boundary of that Republic. Its jurisdiction had been extended and exercised beyond the Nueces. The country between that river and the Del Norte had been represented in the Congress and in the convention of Texas, had thus taken part in the act of annexation itself, and is now included within one of our Congressional districts. Our own Congress had, moreover, with great unanimity, by the act approved December 31, 1845, recognized the country beyond the Nueces as a part of our territory by including it within our own revenue system, and a revenue officer to reside within that district has been appointed by and with the advice and consent of the Senate. It became, therefore, of urgent necessity to provide for the defense of that portion of our country. Accordingly, on the 13th of January last instructions were issued to the general in command of these troops to occupy the left bank of the Del Norte. This river, which is the southwestern boundary of the State of Texas, is an exposed frontier. From this quarter invasion was threatened; upon it and in its immediate vicinity, in the judgment of high military experience, are the proper stations for the protecting forces of the Government. In addition to this important consideration, several other occurred to induce this movement. Among these are the facili-

[6]James D. Richardson, comp., *Messages and Papers of the Presidents, 1789–1897* (Washington, 1897), IV, 440–443.

ties afforded by the ports at Brajor Santiago and the mouth of the Del Norte for the reception of supplies by sea, the stronger and more healthful military positions, the convenience for obtaining a ready and more abundant supply of provisions, water, fuel, and forage, and the advantages which are afforded by the Del Norte in forwarding supplies to such posts as may be established in the interior and upon the Indian frontier.

The movement of the troops to the Del Norte was made by the commanding general under positive instructions to abstain from all aggressive acts toward Mexico or Mexican citizens and to regard the relations between that Republic and the United States as peaceful unless she should declare war or commit acts of hostility indicative of a state of war. . . .

The Mexican forces at Matamoras assumed a belligerent attitude, and on the 12th of April General Ampudia, then in command, notified General Taylor to break up his camp within twenty-four hours and to retire beyond the Nueces River, and in the event of his failure to comply with these demands announced that arms, and arms alone, must decide the question. But no open act of hostility was committed until the 24th of April. On that day General Arista, who had succeeded to the command of the Mexican forces, communicated to General Taylor that "he considered hostilities commenced and should prosecute them." A party of dragoons of 63 men and officers were on the same day dispatched from the American camp up the Rio del Norte, on its left bank, to ascertain whether the Mexican troops had crossed or were preparing to cross the river, "became engaged with a large body of these troops, and after a short affair, in which some 16 were killed and wounded, appear to have been surrounded and compelled to surrender." . . .

The cup of forbearance had been exhausted even before the recent information from the frontier of the Del Norte. But now after reiterated menaces, Mexico has passed the boundary of the United States, has invaded our territory and shed American blood upon American soil. She has proclaimed that hostilities have commenced, and that the two nations are now at war.

As war exists, and, notwithstanding all our efforts to avoid it, exists by the act of Mexico herself, we are called upon by every consideration of duty and patriotism to vindicate with decision the honor, the rights and the interests of our country. . . .

In further vindication of our rights and defense of our territory, I invoke the prompt action of Congress to recognize the existence of the war, and to place at the disposition of the Executive the means of prosecuting the war with vigor, and thus hastening the restoration of peace.

READING NO. 7

LEWIS CASS, LETTER TO
A. O. P. NICHOLSON[7]

Hopeful for the Democratic Party nomination for the presidency in 1848, Lewis Cass of Michigan put forward a compromise solution to the extreme positions of congressional prohibition of and non-interference with slavery in the territories.

γ   γ   γ

In various respects, the Territories differ from the States. Some of their rights are inchoate, and they do not possess the peculiar attributes of sovereignty. Their relation to the general government is very imperfectly defined by the Constitution, and it will be found upon examination, that in that instrument the only grant of power concerning them is conveyed in the phrase, "Congress shall have the power to dispose of and make all needful rules and regulations respecting the territory and other property belonging to the United States." Certainly this phraseology is very loose, if it were designed to include in the grant the whole power of legislation over persons as well as things. . . . But the lives and persons of our citizens, with the vast variety of objects connected with them, can not be controlled by an authority which is merely called into existence for the purpose of *making rules and regulations for the disposition and management of property*.

But certain it is that the principle of interference should not be carried beyond the necessary implication which produces it. It should be limited to the creation of proper governments for new countries acquired or settled, and to the necessary provision for their eventual admission into the Union; leaving, in the meantime, the people inhabiting them to regulate their internal concerns in their own way. They are just as capable of doing so as the

---

[7]Greeley and Cleveland, *A Political Textbook*, 179–181. Lewis Cass to A. O. P. Nicholson, Dec. 24, 1847.

people of the States; and they can do so, at any rate, as soon as their political independence is recognized by admission into the Union. During this temporary condition, it is hardly expedient to call into exercise a doubtful and invidious authority, which questions the intelligence of a respectable portion of our citizens, and whose limitation, whatever it may be, will be rapidly approaching its termination—an authority which would give to Congress despotic power, uncontrolled by the Constitution, over most important sections of our common country. For, if the regulation of master and servant may be regulated or annihilated by its legislation, so may the relation of husband and wife, parent and child, and of any other condition which our institutions and the habits of our society recognize. . . .

Briefly, then, I am opposed to the exercise of any jurisdiction by Congress over this matter, and I am in favor of leaving to the people of any territory which may be hereafter acquired, the right to regulate it for themselves under the general principles of the Constitution. Because—

1. I do not see in the Constitution any grant of the requisite power to Congress; and I am not disposed to extend a doubtful precedent beyond its necessity,—the establishment of territorial governments when needed,—leaving to the inhabitants all the rights compatible with the relations they bear to the Confederation.

2. Because I believe this measure, if adopted, would weaken, if not impair, the union of the States, and would sow seeds of future discord, which would grow up and ripen into an abundant harvest of calamity.

3. Because I believe a general conviction that such a proposition would succeed, would lead to an immediate withholding of the supplies, and thus to a dishonorable termination of the war. I think no dispassionate observer at the seat of government can doubt this result.

4. If, however, in this I am under a misapprehension, I am under none in the practical operation of this restriction, if adopted by Congress, upon a treaty of peace making acquisition of Mexican territory. Such a treaty would be rejected, just as certainly as presented to the Senate. More than one-third of that body would vote against it, viewing such a principle as an exclusion of the citizens of the slave-holding States from a

participation in the benefits acquired by the treasure and exertions of all, and which should be common to all. . . .

5. But after all, it seems to be generally conceded that this restriction, if carried into effect, could not operate upon any State to be formed from newly-acquired territory. The well known attributes of sovereignty, recognized by us as belonging to the State governments, would sweep before them any such barrier, and would leave to the people to express and exert their will at pleasure. Is the object, then, of temporary exclusion for so short a period as the duration of the territorial government, worth the price at which it would be purchased?—worth the discord it would engender, the trial to which it would expose our Union, and the evils that would be the certain consequences, let that trial result as it might? . . .

. . . The Wilmot proviso seeks to take from its legitimate tribunal a question of domestic policy, having no relation to the Union, as such, and to transfer it to another created by the people for a special purpose, and foreign to the subject matter involved in this issue. By going back to our true principles, we go back to the road of peace and safety. Leave it to the people, who will be affected by this question, to adjust it upon their own responsibility, and in their own manner, and we shall render another tribute to the original principles of our government, and furnish another guarantee for its permanence and prosperity.

READING NO. 8

MASSACHUSETTS LEGISLATURE, RESOLUTIONS ON THE WAR WITH MEXICO[8]

Adopting the view that the "Slave Power" lay behind the Mexican War, the Massachusetts legislature in 1847 passed resolutions against a war allegedly intended to extend slavery and enhance the Slave Power, and control the free states.

γ   γ   γ

It is a War to Strengthen the "Slave Power." But it is not merely proposed to open new markets for slavery: it is also designed to confirm and fortify the "Slave Power." . . . Slavery is odious as an institution, if viewed in the light of morals and Christianity. On this account alone we should refrain from rendering it any voluntary support. But it has been made the basis of a political combination, to which has not inaptly been applied the designation of the "Slave Power." The slaveholders of the country—who are not supposed to exceed 200,000 or at most 300,000 in numbers—by the spirit of union which animates them, by the strong sense of a common interest, and by the audacity of their leaders, have erected themselves into a new "estate," as it were, under the Constitution.

The object of the bold measure of annexation was not only to extend slavery, but to strengthen the "Slave Power." The same object is now proposed by the Mexican war. This is another link in the gigantic chain by which our country and the Constitution are to be bound to the "Slave Power." This has been proclaimed in public journals. The following passage from the *Charleston* (S. C.) *Courier* avows it: "Every battle fought in Mexico, and every dollar spent there, but insures the acquisition of territory which must widen the field of Southern enterprise and power in future. And the final result will be to readjust the balance of

[8]*Old South Leaflets*, Vol. 6, No. 132, 137*ff.*

power in the confederacy, so as to give us control over the operations of government in all time to come."

It is a War Against the Free States. Regarding it as a war to strengthen the "Slave Power," we are conducted to a natural conclusion, that it is virtually, and in its consequences, a war against the free States of the Union. Conquest and robbery are attempted in order to obtain a political control at home; and distant battles are fought, less with a special view of subjugating Mexico than with the design of overcoming the power of the free States, under the Constitution. . . .

Criminality of the War. And it is also a violation of the fundamental law of Heaven, of that great law of Right which is written by God's own finger on the heart of man. . . . The war is a crime, and all who have partaken in the blood of its well-fought fields have aided in its perpetration. . . .

Resolves. Concerning the Mexican War, and the Institution of Slavery.

Resolved, That the present war with Mexico has its primary origin in the unconstitutional annexation to the United States of the foreign State of Texas, while the same was still at war with Mexico; that it was unconstitutionally commenced by the order of the President, to General Taylor, to take military possession of territory in dispute between the United States and Mexico, and in the occupation of Mexico; and that it is now waged in-gloriously,—by a powerful nation against a weak neighbor,—unnecessarily and without just cause, at immense cost of trea-sure and life, for the dismemberment of Mexico, and for the conquest of a portion of her territory, from which slavery has already been excluded, with the triple object of extending slav-ery, of strengthening the "Slave Power," and of obtaining the control of the Free States, under the Constitution of the United States.

Resolved, That such a war of conquest so hateful in its objects, so wanton, unjust, and unconstitutional in its origin and charac-ter, must be regarded as a war against freedom, against human-ity, against justice, against the Union, against the Constitution, and against the Free States. . . .

Resolved, That our attention is directed anew to the wrong and "enormity" of slavery, and to the tyranny and usurpation of the

"Slave Power," as displayed in the history of our country, particularly in the annexation of Texas, and the present war with Mexico; . . . and a just self-defence, make it specially incumbent on the people of the free States to co-operate in strenuous exertions to restrain and overthrow the "Slave Power."

READING NO. 9

ROBERT TOOMBS, SPEECH IN THE HOUSE OF REPRESENTATIVES, 1849[9]

The Wilmot Proviso's principle that Congress could outlaw slavery in the new territories won favor in the House, alarming Robert Toombs of Georgia. During the speakership crisis of 1849; he threatened disunion if Congress prohibited slavery in the territories or the District of Columbia.

γ   γ   γ

Mr. Toombs said the difficulties in the way of the organization of this House are apparent and well understood here, and should be understood by the country. A great sectional question lies at the foundation of all these troubles. . . .

It seems, from the remarks of the gentleman from New York, that we are to be intimidated by eulogies upon the Union, and denunciations of those who are not ready to sacrifice national honor, essential interests, and constitutional rights, upon its altar. Sir, I have as much attachment to the Union of these States, under the Constitution of our fathers, as any freeman ought to have, I am ready to concede and sacrifice for it whatever a just and honorable man ought to sacrifice—I will do no more. I have not heeded the aspersions of those who did not understand, or desired to misrepresent, my conduct or opinions in relation to these questions, which, in my judgment, so vitally affect it. The time has come when I shall not only utter them, but make them the basis of my political action here. I do not, then, hesitate to avow before this House and the country, and in the presence of the living God, that if by your legislation you seek to drive us from the territories of California and New Mexico, purchased by the common blood and treasure of the whole people, and to abolish slavery in this District, thereby attempting to fix a national degradation upon half the States of this Confederacy, *I*

---

[9]*Congressional Globe*, 31st Cong., 1st sess., 27–28.

am for disunion; and if my physical courage be equal to the maintenance of my convictions of right and duty, I will devote all I am and all I have on earth to its consummation. From 1787 to this hour the people of the South have asked nothing but justice—nothing but the maintenance of the principles and the spirit which controlled our fathers in the formation of the Constitution. Unless we are unworthy of our ancestors, we will never accept less as a condition of union. . . . The Territories are the common property of the people of the United States, purchased by their common blood and treasure. You are their common agents; it is your duty, while they are in a territorial state, to remove all impediments to their free enjoyment by all sections and people of the Union, the slaveholder and the non-slaveholder. You have given the strongest indications that you will not perform this trust—that you will appropriate to yourselves all of this Territory, perpetrate all these wrongs which I have enumerated; yet with these declarations on your lips, when southern men refused to act in party caucuses with you, in which you have a controlling majority—when we ask the simplest guarantee for the future—we are denounced out of doors as recusants and factionists, and indoors we are met with the cry of "Union, Union."

READING NO. 10

JOHN C. CALHOUN, ADDRESS OF THE SOUTHERN DELEGATES IN CONGRESS[10]

The leading spokesman of the South, Senator John C. Calhoun, penned the address which described the calamities that emancipation would bring on the South.

γ   γ   γ

If the determination avowed by the North to monopolize all the territories, to the exclusion of the South, should be carried into effect, that of itself would, at no distant day, add to the North a sufficient number of States to give her three-fourths of the whole; when, under the color of an amendment of the Constitution, she would emancipate our slaves, however opposed it might be to its true intent.

To destroy the existing relation between the free and servile races at the South would lead to consequences unparalleled in history. They cannot be separated, and cannot live together in peace, or harmony, or to their mutual advantage, except in their present relation. Under any other, wretchedness, and misery, and desolation would overspread the whole South. The example of the British West Indies, as blighting as emancipation has proved to them, furnishes a very faint picture of the calamities it would bring on the South. . . .

Very different would be the circumstances under which emancipation would take place with us. If it ever should be effected, it will be through the agency of the Federal Government, controlled by the dominant power of the Northern States of the Confederacy, against the resistance and struggle of the Southern. It can then only be effected by the prostration of the white race; and that would necessarily engender the bitterest feelings of hostility between them and the North. But the reverse would be the case between the blacks of the South and the people of the

[10]Cralle, ed., *Works*, VI, 308–311.

North. Owing their emancipation to them, they would regard them as friends, guardians, and patrons, and center, accordingly, all their sympathy in them. The people of the North would not fail to reciprocate and to favor them, instead of the whites. Under the influence of such feelings, and impelled by fanaticism and love of power, they would not stop at emancipation. Another step would be taken—to raise them to a political and social equality with their former owners, by giving them the right of voting and holding public offices under the Federal Government. We see the first step toward it in the bill already alluded to—to vest the free blacks and slaves with the right to vote on the question of emancipation in this District. *But when once raised to an equality, they would become the fast political associates of the North, acting and voting with them on all questions, and by this political union between them, holding the white race at the South in complete subjection.*

READING NO. 11

THE TEXAS AND NEW MEXICO ACT AND THE FUGITIVE SLAVE ACT[11]

The Texas and New Mexico Act of 1850 in addition to settling the Texas Boundary question incorporated the new compromise principle of popular sovereignty. At the same time, Southerners secured a new stringent fugitive slave law.

γ γ γ

2. THE TEXAS AND NEW MEXICO ACT
September 9, 1850

Sec. 2. . . . all that portion of the Territory of the United States bounded as follows (boundaries) . . . is hereby erected into a temporary government, by the name of the Territory of New Mexico: *Provided,* That nothing in this act contained shall be construed to inhibit the government of the United States from dividing said Territory into two or more Territories, in such manner and at such times as Congress shall deem convenient and proper, or from attaching any portion thereof to any other Territory or State: *And provided, further,* That, when admitted as a State, the said Territory, or any portion of the same, shall be received into the Union, with or without slavery, as their constitution may prescribe at the time of their admission.

4. FUGITIVE SLAVE ACT
(September 18, 1850)

Sec. 5. . . . all good citizens are hereby commanded to aid and assist in the prompt and efficient execution of this law, whenever their services may be required, as aforesaid, for that purpose; and said warrants shall run, and be executed by said officers, any where in the State within which they are issued.

SEC. 6. That when a person held to service or labor in any State or Territory of the United States, has heretofore or shall hereafter escape into another State or Territory of the United

---

[11]*U.S. Statutes at Large,* IX, 446*ff.* and 462*ff.*

States, the person or persons to whom such service or labor may be due, . . . may pursue and reclaim such fugitive person, . . . causing such person to be taken, forthwith before such court, judge, or commissioner, whose duty it shall be to hear and determine the case of such claimant in a summary manner; and upon satisfactory proof being made, . . . of the identity of the person whose service or labor is claimed to be due as aforesaid, that the person so arrested does in fact owe service or labor to the person or persons claiming him or her, in the State or Territory. . . to make out and deliver to such claimant, his or her agent or attorney, a certificate setting forth the substantial facts as to the service or labor due from such fugitive to the claimant, and of his or her escape from the State of Territory in which he or she was arrested, with authority to such claimant, . . . to use such reasonable force and restraint as may be necessary, under the circumstances of the case, to take and remove such fugitive person back to the State or Territory whence he or she may have escaped as aforesaid. In no trial or hearing under this act shall the testimony of such alleged fugitive be admitted in evidence; and the certificates in this and the first [fourth] section mentioned, shall be conclusive of the right of the person or persons in whose favor granted, to remove such fugitive to the State or Territory from which he escaped, and shall prevent all molestation of such person or persons by any process issued by any court, judge, magistrate, or other person whomsoever.

SEC. 7. That any persons who shall knowingly and willingly obstruct, hinder, or prevent such claimant, . . . be subject to a fine not exceeding one thousand dollars, and imprisonment not exceeding six months . . . ; and shall moreover forfeit and pay, by way of civil damages to the party injured by such illegal conduct, the sum of one thousand dollars, for each fugitive so lost as aforesaid. . . .

SEC. 9. That, upon affidavit made by the claimant of such fugitive, . . . that he has reason to apprehend that such fugitive will be rescued by force from his or their possession before he can be taken beyond the limits of the State in which the arrest is made, it shall be the duty of the officer making the arrest to retain such fugitive in his custody, and to remove him to the State whence he fled, and there to deliver him to said claimant, his agent, or attorney. . . .

Sec. 10. That when any person held to service or labor in any State or Territory, or in the District of Columbia, shall escape therefrom, the party to whom such service or labor shall be due, . . . may apply to any court of record therein, . . . and make satisfactory proof to such court, . . . of the escape aforesaid, and that the person escaping owed service or labor to such party. . . . And the said court commissioner, judge, or other person authorized by this act to grant certificates to claimants of fugitives, shall, upon the production of the record and other evidences aforesaid, grant to such claimant a certificate of his right to take any such person identified and proved to be owing service or labor as aforesaid, which certificate shall authorize such claimant to seize or arrest and transport such person to the State or Territory from which he escaped. . . .

READING NO. 12

THE GEORGIA PLATFORM, 1850[12]

Following the Compromise of 1850 a Georgia convention accepted the compromise, withholding full approval and announcing the terms on which Georgia would remain in the Union.

γ   γ   γ

To the end that the position of this State may be clearly apprehended by her Confederates of the South and of the North, and that she may be blameless of all future consequences—

Be it resolved by the people of Georgia in Convention assembled, First. That we hold the American Union secondary in importance only to the rights and principles it was designed to perpetuate. That past associations, present fruition, and future prospects, will bind us to it so long as it continues to be the safeguard of those rights and principles.

Second. That if the thirteen original Parties to the Compact, bordering the Atlantic in a narrow belt, while their separate interests were in embryo, their peculiar tendencies scarcely developed, their revolutionary trials and triumphs still green in memory, found Union impossible without compromise, the thirty-one of this day may well yield somewhat in the conflict of opinion and policy, to preserve that Union which has extended the sway of Republican Government over a vast wilderness to another ocean, and proportionately advanced their civilization and national greatness.

Third. That in this spirit the State of Georgia has maturely considered the action of Congress, embracing a series of measures for the admission of California into the Union, the organization of Territorial Governments for Utah and New Mexico, the establishment of a boundary between the latter and the State of Texas, the suppression of the slave-trade in the District of Columbia, and the extradition of fugitive slaves, and (connected

[12]A. H. Stephens, *The War between the States* (Philadelphia, 1868), II, app. B.

with them) the rejection of propositions to exclude slavery from the Mexican Territories, and to abolish it in the District of Columbia; and, whilst she does not wholly approve, will abide by it as a permanent adjustment of this sectional controversy.

Fourth. That the State of Georgia, in the judgment of this Convention, will and ought to resist, even (as a last resort) to a disruption of every tie which binds her to the Union, any future Act of Congress abolishing Slavery in the District of Columbia, without the consent and petition of the slaveholders thereof, or any Act abolishing Slavery in places within the slave-holding States, purchased by the United States for the erection of forts, magazines, arsenals, dock-yards, navy-yards, and other like purposes; or in any Act suppressing the slave-trade between slave-holding States; or in any refusal to admit as a State any Territory applying because of the existence of Slavery therein; or in any Act prohibiting the introduction of slaves into the Territories of Utah and New Mexico; or in any Act repealing or materially modifying the laws now in force for the recovery of fugitive slaves.

Fifth. That it is the deliberate opinion of this Convention, that upon the faithful execution of the Fugitive Slave Bill by the proper authorities, depends the preservation of our much loved Union.

READING NO. 13

HARRIET BEECHER STOWE, *UNCLE TOM'S CABIN*[13]

In her sensational novel, Uncle Tom's Cabin, *Harriet Beecher Stowe personified good and evil in the characters of Uncle Tom, the pious black victim of slavery, and Simon Legree, the cruel white master.*

γ　　　　　γ　　　　　γ

Mr. Simon Legree, Tom's master, had purchased slaves at one place and another, in New Orleans, to the number of eight, and driven them, handcuffed, in couples of two and two, down to the good steamer Pirate, which lay at the levee, ready for a trip up the Red River.

Having got them fairly on board, and the boat being off, he came round, with that air of efficiency which ever characterized him, to take a review of them. Stopping opposite to Tom, who had been attired for sale in his best broadcloth suit, with well-starched linen and shining boots, he briefly expressed himself as follows:—

"Stand up."

Tom stood up.

"Take off that stock!" and, as Tom, encumbered by his fetters, proceeded to do it, he assisted him, by pulling it, with no gentle hand, from his neck, and putting it in his pocket.

Legree now turned to Tom's trunk, which, previous to this, he had been ransacking, and, taking from it a pair of old pantaloons and a dilapidated coat, which Tom had been wont to put on about his stable-work, he said, liberating Tom's hands from the handcuffs, and pointing to a recess in among the boxes,—

"You go there, and put these on."

Tom obeyed, and in a few moments returned.

"Take off your boots," said Mr. Legree.

[13]Harriet Beecher Stowe, *Uncle Tom's Cabin* (Boston, 1889), 376–379.

Tom did so.

"There," said the former, throwing him a pair of coarse stout shoes, such as were common among the slaves, "put these on."

In Tom's hurried exchange, he had not forgotten to transfer his cherished Bible to his pocket. It was well he did so; for Mr. Legree, having refitted Tom's handcuffs, proceeded deliberately to investigate the contents of his pockets. He drew out a silk handkerchief, and put it into his own pocket. Several little trifles, which Tom had treasured, chiefly because they had amused Eva, he looked upon with a contemptuous grunt, and tossed them over his shoulder into the river.

Tom's Methodist hymn-book, which, in his hurry, he had forgotten, he now held up and turned over.

"Humph! pious, to be sure. So, what's yer name,—you belong to the church, eh?"

"Yes, Mas'r," said Tom, firmly.

"Well, I'll soon have *that* out of you. I have non o' yer bawling, praying, singing niggers on my place; so remember. Now, mind yourself," he said, with a stamp and a fierce glance of his gray eye, directed at Tom, "*I'm* your church now! You understand,—you've got to be as I say."

Something within the silent black man answered *No!* and, as if repeated by an invisible voice, came the words of an old pro-phetic scroll, as Eva had often read them to him,—"Fear not! for I have redeemed thee. I have called thee by my name. Thou art MINE!"

But Simon Legree heard no voice. That voice is one he never shall hear. He only glared for a moment on the downcast face of Tom, and walked off. He took Tom's trunk, which contained a very neat and abundant wardrobe, to the forecastle, where it was soon surrounded by various hands of the boat. With much laughing, at the expense of niggers who tried to be gentlemen, the articles very readily were sold to one and another, and the empty trunk finally put up at auction. It was a good joke, they all thought, especially to see how Tom looked after his things, as they were going this way and that; and then the auction of the trunk, that was funnier than all, and occasioned abundant witti-cisms.

This little affair being over, Simon sauntered up again to his property.

"Now, Tom, I've relieved you of any extra baggage, you see. Take mighty good care of them clothes. It'll be long enough 'fore you get more. I go in for making niggers careful; one suit has to do for one year, on my place."

Simon next walked up to the place where Emmeline was sitting, chained to another woman.

"Well, my dear," he said, chucking her under the chin, "keep up your spirits."

The involuntary look of horror, fright, and aversion with which the girl regarded him, did not escape his eye. He frowned fiercely.

"None o' your shines, gal! you's got to keep a pleasant face, when I speak to ye—d' ye hear? And you, you old yellow poco moonshine!" he said, giving a shove to the mulatto woman to whom Emmeline was chained, "don't you carry that sort of face! You's got to look chipper, I tell ye!"

"I say, all on ye," he said, retreating a pace or two back, "look at me,—look at me,—look me right in the eye,—*straight,* now!" said he, stamping his foot at every pause.

As by a fascination, every eye was now directed to the glaring greenish-gray eye of Simon.

"Now," said he, doubling his great, heavy fist into something resembling a blacksmith's hammer, "d' ye see this fist? Heft it!" he said, bringing it down on Tom's hand. "Look at these yer bones! Well, I tell ye this yer fist has got as hard as iron *knocking down niggers.* I never see the nigger, yet, I couldn't bring down with one crack," said he, bringing his fist down so near to the face of Tom that he winked and drew back. "I don't keep none o' yer cussed overseers; I does my own overseeing; and I tell you things *is* seen to. You's every one on ye got to toe the mark, I tell ye; quick,—straight,—the moment I speak. That's the way to keep in with me. Ye won't find no soft spot in me, nowhere. So, now, mind yerselves; for I don't show no mercy!"

The women involuntarily drew in their breath, and the whole gang sat with downcast, dejected faces. Meanwhile, Simon turned on his heel, and marched up to the bar of the boat for a dram.

READING NO. 14

WENDELL PHILLIPS, PHILOSOPHY OF THE ABOLITION MOVEMENT[14]

The great abolitionist orator Wendell Phillips, recognizing the unpopularity of his cause, in 1853 explained and defended the abolition movement to a Northern audience.

γ   γ   γ

Every thoughtful and unprejudiced mind must see that such an evil as slavery will yield only to the most radical treatment. If you consider the work we have to do, you will not think us needlessly aggressive, or that we dig down unnecessarily deep in laying the foundations of our enterprise. A money power of two thousand millions of dollars, as the prices of slaves now range, held by a small body of able and desperate men; that body raised into a political aristocracy by special constitutional provisions; cotton, the product of slave labor, forming the basis of our whole foreign commerce, and the commercial class thus subsidized; the press bought up, the pulpit reduced to vassalage, the heart of the common people chilled by a bitter prejudice against the black race; our leading men bribed, by ambition, either to silence or open hostility;—in such a land, on what shall an Abolitionist rely? On a few cold prayers, mere lip-service, and never from the heart? On a church resolution, hidden often in its records, and meant only as a decent cover for servility in daily practice? On political parties, with their superficial influence at best, and seeking ordinarily only to use existing prejudices to the best advantage? Slavery has deeper root here than any aristocratic institution has in Europe; and politics is but the common pulse-beat, of which revolution is the fever-spasm. Yet we have seen European aristocracy survive storms which seemed to reach down to the primal strata of European life. Shall we, then,

---

[14]Wendell Phillips, *Speeches, Lectures, and Letters by Wendell Phillips*, (Boston, 1863), 98*ff*.

trust to mere politics, where even revolution has failed? How shall the stream rise above its fountain? Where shall our church organizations or parties get strength to attack their great parent and moulder, the Slave Power? Shall the thing formed say to him that formed it, Why hast thou made me thus? The old jest of one who tried to lift himself in his own basket, is but a tame picture of the man who imagines that, by working solely through existing sects and parties, he can destroy slavery. Mechanics say nothing but an earthquake, strong enough to move all Egypt, can bring down the Pyramids.

Experience has confirmed these views. The Abolitionists who have acted on them have a "short method" with all unbelievers. They have but to point to their own success, in contrast with every other man's failure. To waken the nation to its real state, and chain it to the consideration of this one duty, is half the work. So much we have done. Slavery has been made the question of this generation. To startle the South to madness, so that every step she takes, in her blindness, is one step more toward ruin, is much. This we have done. Witness Texas and the Fugitive Slave Law. To have elaborated for the nation the only plan of redemption, pointed out the only exodus from this "sea of troubles," is much. This we claim to have done in our motto of IMMEDIATE, UNCONDITIONAL EMANCIPATION ON THE SOIL. The closer any statesmanlike mind looks into the question, the more favor our plan finds with it. The Christian asks fairly of the infidel, "If this Religion be not from God, how do you explain its triumph, and the history of the first three centuries?" Our question is similar. If our agitation has not been wisely planned and conducted, explain for us the history of the last twenty years! Experience is a safe light to walk by, and he is not a rash man who expects success in future from the same means which have secured it in times past.

READING NO. 15

GEORGE F. HOLMES, A REVIEW OF UNCLE TOM'S CABIN[15]

In a devastating critique Professor George F. Holmes of the University of Virginia dismissed Uncle Tom's Cabin *as "philanthropic twaddle," "misguided," "pernicious," and "willful slander."*

γ   γ   γ

It should be observed that the whole tenor of this pathetic tale derives most of its significance and colouring from a distorted representation or a false conception of the sentiments and feelings of the slave. It presupposes an identity of sensibilities between the races of the free and the negroes, whose cause it pretends to advocate. It takes advantage of this presumption, so suspiciously credited where slavery is unknown, to arouse sympathies for what might be grievous misery to the white man, but is none to the differently tempered black. Every man adapts himself and his feelings more or less to the circumstances of his condition: without this wise provision of nature life would be intolerable to most of us. Every race in like manner becomes habituated to the peculiar accidents of its particular class; even the Paria may be happy. Thus what would be insupportable to one race, or one order of society, constitutes no portion of the wretchedness of another. The joys and the sorrows of the slave are in harmony with his position, and are entirely dissimilar from what would make the happiness, or misery, of another class. It is therefore an entire fallacy, or a criminal perversion of truth, according to the motive of the writer, to attempt to test all situations by the same inflexible rules, and to bring to the judgment of the justice of slavery the prejudices and opinions which have been formed when all the characteristics of slavery are not known but imagined.

---

[15] "Uncle Tom's Cabin," *Southern Literary Messenger*, XVIII(December 1852), 721*ff.*

The proposition, then, which may be regarded as embodying the peculiar essence of Uncle Tom's Cabin, is a palpable fallacy, and inconsistent with all social organization. Granting, therefore, all that could be asked by our adversaries, it fails to furnish any proof whatever of either the inquity or the enormity of slavery. If it was capable of proving anything at all, it would prove too much. It would demonstrate that all order, law, government, society was a flagrant and unjustifiable violation of the rights, and mockery of the feelings of man and ought to be abated as a public nuisance. The hand of Ishmael would thus be raised against every man, and every man's hand against him. To this result, indeed, both the doctrines and practices of the higher-law agitators at the North, and as set forth in this portentous book of sin, unquestionably tend: and such a conclusion might naturally be anticipated from their sanctimonious professions. The fundamental position, then, of these dangerous and dirty little volumes is a deadly blow to all the interests and duties of humanity, and is utterly impotent to show any inherent vice in the institution of slavery which does not also appertain to all other institutions whatever. But we will not be content to rest here: we will go a good bow-shot beyond this refutation, though under no necessity to do so; and we maintain that the distinguishing characteristic of slavery is its tendency to produce effects exactly opposite to those laid to its charge; to diminish the amount of individual misery in the servile classes; to mitigate and alleviate all the ordinary sorrows of life; to protect the slaves against want as well as against material and mental suffering; to prevent the separation and dispersion of families; and to shield them from the frauds, the crimes, and the casualties of others, whether masters or fellow-slaves, in a more eminent degree than is attainable under any other organization of society, where slavery does not prevail. This is but a small portion of the peculiar advantages to the slaves themselves resulting from the institution of slavery, but these suffice for the present, and furnish a most overwhelming refutation of the philanthropic twaddle of this and similar publications. . . .

We dismiss Uncle Tom's Cabin with the conviction and declaration that every holier purpose of our nature is misguided, every charitable sympathy betrayed, every loftier sentiment polluted, every moral purpose wrenched to wrong, and every patriotic feeling outraged, by its criminal prostitution of the high functions of the imagination to the pernicious intrigues of sectional animosity, and to the petty calumnies of willful slander.

READING NO. 16

POPULATION, REPORT ON
THE EIGHTH CENSUS[16]

*The United States Census Bureau in 1860 described the huge
growth of population in the preceding decade and its distribution
over the nation.*

γ   γ   γ

Though the number of States has increased during the last
decenial period from thirty-one to thirty-four, and five new
Territories have been organized, the United States has received
no accessions of territory within that term, except a narrow strip
to the southward of the Colorado river, along the Mexican line,
not yet inhabited. As general good health prevailed, and peace
reigned throughout the country, there was no apparent cause of
disturbance or interruption to the natural progress of population.
It is true that the very large immigration from Europe, together
with an influx of considerable magnitude from Asia to California, has added largely to the augmentation which the returns
show to have taken place during the decade.

In comparing the gain of any class of the population, or of the
whole of it, one decade with another, the rate per cent. is not a
full test of advancement. The *rate* of gain necessarily diminishes
with the density of population, while the absolute increase
continues unabated. The actual increase of the entire free and
slave population from 1850 to 1860, omitting the Indian tribes,
was 8,225,464, and the rate per cent. is set down at 35.46; while
from 1840 to 1850 the positive increment of all classes were
6,112,423, yet the ratio of gain was 35.87 per cent. . . . No more
striking evidence can be given of the rapid advancement of our
country in the first element of national progress than that the
increase of its inhabitants during the last ten years is greater by

[16]U.S. Bureau of the Census, *Preliminary Report on the Eighth Census* (Washington, 1862), 3*ff.*

more than 1,000,000 of souls than the whole population in 1810, and nearly as great as the entire number of people in 1820. That the whole of this gain is not from natural increase, but is, in part, derived from the influx of foreigners seeking here homes for themselves and their children, is a fact which may justly enhance rather than detract from the satisfaction wherewith we should regard this augmentation of our numbers.

Thus far in our history no State has declined in population. Vermont has remained nearly stationary, and is saved from a positive loss of inhabitants by only one-third of one per cent. New Hampshire, likewise, has gained but slowly, her increment being only 8,097, or two and one-half per cent. on that of 1850. Maine has made the satisfactory increase of 45,110, or 7.74 per cent. The old agricultural States may be said to be filled up, so far as regards the resources adapted to a rural population in the present condition of agricultural science. The conditions of their increase undergo a change upon the general occupation and allotment of their areas. Manufactures and commerce, then, come in to supply the means of subsistence to an excess of inhabitants beyond what the ordinary cultivation of the soil can sustain. This point in the progress of population has been reached, and, perhaps, passed in most, if not all, of the New England States. But while statistical science may demonstrate within narrow limits the number of persons who may extract a subsistence from each square mile of arable land, it cannot compute with any reasonable approach to certainty the additional population, resident on the same soil, which may obtain its living by the thousand branches of artificial industry which the demands of society and civilization have created.

South Carolina has gained during the decade 35,201 inhabitants of all conditions, equal to 5.27 per cent. Of this increase 16,825 are whites, and the remainder free colored and slaves. It is perhaps a little remarkable that the relative increase of the free colored class in this State was more considerable than that of any other. As their number, 9914, is so small as to excite neither apprehension or jealousy among the white race, the increase is probably due both to manumission and natural causes. This State has made slower progress during the last term than any other in the south, having advanced only from 27.28 to 28.72 inhabitants to the square mile. . . .

Turning now to the States which have made the most rapid advance, we find that New York has increased from 3,097,394 to 3,880,735, exhibiting an augmentation of 783,341 inhabitants, being at the rate of 25.29 per cent. The free colored population has fallen off 64 since 1850, a diminution to be accounted for probably by the operation of the fugitive slave law, which induced many colored persons to migrate further north.

The gain of Pennsylvania has been in round numbers 595,000. In that State the free colored have increased about 3,000. The greater mildness of the climate and a milder type of the prejudices connected with this class of population, the result of benevolent influences and its proximity to the slaveholding States, may account for the fact that this race holds its own in Pennsylvania, while undergoing a diminution in the State next adjoining on the north.

Minnesota was chiefly unsettled territory at the date of the Seventh Census; its large present population, as shown by the returns, is therefore nearly clear gain.

The vast region of Texas ten years since was comparatively a wilderness. It has now a population of over 600,000, and the rate of its increase is given as 184 per cent.

Illinois presents the most wonderful example of great, continuous, and healthful increase. In 1830 Illinois contained 157,445 inhabitants; in 1840, 476,183; in 1850, 851,470; in 1860, 1,711,951. The gain during the last decade was, therefore, 860,481, or 101.06 per cent. So large a population, more than doubling itself in ten years, by the regular course of settlement and natural increase, is without a parallel. The condition to which Illinois has attained under the progress of the last thirty years is a monument of the blessings of industry, enterprise, peace, and free institutions.

The growth of Indiana in population, though less extraordinary than that of her neighboring State, has been most satisfactory, her gain during the decade having been 362,000, or more than thirty-six per cent. upon her number in 1850.

Michigan, Wisconsin, and Iowa have participated to the full extent in the surprising development of the northwest. The remarkable healthfulness of the climate of that region seems to more than compensate for its rigors, and the fertility of the new soil leads men eagerly to contend with and overcome the harshness of the elements. The energies thus called into action have, in a few years, made the States of the northwest the granary of Europe, and that section of our Union which, within the recollection of living men, was a wilderness is now the chief source of supply in seasons of scarcity for the suffering millions of another continent.

Looking cursorily over the returns, it appears that the fifteen slaveholding States contain 12,240,000 inhabitants, of whom 8,039,000 are whites, 251,000 free colored persons, and 3,950,000 are slaves. The actual gain of the whole population in those States from 1850 to 1860, was 2,627,000, equal to 27.33 per cent. The slaves advanced in numbers 749,931 or 23.44 per cent. This does not include the slaves of the District of Columbia, who decreased 502 in the course of the ten years. The nineteen free States and seven Territories, together with the federal District, contained, according to the Eighth Census, 19,201,546 persons, including 27,749 Indians; of whom 18,936,579 were white, and 237,218 free colored. The increase of both classes was 5,598,603, or 41.24 per cent. No more satisfactory indication of the advancing prosperity of the country could be desired than this general and remarkable progress in population. North and south we find instances of unprecedented gains, as in the case of Illinois, just adverted to. In the southwest the great State of Missouri has increased by the number of 500,000 inhabitants, which is within a fraction of 74 per cent. It is due to candor to state that the marked disproportion between the rate of gain in the north and south respectively, is manifestly to some extent caused by the larger number of immigrants who settle in the former section, on account of congeniality of climate, the variety of occupation, the dignity wherewith respectable employment is invested, and the freedom of labor.

READING NO. 17

THE KANSAS-NEBRASKA ACT[17]

The act defined the boundaries of two new territories, repealed the 1820 guarantee of "forever" prohibiting slavery in the Northern Louisiana Territory, and substituted the new principle of popular sovereignty.

ϒ   ϒ   ϒ

Be it enacted . . . , That all that part of the territory of the United States included within the following limits . . . is hereby created into a temporary government by the name of the Territory of Nebraska; and when admitted as a State or States, the said Territory, or any portion of the same, shall be received into the Union with or without slavery, as their constitution may prescribe at the time of their admission: . . .

SEC. 14. *And be it further enacted,* . . . That the Constitution, and all laws of the United States which are not locally inapplicable, shall have the same force and effect within the said Territory of Nebraska as elsewhere within the United States, except the eighth section of the act preparatory to the admission of Missouri into the Union, approved March 6, 1820, which, being inconsistent with the principle of non-intervention by Congress with slavery in the States and Territories, as recognized by the legislation of eighteen hundred and fifty, commonly called the Compromise Measures, is hereby declared inoperative and void; it being the true intent and meaning of this act not to legislate slavery into any Territory or State, nor to exclude it therefrom, but to leave the people thereof perfectly free to form and regulate their domestic institutions in their own way, subject only to the Constitution of the United States: *Provided,* That nothing herein contained shall be construed to revive or put in force any law or regulation which may have existed prior to the act of March 6, 1820, either protecting, establishing, prohibiting, or abolishing slavery. . . .

---

[7]U.S. Statutes at Large, X, 277*ff.*

SEC. 19. *And be it further enacted,* That all that part of the Territory of the United States included within the following limits, except such portions thereof as are hereinafter expressly exempted from the operations of this act, to wit, beginning at a point on the western boundary of the State of Missouri, where the thirty-seventh parallel of north latitude crosses the same; thence west on said parallel to the eastern boundary of New Mexico; thence north on said boundary to latitude thirty-eight; thence following said boundary westward to the east boundary of the Territory of Utah, on the summit of the Rocky Mountains; thence northward on said summit to the fortieth parallel of latitude; thence east on said parallel to the western boundary of the State of Missouri; thence south with the western boundary of said State to the place of beginning, be, and the same is hereby, created into a temporary government by the name of the Territory of Kansas; and when admitted as a State or States, the said Territory, or any portion of the same, shall be received into the Union with or without slavery, as their constitution may prescribe at the time of their admission: . . .

READING NO. 18

APPEAL OF THE INDEPENDENT DEMOCRATS[18]

*The Kansas-Nebraska Act, passed by a Democratic adminis-
tration, shattered old party allegiances and provoked an angry
response from "independent Democrats."*

γ   γ   γ

As Senators and Representatives in the Congress of the United
States it is our duty to warn our constituents, whenever imminent danger menaces the freedom of our institutions or the
permanency of the Union. . . .

At the present session a new Nebraska bill has been reported
by the Senate Committee on Territories, which, should it unhap-
pily receive the sanction of Congress, will open all the unorganized Territories of the Union to the ingress of slavery.

We arraign this bill as a gross violation of a sacred pledge; as a
criminal betrayal of precious rights; as part and parcel of an
atrocious plot to exclude from a vast unoccupied region immigrants from the Old World and free laborers from our own States,
and convert it into a dreary region of despotism, inhabited by
masters and slaves. . . .

This immense region, occupying the very heart of the North
American Continent, and larger, by thirty-three thousand square
miles, than all the existing free States—including California
. . . this immense region the bill now before the Senate, without
reason and without excuse, but in flagrant disregard of sound
policy and sacred faith, purposes to open to slavery. . . .

We confess our total inability properly to delineate the character or describe the consequences of this measure. Language fails
to express the sentiments of indignation and abhorrence which it
inspires; and no vision less penetrating and comprehensive than
that of the All-Seeing can reach its evil issues. . . .

---

[18]J. W. Schuckers, *The Life and Public Services of Salmon P. Chase* (New York,
1874), 140*ff.*

191

We appeal to the people. We warn you that the dearest interests of freedom and the Union are in imminent peril. Demagogues may tell you that the Union can be maintained only by submitting to the demands of slavery. We tell you that the Union can only be maintained by the full recognition of the just claims of freedom and man. The Union was formed to establish justice and secure the blessings of liberty. When it fails to accomplish these ends it will be worthless, and when it becomes worthless it cannot long endure.

We entreat you to be mindful of that fundamental maxim of Democracy—EQUAL RIGHTS AND EXACT JUSTICE FOR ALL MEN. Do not submit to become agents in extending legalized oppression and systematized injustice over a vast territory yet exempt from these terrible evils.

We implore Christians and Christian ministers to interpose. Their divine religion requires them to behold in every man a brother, and to labor for the advancement and regeneration of the human race.

Whatever apologies may be offered for the toleration of slavery in the States, none can be offered for its extension into Territories where it does not exist, and where that extension involves the repeal of ancient law and the violation of solemn compact. Let all protest, earnestly and emphatically, by correspondence, through the press, by memorials, by resolutions of public meetings and legislative bodies, and in whatever other mode may seem expedient, against this enormous crime.

For ourselves, we shall resist it by speech and vote, and with all the abilities which God has given us. Even if overcome in the impending struggle, we shall not submit. We shall go home to our constituents, erect anew the standard of freedom, and call on the people to come to the rescue of the country from the domination of slavery. We will not despair; for the cause of human freedom is the cause of God.

S. P. Chase
Charles Sumner
J. R. Giddings
Edward Wade
Gerritt Smith
Alexander De Witt.

READING NO. 19

THE OSTEND MANIFESTO[19]

Responding to expansionist sentiment, three United States ministers issued the notorious manifesto justifying taking Cuba from Spain.

γ　　　　γ　　　　γ

Aix la Chapelle, October 18, 1854.

Sir:—The undersigned, in compliance with the wish expressed by the President in the several confidential despatches you have addressed to us, respectively, to that effect, have met in conference, first at Ostend, in Belgium, on the 9th, 10th, and 11th instant, and then at Aix la Chapelle, in Prussia, on the days next following, up to the date hereof. . . .

We have arrived at the conclusion, and are thoroughly convinced, that an immediate and earnest effort ought to be made by the government of the United States to purchase Cuba from Spain at any price for which it can be obtained, not exceeding the sum of $—. . . .

But if Spain, dead to the voice of her own interest, and actuated by stubborn pride and a false sense of honor, should refuse to sell Cuba to the United States, then the question will arise, What ought to be the course of the American government under such circumstances? Self-preservation is the first law of nature, with States as well as with individuals. All nations have, at different periods, acted upon this maxim. Although it has been made the pretext for committing flagrant injustice, as in the partition of Poland and other similar cases which history records, yet the principle itself, though often abused, has always been recognized. . . .

Our past history forbids that we should acquire the island of Cuba without the consent of Spain, unless justified by the great law of self-preservation. We must, in any event, preserve our own conscious rectitude and our own self-respect.

[19]U. S. 33rd Congress, 2nd sess., *House Executive Doc*. No. 93.

Whilst pursuing this course we can afford to disregard the censures of the world, to which we have been so often and so unjustly exposed.

After we shall have offered Spain a price for Cuba far beyond its present value, and this shall have been refused, it will then be time to consider the question, does Cuba, in the possession of Spain, seriously endanger our internal peace and existence of our cherished Union?

Should this question be answered in the affirmative, then, by every law, human and divine, we shall be justified in wresting it from Spain if we possess the power; and this upon the very same principle that would justify an individual in tearing down the burning house of his neighbor if there were no other means of preventing the flames from destroying his own home.

Under such circumstances we ought neither to count the cost nor regard the odds which Spain might enlist against us. We forbear to enter into the question, whether the present condition of the island would justify such a measure? We should, however, be recreant to our duty, be unworthy of our gallant forefathers, and commit base treason against our posterity, should we permit Cuba to be Africanized and become a second St. Domingo, with all its attendant horrors to the white race, and suffer the flames to extend to our own neighboring shores seriously to endanger or actually to consume the fair fabric of our Union.

We fear that the course and current of events are rapidly tending towards such a catastrophe. We, however, hope for the best, though we ought certainly to be prepared for the worst. . . .

Yours, very respectfully,

James Buchanan.

J. Y. Mason.

Pierre Soulé.

Hon. Wm. L. Marcy, Secretary of State.

READING NO. 20

ABRAHAM LINCOLN, SPEECH AT PEORIA, ILLINOIS, 1854[20]

In a reply to a speech by Stephen A. Douglas, Abraham Lincoln branded repeal of the Missouri Compromise as wrong, acknowledged a constitutional right to reclaiming fugitive slaves, and urged Americans North and South to oppose the new principle.

γ γ γ

This is the *repeal* of the Missouri Compromise. . . .

I think, and shall try to show, that it is wrong; wrong in its direct effect, letting slavery into Kansas and Nebraska—and wrong in its prospective principle, allowing it to spread to every other part of the wide world, where men can be found inclined to take it.

This *declared* indifference, but as I must think, covert *real* zeal for the spread of slavery, I cannot but hate. I hate it because of the monstrous injustice of slavery itself. I hate it because it deprives our republican example of its just influence in the world. . . .

Before proceeding, let me say I think I have no prejudice against the Southern people. They are just what we would be in their situation. If slavery did not now exist amongst them, they would not introduce it. If it did now exist amongst us, we should not instantly give it up.

When they remind us of their constitutional rights, I acknowledge them, not grudgingly, but fully, and fairly; and I would give them any legislation for the reclaiming of their fugitives, which should not, in its stringency, be more likely to carry a free man into slavery, than our ordinary criminal laws are to hang an innocent one.

---

[20]Roy P. Basler *et al.*, eds., *The Collected Works of Abraham Lincoln* (9 vols., New Brunswick, N. J., 1953–1955), II, 247*ff.*

But all this, to my judgment, furnishes no more excuse for permitting slavery to go into our own free territory, than it would for reviving the African slave trade by law. The law which forbids the bringing of slaves *from* Africa; and that which has so long forbid the taking them *to* Nebraska, can hardly be distinguished on any moral principle; and the repeal of the former could find quite as plausible excuses as that of the latter.

Fellow countrymen—Americans south, as well as north, shall we make no effort to arrest this? Already the liberal party throughout the world, express the apprehension "that the one retrograde institution in America, is undermining the principles of progress, and fatally violating the noblest political system the world ever saw." This is not the taunt of enemies, but the warning of friends. Is it quite safe to disregard it—to despise it? Is there no danger to liberty itself, in discarding the earliest practice, and first precept of our ancient faith? In our greedy chase to make profit of the negro, let us beware, lest we "cancel and tear to pieces" even the white man's charter of freedom.

Our republican robe is soiled, and trailed in the dust. Let us repurify it. Let us turn and wash it white, in the spirit, if not the blood, of the Revolution. Let us turn slavery from its claims of "moral right," back upon its existing legal rights, and its arguments of "necessity." Let us return it to the position our fathers gave it; and there let it rest in peace. Let us readopt the Declaration of Independence, and with it, the practices, and policy, which harmonize with it. Let North and South—let all Americans—let all lovers of liberty everywhere—join in the great and good work. If we do this, we shall not only have saved the Union; but we shall have so saved it, as to make, and to keep it, forever worthy of the saving. We shall have so saved it, that the succeeding millions of free happy people, the world over, shall rise up, and call us blessed, to the latest generations. . . .

READING NO. 21

MASSACHUSETTS PERSONAL LIBERTY ACT, 1855[21]

Scene of Anthony Burns's forced return to slavery, Massachusetts reacted with a severe personal liberty law aimed at withdrawing state support from the return of fugitive slaves. It aggravated North-South relations.

γ   γ   γ

Sec. 6. If any claimant shall appear to demand the custody or possession of the person for whose benefit such writ is sued out, such claimant shall state in writing the facts on which he relies, with precision and certainty; and neither the claimant of the alleged fugitive, nor any person interested in his alleged obligation to service or labor, nor the alleged fugitive, shall be permitted to testify at the trial of the issue; and no confessions, admissions or declarations of the alleged fugitive against himself shall be given in evidence. Upon every question of fact involved in the issue, the burden of proof shall be on the claimant, and the facts alleged and necessary to be established, must be proved by the testimony of at least two credible witnesses, or other legal evidence equivalent thereto, and by the rules of evidence known and secured by the common law, . . .

Sec. 11. Any person who shall act as counsel or attorney for any claimant of any alleged fugitive from service or labor, under or by virtue of the acts of congress mentioned in the ninth section of this act, shall be deemed to have resigned any commission from the Commonwealth that he may possess, and he shall be thereafter incapacitated from appearing as counsel or attorney in the courts of this Commonwealth. . . .

Sec. 14. Any person holding any judicial office under the constitution or laws of this Commonwealth, who shall continue, for ten

---

[21]*Acts and Resolves Passed by the General Court of Massachusetts in the Year 1855,* 924 *ff.*

days after the passage of this act, to hold the office of United
States commissioner, or any office . . . which qualifies him to
issue any warrant or other process . . . under the [Fugitive Slave
Acts] shall be deemed to have violated good behavior, to have
given reason for the loss of public confidence, and furnished
sufficient ground either for impeachment or for removal by
address.

Sec. 15. Any sheriff, deputy sheriff, jailer, coroner, constable, or
other officer of this Commonwealth, or the police of any city or
town, or any district, county, city or town officer, or any officer
or other member of the volunteer militia of this Commonwealth,
who shall hereafter arrest . . . any person for the reason that he is
claimed or adjudged to be a fugitive from service or labor, shall
be punished by fine . . . and by imprisonment. . . .

Sec. 16. The volunteer militia of the Commonwealth shall not act
in any manner in the seizure . . . of any person for the reason that
he is claimed or adjudged to be a fugitive from service or
labor. . . .

Sec. 19. No jail, prison, or other place of confinement belonging
to, or used by, either the Commonwealth of Massachusetts or any
county therein, shall be used for the detention or imprisonment
of any person accused or convicted of any offence created by [the
Federal Fugitive Slave Acts] . . . or accused or convicted of
obstructing or resisting any process, warrant, or order issued
under either of said acts, or of rescuing, or attempting to rescue,
any person arrested or detained under any of the provisions of
either of the said acts. . . .

READING NO. 22

STEPHEN A. DOUGLAS, SPEECH IN THE SENATE, 1856[22]

Speaking in behalf of an enabling act for Kansas territory, Stephen A. Douglas criticized outside interference in the territory's affairs and upheld "the cardinal principles of self-government, non-intervention, and State equality."

γ   γ   γ

This brings us to the direct and distinct issue between the majority and minority reports—between the supporters and the opponents of the principles involved in the Kansas-Nebraska act. The one affirms the principles of non-intervention from without, and self-government within, the Territories, in strict obedience to the Constitution of the United States; while the other insists that the domestic affairs and internal concerns of the Territories may be controlled by associations and corporations from abroad, under the authority of the Legislatures of the several States, or of Congress, as they may be able to gain the political ascendency over the one or the other. In the prosecution of this line of policy, the opponents of the principles involved in the Kansas-Nebraska act, having failed to accomplish their purposes in the Halls of Congress and under the forms of the Constitution, immediately organized themselves into an emigrant aid association in this city, and through their friends and co-laborers obtained acts of incorporation from the Legislature of Massachusetts, with a capital of five millions of dollars in one instance and one million of dollars in another, to enable them there to accomplish indirectly what they'had found themselves unable to do by the action of Congress. With them it was a great point gained, if, by an organized system of foreign interference, under color of a legislative enactment, they could draw after it a counter movement in conflict with it, and thus produce violence and bloodshed as "the

[22]*Congressional Globe*, 34th Cong., 1st sess., 693.

natural, and perhaps unavoidable, consequence of the experiment," and charge the odium of the whole upon the Nebraska bill and its supporters, as a fulfillment of the predictions which they had made and were resolved should be realized as political capital in the approaching presidential election. They have succeeded by this system of foreign interference in producing violence, and bloodshed, and rebellion in Kansas; and it now only remains to be seen whether the minority report shall be equally successful in convincing the people that "the natural, and perhaps unavoidable, consequences" of their own action are justly chargeable to "the vice of a mistaken law," the principles and provisions of which were intended to be outraged and brought into disrepute by these very proceedings.

When the time shall arrive, and I trust it is near at hand, that the cardinal principles of self-government, non-intervention and State equality, shall be recognized as irrevocable rules of action, binding on all good citizens who regard, and are willing to obey, the Constitution as the supreme law of the land, there will be an end of the slavery controversy in Congress and between the different sections of the Union. The occupation of political agitators whose hopes of position and promotion depend upon their capacity to disturb the peace of the country will be gone. The controversy, if continued, will cease to be a national one— will dwindle into a mere local question, and will affect those only who, by their residence in the particular State or Territory, are interested in it, and have the exclusive right to control it. What right has any State or Territory of this Union to pass any law or do any act with the view of controlling or changing the domestic institutions of any other State or Territory? Do you not recognize an imperative obligation resting on the United States to observe entire and perfect neutrality towards all foreign States with which we are at peace, in respect to their domestic institutions and internal affairs? Has that obligation any higher source of authority than that spirit of comity which all civilized nations acknowledge to be binding on all friendly Powers? Are not the different parts of this Union composed of friendly powers? Are they not all at peace with each other, and hence under an obligation to preserve a friendly forbearance and generous comity quite as sacred and imperative as that to which all foreign States, at peace with each other, acknowledge their obligation to yield implicit obedience? Have you not passed neutrality laws, and exerted the whole executive authority of the Government, including the Army and Navy, to enforce them, in restraining our citizens from interfering with the internal affairs of foreign States and their Territories? Are not the different States and Territories of this Union under the same obligation towards each other? Indeed, does not the Constitution of the United States impose an additional and higher obligation than it is possible for the laws of nations to enjoin on foreign States? How can we hope to preserve peace and fraternal feeling between the different portions of this Union unless we are willing to yield obedience to a principle so just in itself, so fair towards all, that no one can complain of its operation—a principle distinctly recognized by all civilized countries as a fundamental article in the laws of nations, for the reason that the peace of the world could not be preserved for a single day without its observance?

READING NO. 23

WILLIAM PHILLIPS, THE SACK OF LAWRENCE[23]

A correspondent for Horace Greeley's anti-slavery New York
Tribune, *William Phillips reported on the notorious pro-slavery
raid on Lawrence, Kansas.*

γ　　　　　γ　　　　　γ

The army of invasion formed into line and marched into
Lawrence. A motley-looking crew they were; many of them had
red flannel shirts, with curious border ruffian devices on them,
so that they could be recognized by their friends in travelling.
This scarlet uniform gave them some little the appearance of the
"red coats;" and certainly never did such "tories" march to
desecrate American soil, or trample under foot the rights of
American freemen. . . .

The first place attacked was the printing office of the "*Free
State.*" It was in the second story of a concrete building. There
was a store below. One of the ruffian officers entered the store
and demanded of the proprietor if there was a mine under the
building to blow it up. The merchant assured him there was not,
when the interrogator told him that they were going up into the
printing office, and that if anything happened he would hold him
responsible. The "posse" or ruffians, either or both, entered the
office of the *Free State*, and the work of demolition commenced.
The press and other articles were first broken, so as to be
rendered perfectly useless, and then thrown into the Kansas
river. As this was some distance to carry the articles, they got
tired of it, and began throwing the remainder in the street. Books
and papers were thrown in the street. . . .

The office of the other paper in Lawrence, the *Herald of
Freedom*, was entered by the Carolinians, shortly after the

[23]William Phillips, *The Conquest of Kansas by Missouri and Her Allies* (Boston, 1856), 296*ff.*

compatriots had commenced the work of demolition in the *Free State* office. . . . In the *Herald of Freedom* office the same reckless work of destruction went on. The presses were broken in a thorough and *enlightened* manner, which showed the hand or the direction of a practical printer, the fragments being perfectly useless. Books and papers were thrown out in the street, or stolen. Several members of the posse were marching about the streets with books stuck on the points of their bayonets. Others were tearing books to shreds, but the more prudent carried them off.

The next step in the process was the destruction of the hotel. The enemy planted their artillery in front of the hotel, one hundred and fifty feet distant from it, across Massachusetts-street. The hotel was a very large building, three full stories high besides the basement; it seemed almost impossible that they could miss it. The proprietor of the establishment, Mr. Eldrige, was notified by Jones to remove his furniture in a certain time. This Mr. Eldrige said he could not do. Some of the posse went to work and began to carry articles of furniture out into the street; but they very soon got weary of this, and found a task more congenial. They discovered the wines and liquors, a good stock of which was on hand, and, helping themselves freely to these and to eatables and cigars, the heroes of this gallant campaign were soon in an interesting condition.

. . . Some fifty rounds were fired, when, finding it slow business, the hotel looking, externally, little the worse for it, they undertook to blow it up. Four kegs of gunpowder were placed in it, but only two of them exploded, and they made little report, and still less impression on the walls; but fire was communicated to the building in several places, and it was soon a magnificent sea of flame. . . .

And now commenced a scene of wild and reckless pillage. When the citizens of Lawrence had left their homes, those who could locked them; but locks and bolts were small security; when the marauders could not enter by the doors, they got in by the windows. All the money and jewelry that could be found was taken, and also clothing. In fact, they took everything they wanted, or could carry away. Much of what they could not take, they destroyed. . . .

The closing act was the burning of Governor Robinson's

dwelling, which stood upon the brow of Mount Oread. This had been plundered through the day, and at night it was set on fire; and the pyramid of flame from the mount lighted up the pathway of the retreating army.

Besides the plundering in town, these men both before and after the 21st, went about the country, and plundered many houses. It is supposed that not less than two hundred horses were taken, in and around Lawrence. There were also frightful stories of outrages, and of women being ravished. Such cases there may have been, but rare. There were villains in that posse who were certainly none too good for it.

READING NO. 24

REPUBLICAN NATIONAL PLATFORM, 1856[24]

Proclaiming its adherence to old republican principles, the Republican Party platform in 1856 concentrated on securing freedom in the territories, while hitting at the Democrats' policies in Kansas and Cuba and favoring internal improvements by the federal government.

γ γ γ

This Convention of Delegates, assembled in pursuance of a call addressed to the people of the United States, without regard to past political differences or divisions, who are opposed to the repeal of the Missouri Compromise; to the policy of the present Administration; to the extension of Slavery into Free Territory; in favor of the admission of Kansas as a Free State; of restoring the action of the Federal Government to the principles of Washington and Jefferson; and for the purpose of presenting candidates for the offices of President and Vice-President, do

Resolve: That the maintenance of the principles promulgated in the Declaration of Independence, and embodied in the Federal Constitution are essential to the preservation of our Republican institutions, and that the Federal Constitution, the rights of the States, and the union of the States, must and shall be preserved.

Resolved: That, with our Republican fathers, we hold it to be a self-evident truth, that all men are endowed with the inalienable right to life, liberty, and the pursuit of happiness, and that the primary object and ulterior design of our Federal Government were to secure these rights to all persons under its exclusive jurisdiction; that, as our Republican fathers, when they had abolished Slavery in all our National Territory, ordained that no person shall be deprived of life, liberty, or property, without due process of law, it becomes our duty to maintain this provision of

[24]Greeley and Cleveland, *Political Textbook*, 22–23.

the Constitution against all attempts to violate it for the purpose of establishing Slavery in the Territories of the United States by positive legislation, prohibiting its existence or extension therein. That we deny the authority of Congress, of a Territorial Legislation, of any individual, or association of individuals, to give legal existence to Slavery in any Territory of the United States, while the present Constitution shall be maintained.

Resolved: That the Constitution confers upon Congress sovereign powers over the Territories of the United States for their government; and that in the exercise of this power, it is both the right and the imperative duty of Congress to prohibit in the Territories those twin relics of barbarism—Polygamy, and Slavery.

Resolved: That while the Constitution of the United States was ordained and established by the people, in order to "form a more perfect union, establish justice, insure domestic tranquility, provide for the common defense, promote the general welfare, and secure the blessings of liberty," and contain ample provision for the protection of the life, liberty, and property of every citizen, the dearest Constitutional rights of the people of Kansas have been fraudulently and violently taken from them;

Their Territory has been invaded by an armed force;

Spurious and pretended legislative, judicial, and executive officers have been set over them, by whose usurped authority, sustained by the military power of the government, tyrannical and unconstitutional laws have been enacted and enforced;

The right of the people to keep and bear arms has been infringed;

Test oaths of an extraordinary and entangling nature have been imposed as a condition of exercising the right of suffrage and holding office;

The right of an accused person to a speedy and public trial by an impartial jury has been denied;

The right of the people to be secure in their persons, houses, papers, and effects, against unreasonable searches and seizures, has been violated;

They have been deprived of life, liberty, and property without due process of law;

That the freedom of speech and of the press has been abridged;

The right to choose their representatives has been made of no effect;

Murders, robberies, and arsons have been instigated and encouraged, and the offenders have been allowed to go unpunished;

That all these things have been done with the knowledge, sanction, and procurement of the present National Administration; and that for this high crime against the Constitution, the Union, and humanity, we arraign that Administration, the President, his advisers, agents, supporters, apologists, and accessories, either *before* or *after* the fact, before the country and before the world; and that it is our fixed purpose to bring the actual perpetrators of these atrocious outrages and their accomplices to a sure and condign punishment thereafter.

Resolved, That Kansas should be immediately admitted as a state of this Union, with her present Free Constitution, as at once the most effectual way of securing to her citizens the enjoyment of the rights and privileges to which they are entitled, and of ending the civil strife now raging in her territory.

Resolved, That the highwayman's plea, that "might makes right," embodied in the Ostend Circular, was in every respect unworthy of American diplomacy, and would bring shame and dishonor upon any Government or people that gave it their sanction.

Resolved, That a railroad to the Pacific Ocean by the most central and practicable route is imperatively demanded by the interests of the whole country, and that the Federal Government ought to render immediate and efficient aid in its construction, and as an auxiliary thereto, to the immediate construction of an emigrant road on the line of the railroad.

Resolved, That appropriations by Congress for the improvement of rivers and harbors, of a national character, required for the accommodation and security of our existing commerce, are authorized by the Constitution, and justified by the obligation of the Government to protect the lives and property of its citizens.

Resolved, That we invite the affiliation and cooperation of the men of all parties, however differing from us in other respects, in support of the principles herein declared; and believing that the spirit of our institutions as well as the Constitution of our country, guarantees liberty of conscience and equality of rights among citizens, we oppose all legislation impairing their security.

READING NO. 25

DRED SCOTT V. SANDFORD[25]

In the Dred Scott decision Chief Justice Roger B. Taney discussed the questions whether a Negro could become a citizen of the United States, whether slaves were property, and whether Congress could prohibit the holding of slaves in the territories.

γ   γ   γ

TANEY, C. J. . . . There are two leading questions presented by the record:

1. Had the Circuit Court of the United States jurisdiction to hear and determine the case between these parties? And,

2. If it had jurisdiction, is the judgment it has given erroneous or not?

It becomes necessary, therefore, to determine who were citizens of the several States when the Constitution was adopted. And in order to do this, we must recur to the governments and institutions of the thirteen Colonies, when they separated from Great Britain and formed new sovereignties. . . . We must inquire who, at that time, were recognized as the people or citizens of a State. . . .

In the opinion of the court, the legislation and histories of the times, and the language used in the Declaration of Independence, show, that neither the class of persons who had been imported as slaves, nor their descendants, whether they had become free or not, were then acknowledged as a part of the people, nor intended to be included in the general words used in that memorable instrument.

It is difficult at this day to realize the state of public opinion in relation to that unfortunate race, which prevailed in the civilized and enlightened portions of the world at the time of the Declaration of Independence, and when the Constitution of the United States was framed and adopted. . . .

[25]19 Howard, 393 (1857)

They had for more than a century before been regarded as beings of an inferior order; and altogether unfit to associate with the white race, either in social or political relations; and so far inferior that they had no rights which the white man was bound to respect; and that the negro might justly and lawfully be reduced to slavery for his benefit. . . . This opinion was at that time fixed and universal in the civilized portion of the white race. It was regarded as an axiom in morals as well as in politics, which no one thought of disputing, or supposed to be open to dispute; and men in every grade and position in society daily and habitually acted upon it in their private pursuits, as well as in matters of public concern, without doubting for a moment the correctness of this opinion. . . .

And upon a full and careful consideration of the subject, the court is of opinion that, upon the facts stated in the plea in abatement, Dred Scott was not a citizen of Missouri within the meaning of the Constitution of the United States, and not entitled as such to sue in its courts; and, consequently, that the Circuit Court had no jurisdiction of the case, and that the judgment on the plea in abatement is erroneous. . . .

. . . if the Constitution recognizes the right of property of the master in a slave, and makes no distinction between that description of property and other property owned by a citizen, no tribunal, acting under the authority of the United States, whether it be legislative, executive, or judicial, has a right to draw such a distinction, or deny to it the benefit of the provisions and guarantees which have been provided for the protection of private property against the encroachments of the Government.

Now . . . the right of property in a slave is distinctly and expressly affirmed in the Constitution. The right to traffic in it, like an ordinary article of merchandise and property, was guaranteed to the citizens of the United States, in every State that might desire it, for twenty years. And the Government in express terms is pledged to protect it in all future time, if the slave escapes from his owner. . . . And no word can be found in the Constitution which gives Congress a greater power over slave property, or which entitles property of that king to less protection than property of any other description. The only power conferred is the power coupled with the duty of guarding and protecting the owner in his rights.

Upon these considerations, it is the opinion of the court that the Act of Congress which prohibited a citizen from holding and owning property of this kind in the territory of the United States north of the line therein mentioned, is not warranted by the Constitution, and is therefore void; and that neither Dred Scott himself, nor any of his family, were made free by being carried into this territory; even if they had been carried there by the owner, with the intention of becoming a permanent resident. . . .

Upon the whole, therefore, it is the judgment of this court, that it appears by the record before us that the plaintiff in error is not a citizen of Missouri, in the sense in which that word is used in the Constitution; and that the Circuit Court of the United States, for that reason, had no jurisdiction in the case, and could give no judgment in it.

Its judgment for the defendant must, consequently, be reversed, and a mandate issued directing the suit to be dismissed for want of jurisdiction.

WAYNE, J., NELSON, J., GRIER, J., DANIEL, J., CAMPBELL, J., AND CATRON, J., filed separate concurring opinions. McLEAN, J. and CURTIS, J. dissented.

READING NO. 26

FREDERICK DOUGLASS ON THE DRED SCOTT DECISION[26]

Angrily, Frederick Douglass spoke out against the Supreme Court's denial of citizens' rights to blacks and the advance of the Slave Power.

γ　　　　　γ　　　　　γ

We are now told, in tones of lofty exultation, that the day is lost—all lost—and that we might as well give up the struggle. The highest authority has spoken. The voice of the Supreme Court has gone out over the troubled waves of the National Conscience, saying peace, be still. This infamous decision of the slaveholding wing of the Supreme Court maintains that slaves are within the contemplation of the Constitution of the United States, property; that slaves are property in the same sense that horses, sheep, and swine are property; that the old doctrine that slavery is a creature of local law is false; that the right of the slaveholder to his slave does not depend upon the local law, but is secured wherever the Constitution of the United States extends; that Congress has no right to prohibit slavery anywhere; that slavery may go in safety anywhere under the star-spangled banner; that colored persons of African descent have no rights that white men are bound to respect; that colored men of African descent are not and cannot be citizens of the United States. . . .

The Supreme Court of the United States is not the only power in this world. It is very great, but the Supreme Court of the Almighty is greater. Judge Taney can do many things, but he cannot perform impossibilities. He cannot bail out the ocean, annihilate this firm old earth, or pluck the silvery star of liberty from our Northern sky. He may decide, and decide again; but he

[26]Frederick Douglass, *Two Speeches by Frederick Douglass* (Rochester, N. Y., 1857), 31*ff*.

cannot reverse the decision of the Most High. He cannot change the essential nature of things—making evil good, and good, evil.

Happily for the whole human family, their rights have been defined, declared, and decided in a court higher than the Supreme Court. . . . Such a decision cannot stand. God will be true though every man be a liar. We can appeal from this hell-black judgment of the Supreme Court, to the court of common sense and common humanity. We can appeal from man to God. If there is no justice on earth, there is yet justice in heaven. You may close your Supreme Court against the black man's cry for justice, but you cannot, thank God, close against him the ear of a sympathizing world, nor shut up the Court of Heaven. All that is merciful and just, on earth and in Heaven, will execrate and despise this edict of Taney.

If it were at all likely that the people of these free States would tamely submit to this demoniacal judgment, I might feel gloomy and sad over it, and possibly it might be necessary for my people to look for a home in some other country. But as the case stands, we have nothing to fear. In one point of view, we, the abolitionists and colored people, should meet this decision, unlooked for and monstrous as it appears, in a cheerful spirit. This very attempt to blot out forever the hopes of an enslaved people may be one necessary link in the chain of events preparatory to the downfall, and complete overthrow of the whole slave system. . . .

Step by step we have seen the slave power advancing; poisoning, corrupting, and perverting the institutions of the country; growing more and more haughty, imperious, and exacting. The white man's liberty has been marked out for the same grave with the black man's. The ballot box is desecrated, God's law set at nought, armed legislators stalk the halls of Congress, freedom of speech is beaten down in the Senate. The rivers and highways are infested by border ruffians, and white men are made to feel the iron heel of slavery. This ought to arouse us to kill off the hateful thing. They are solemn warnings to which the white people, as well as the black people, should take heed.

If these shall fail, judgment, more fierce or terrible, may come. The lightning, whirlwind, and earthquake may come. Jefferson said that he trembled for his country when he reflected that God is just, and his justice cannot sleep forever. The time may come when even the crushed worm may turn under the tyrant's feet. Goaded by cruelty, stung by a burning sense of wrong, in an awful moment of depression and desperation, the bondman and bondwoman at the South may rush to one wild and deadly struggle for freedom. Already slaveholders go to bed with bowie knives, and apprehend death at their dinners. Those who enslave, rob, and torment their cooks, may well expect to find death in their dinner-pots.

READING NO. 27

JAMES H. HAMMOND, IN
THE U.S. SENATE, 1858[27]

*James H. Hammond, United States senator from South Caro-
lina, in this speech boldly asserted, "Cotton is king," and slaves
were "the very mud-sills of society."*

γ   γ   γ

But if there were no other reason why we should never have a
war, would any sane nation make war on cotton? Without firing a
gun, without drawing a sword, when they make war on us we can
bring the whole world to our feet. The South is perfectly competent to go on, one, two, or three years without planting a seed of
cotton. I believe that if she was to plant but half her cotton, it
would be an immense advantage to her. I am not so sure that after
three years' cessation she would come out stronger than ever she
was before and better prepared to enter afresh upon her great
career of enterprise. What would happen if no cotton was furnished for three years? I will not stop to depict what every one
can imagine, but this is certain: old England would topple
headlong and carry the whole civilized world with her. No, sir,
you dare not make war on cotton. No power on earth dares make
war upon it. Cotton is king. Until lately the Bank of England was
king, but she tried to put her screws as usual, the fall before last,
upon the cotton crop, and was utterly vanquished. The last power
has been conquered. Who can doubt it that has looked at recent
events? When the abuse of credit had destroyed credit and
annihilated confidence, when thousands of the strongest commercial houses in the world were coming down, and hundreds of
millions of dollars of supposed property evaporating in thin air,
when you came to a dead lock, and revolutions were threatened,
what brought you up? Fortunately for you it was the commence-
ment of the cotton season, and we have poured in upon you one

[27]*Congressional Globe*, 35th Cong., 1st sess., 961–962.

million six hundred thousand bales of cotton just at the crisis to save you from sinking. That cotton, but for the bursting of your speculative bubbles in the North, which produced the whole of this convulsion, would have brought us $100,000,000. We have sold it for $65,000,000, and saved you. Thirty-five million dollars we, the slaveholders of the South, have put into the charity box of your magnificent financiers, your cotton lords, your merchant princes.

But, sir, the greatest strength of the South arises from the harmony of her political and social institutions. This harmony gives her a frame of society, the best in the world, and an extent of political freedom, combined with entire security, such as no other people ever enjoyed upon the face of the earth. Society precedes government; creates it, and ought to control it; but as far as we can look back in historic times we find the case different; for government is no sooner created than it becomes too strong for society, and shapes and molds, as well as controls it. In later centuries the progress of civilization and of intelligence has made the divergence so great as to produce civil wars and revolutions; and it is nothing now but the want of harmony between governments and societies which occasions all the uneasiness and trouble and terror that we see aboard. It was this that brought on the American Revolution. We threw off a Government not adapted to our social system, and made one for ourselves. The question is, how far have we succeeded? The South, so far as that is concerned, is satisfied, content, happy, harmonious, and prosperous.

In all social systems there must be a class to do the mean duties, to perform the drudgery of life. That is, a class requiring but a low order of intelligence and but little skill. Its requisites are vigor, docility, fidelity. Such a class you must have, or you would not have that other class which leads progress, refinement, and civilization. It constitutes the very mud-sills of society and of political government; and you might as well attempt to build a house in the air, as to build either the one or the other, except on the mud-sills. Fortunately for the South, she found a race adapted to that purpose to her hand. A race inferior to herself, but eminently qualified in vigor, in docility, in capacity to stand the climate, to answer all her purposes. We use them for the purpose, and call them slaves. We are old-fashioned at the

South yet; it is a word discarded now by ears polite; but I will not characterize that class at the North with that term; but you have it; it is there; it is everywhere; it is eternal.

READING NO. 28

THE LINCOLN-DOUGLAS DEBATES, 1858[28]

Highlights of the Lincoln-Douglas debates were the exchange at Freeport, where Douglas declared slavery could be maintained in the territories only by friendly, local legislation, and the final debates at Alton, where Douglas summed up his stand and Lincoln eloquently denounced slavery as immoral.

γ   γ   γ

1. THE SECOND JOINT DEBATE
Freeport, August 27, 1858
LINCOLN'S OPENING SPEECH AND DOUGLAS'S
REPLY
Mr. Lincoln's Speech

. . . I now proceed to propound to the Judge the interrogatories, so far as I have framed them. I will bring forward a new installment when I get them ready. I will bring them forward now only reaching to number four.

The first one is:

Question 1.—If the people of Kansas shall, by means entirely unobjectionable in all other respects, adopt a State constitution, and ask admission into the Union under it, *before* they have the requisite number of inhabitants according to the English bill,—some ninety-three thousand,—will you vote to admit them?

Q. 2. Can the people of a United States Territory, in any lawful way, against the wish of any citizen of the United States, exclude slavery from its limits prior to the formation of a State constitution?

Q. 3. If the Supreme Court of the United States shall decide that States cannot exclude slavery from their limits, are you in favor of acquiescing in, adopting, and following such decision as a rule of political action?

---

[28]E. E. Sparks, ed., *The Lincoln-Douglas Debates of 1858* (Springfield, Ill., 1908), *passim.*

Q. 4. Are you in favor of acquiring additional territory, in disregard of how such acquisition may affect the nation on the slavery question? . . .

Senator Douglas's Reply

First, he desires to know if the people of Kansas shall form a constitution by means entirely proper and unobjectionable, and ask admission into the Union as a State, before they have the requisite population for a member of Congress, whether I will vote for that admission. . . . I will answer his question. In reference to Kansas, it is my opinion that as she has population enough to constitute a slave State, she has people enough for a free State. I will not make Kansas an exceptional case to the other States of the Union. I hold it to be a sound rule, of universal application, to require a Territory to contain the requisite population for a member of Congress before it is admitted as a State into the Union. I made that proposition in the Senate in 1856, and I renewed it during the last session, in a bill providing that no Territory of the United States should form a constitution and apply for admission until it had the requisite population. On another occasion I proposed that neither Kansas nor any other Territory should be admitted until it had the requisite population. Congress did not adopt any of my propositions containing this general rule, but did make an exception of Kansas. I will stand by that exception. Either Kansas must come in as a free State, with whatever population she may have, or the rule must be applied to all the other Territories alike. I therefore answer at once, that, it having been decided that Kansas has people enough for a slave State, I hold that she has enough for a free State. I hope Mr. Lincoln is satisfied with my answer; . . .

The next question propounded to me by Mr. Lincoln is, Can the people of a Territory in any lawful way, against the wishes of any citizen of the United States, exclude slavery from their limits prior to the formation of a State constitution? I answer emphatically, as Mr. Lincoln has heard me answer a hundred times from every stump in Illinois, that in my opinion the people of a Territory can, by lawful means, exclude slavery from their limits prior to the formation of a State constitution. . . . It matters not what way the Supreme Court may hereafter decide as to the abstract question whether slavery may or may not go into a Territory under the Constitution, the people have the lawful means to introduce it or exclude it as they please, for the reason that slavery cannot exist a day or an hour anywhere, unless it is supported by local police regulations. Those police regulations can only be established by the local legislature; and if the people are opposed to slavery, they will elect representatives to that body who will by unfriendly legislation effectually prevent the introduction of it into their midst. If, on the contrary, they are for it, their legislation will favor its extension. Hence, no matter what the decision of the Supreme Court may be on that abstract question, still the right of the people to make a slave Territory or a free Territory is perfect and complete under the Nebraska Bill. . . .

3. The Seventh Joint Debate
Alton, October 15, 1858
Douglas's Speech, Lincoln's Reply

The issue thus being made up between Mr. Lincoln and myself on three points, we went before the people of the State. During the following seven weeks, between the Chicago speeches and our first meeting at Ottawa, he and I addressed large assemblages of the people in many of the central counties. In my speeches I confined myself closely to those three positions which he had taken, controverting his proposition that this Union could not exist as our fathers made it, divided into free and slave States, controverting his proposition of a crusade against the Supreme Court because of the Dred Scott decision, and controverting his proposition that the Declaration of Independence included and meant the negroes as well as the white men, when it declared all men to be created equal. . . . I took up Mr. Lincoln's three propositions in my several speeches, analyzed them, and pointed out what I believed to be the radical errors contained in them. . . .

Mr. Lincoln's Reply

. . . Now, irrespective of the moral aspect of this question as to whether there is a right or wrong in enslaving a negro, I am still in favor of our new Territories being in such a condition that white men may find a home,—may find some spot where they can better their condition; where they can settle upon new soil and better their condition in life. I am in favor of this, not merely

(I must say it here as I have elsewhere) for our own people who are born amongst us, but as an outlet for *free white people everywhere*—the world over—in which Hans, and Baptiste, and Patrick, and all other men from all the world, may find new homes and better their conditions in life.

I have stated upon former occasions, and I may as well state again, what I understand to be the real issue in this controversy between Judge Douglas and myself. . . . The real issue in this controversy—the one pressing upon every mind—is the sentiment on the part of one class that looks upon the institution of slavery *as a wrong*, and of another class that *does not* look upon it as a wrong. The sentiment that contemplates the institution of slavery in this country as a wrong is the sentiment of the Republican party. It is the sentiment around which all their actions, all their arguments, circle, from which all their propositions radiate. They look upon it as being a moral, social, and political wrong; and while they contemplate it as such, they nevertheless have due regard for its actual existence among us, and the difficulties of getting rid of it in any satisfactory way, and to all the constitutional obligations thrown about it. Yet, having a due regard for these, they desire a policy in regard to it that looks to its not creating any more danger. They insist that it should, as far as may be, *be treated* as a wrong; and one of the methods of treating it as a wrong is to *make provision that it shall grow no larger*. They also desire a policy that looks to a peaceful end of slavery at some time, as being wrong. These are the views they entertain in regard to it as I understand them; and all their sentiments, all their arguments and propositions, are brought within this range. . . .

READING NO. 29

THE DEMOCRATIC (DOUGLAS)
PLATFORM, 1860[29]

The Democratic Party's majority platform in 1860, while reaffirming the slavery stand of 1856, recognized differences within the Party, promised to abide by decisions of the Supreme Court, denounced the North's personal liberty laws, and endorsed a railroad to the Pacific.

γ   γ   γ

1. *Resolved,* That we, the Democracy of the Union in Convention assembled, hereby declare our affirmance of the resolutions unanimously adopted and declare as a platform of principles by the Democratic Convention at Cincinnati, in the year 1856, believing that Democratic principles are unchangeable in their nature, when applied to the same subject matters; and we recommend, as the only further resolutions, the following:

2. Inasmuch as difference of opinion exists in the Democratic party as to the nature and extent of the powers of a Territorial Legislature, and as to the powers and duties of Congress, under the Constitution of the United States, over the institution of slavery within the Territories,

Resolved, That the Democratic party will abide by the decision of the Supreme Court of the United States upon these questions of Constitutional law.

3. *Resolved,* That it is the duty of the United States to afford ample and complete protection to all its citizens, whether at home or abroad, and whether native or foreign born.

4. *Resolved,* That one of the necessities of the age, in a military, commercial, and postal point of view, is speedy communication between the Atlantic and Pacific States; and the Democratic party pledge such Constitutional Government aid as

---

[29]Greeley and Cleveland, comps., *Political Textbook*, 80.

will insure the construction of a Railroad to the Pacific coast, at the earliest practicable period.

5. *Resolved,* That the Democratic party are in favor of the acquisition of the Island of Cuba on such terms as shall be honorable to ourselves and just to Spain.

6. *Resolved,* That the enactments of the State Legislatures to defeat the faithful execution of the Fugitive Slave Law, are hostile in character, subversive of the Constitution, and revolutionary in their effect.

7. *Resolved,* That it is in accordance with the interpretation of the Cincinnati platform, that during the existence of the Territorial Governments the measure of restriction, whatever it may be, imposed by the Federal Constitution on the power of the Territorial Legislature over the subject of the domestic relations, as the same has been, or shall hereafter be finally determined by the Supreme Court of the United States, should be respected by all good citizens, and enforced with promptness and fidelity by every branch of the general government.

READING NO. 30

THE DEMOCRATIC (BRECKINRIDGE) PLATFORM, 1860[30]

The Democratic Party's minority platform in 1860 made quali-fications to the 1856 platform, denounced the North's personal liberty laws, favored acquisition of Cuba, and endorsed a rail-road to the Pacific.

γ　　　　γ　　　　γ

Resolved, That the platform adopted by the Democratic party at Cincinnati be affirmed, with the following explanatory resolu-tions:

1. That the Government of a Territory organized by an act of Congress is provisional and temporary, and during its existence all citizens of the United States have an equal right to settle with their property in the Territory, without their rights, either of person or property, being destroyed or impaired by Congressio-nal or Territorial legislation.

2. That it is the duty of the Federal Government, in all its departments, to protect, when necessary, the rights of persons and property in the Territories, and wherever else its constitu-tional authority extends.

3. That when the settlers in a Territory, having an adequate population, form a State Constitution, the right of sovereignty commences, and being consummated by admission into the Union, they stand on an equal footing with the people of other States, and the State thus organized ought to be admitted into the Federal Union, whether its Constitution prohibits or recognizes the institution of slavery.

Resolved, That the Democratic party are in favor of the acqui-sition of the Island of Cuba, on such terms as shall be honorable to ourselves and just to Spain, at the earliest practicable mo-ment.

[30]*Idem.*

Resolved, That the enactments of State Legislatures to defeat the faithful execution of the Fugitive Slave Law are hostile in character, subversive of the Constitution, and revolutionary in their effect.

Resolved, That the Democracy of the United States recognize it as the imperative duty of this Government to protect the naturalized citizen in all his rights, whether at home or in foreign lands, to the same extent as its native-born citizens.

WHEREAS, One of the greatest necessities of the age, in a political, commercial, postal and military point of view, is a speedy communication between the Pacific and Atlantic coasts. Therefore be it.

Resolved, That the National Democratic party do hereby pledge themselves to use every means in their power to secure the passage of some bill; to the extent of the constitutional authority of Congress, for the construction of a Pacific Railroad from the Mississippi River to the Pacific Ocean, at the earliest practicable moment.

READING NO. 31

THE CONSTITUTIONAL UNION PLATFORM, 1860[31]

Following an old Whig formula, the Constitutional Union platform in 1860 in the interests of party, geographical, and sectional harmony adopted a brief and very general statement.

γ　　　　　γ　　　　　γ

Whereas, Experience has demonstrated that Platforms adopted by the partisan Conventions of the country have had the effect to mislead and deceive the people, and at the same time to widen the political divisions of the country, by the creation and encouragement of geographical and sectional parties; therefore

Resolved, that it is both the part of patriotism and of duty to *recognize* no political principle other than THE CONSTITUTION OF THE COUNTRY, THE UNION OF THE STATES, AND THE ENFORCEMENT OF THE LAWS, and that, as representatives of the Constitutional Union men of the country, in National Convention assembled, we hereby pledge ourselves to maintain, protect, and defend, separately and unitedly, this great principle of public liberty and national safety, against all enemies, at home and abroad; believing that thereby peace may once more be restored to the country; the rights of the People and of the States reestablished, and the Government again placed in that condition of justice, fraternity and equality, which, under the example and Constitution of our fathers, has solemnly bound every citizen of the United States to maintain a more perfect union, establish justice, insure domestic tranquillity, provide for the common defense, promote the general welfare, and secure the blessings of liberty to ourselves and our posterity.

READING NO. 32

THE REPUBLICAN PLATFORM, 1860[32]

The Republicans, again as in 1856 invoking the republican tradition, attributed the nation's success to the Union of the states. They affirmed the power of Congress to maintain freedom —"the normal condition"—in the territories. Their platform reviewed grievances concerning slavery and formulated an economic policy for the future.

γ   γ   γ

Resolved, That we, the delegated representatives of the Republican electors of the United States, in Convention assembled, in discharge of the duty we owe to our constituents and our country, unite in the following declarations:

1. That the history of the nation during the last four years, has fully established the propriety and necessity of the organization and perpetuation of the Republican party, and that the causes which called it into existence are permanent in their nature, and now, more than ever before, demand its peaceful and constitutional triumph.

2. That the maintenance of the principles promulgated in the Declaration of Independence and embodied in the Federal Constitution, "That all men are created equal; that they are endowed by their Creator with certain inalienable rights; that among these are life, liberty and the pursuit of happiness; that to secure these rights, governments are instituted among men, deriving their just powers from the consent of the governed," is essential to the preservation of our Republican institutions; and that the Federal Constitution, the Rights of the States, and the Union of the States must and shall be preserved.

3. That to the Union of the States this nation owes its unprecedented increase in population, its surprising development of material resources, its rapid augmentation of wealth, its happiness at home and its honor abroad; and we hold in abhorrence all

[32]*Idem*, 26–27.

schemes for disunion, come from whatever source they may. And we congratulate the country that no Republican member of Congress has uttered or countenanced the threats of disunion so often made by Democratic members, without rebuke and with applause from their political associates; and we denounce those threats of disunion, in case of a popular overthrow of their ascendency as denying the vital principles of a free government, and as an avowal of contemplated treason, which it is the imperative duty of an indignant people sternly to rebuke and forever silence.

4. That the maintenance inviolate of the rights of the states, and especially the right of each state to order and control its own domestic institutions according to its own judgment exclusively, is essential to that balance of powers on which the perfection and endurance of our political fabric depends; and we denounce the lawless invasion by armed force of the soil of any state or territory, no matter under what pretext, as among the gravest of crimes.

5. That the present Democratic Administration has far exceeded our worst apprehensions, in its measureless subserviency to the exactions of a sectional interest, as especially evinced in its desperate exertions to force the infamous Lecompton Constitution upon the protesting people of Kansas; in construing the personal relations between master and servant to involve an unqualified property in persons; in its attempted enforcement everywhere, on land and sea, through the intervention of Congress and of the Federal Courts, of the extreme pretensions of a purely local interest; and in its general and unvarying abuse of the power intrusted to it by a confiding people.

6. That the people justly view with alarm the reckless extravagance which pervades every department of the Federal Government; that a return to rigid economy and accountability is indispensable to arrest the systematic plunder of the public treasury by favored partisans; while the recent startling developments of frauds and corruptions at the Federal metropolis, show that an entire change of administration is imperatively demanded.

7. That the new dogma that the Constitution, of its own force, carries slavery into any or all of the territories of the United States, is a dangerous political heresy, at variance with the

explicit provisions of that instrument itself, with contemporaneous exposition, and with legislative and judicial precedent; is revolutionary in its tendency, and subversive of the peace and harmony of the country.

8. That the normal condition of all the territory of the United States is that of freedom: That, as our Republican fathers, when they had abolished slavery in all our national territory, ordained that "no persons should be deprived of life, liberty or property without due process of law," it becomes our duty, by legislation, whenever such legislation is necessary, to maintain this provision of the Constitution against all attempts to violate it; and we deny the authority of Congress, of a territorial legislature, or of any individuals, to give legal existence to slavery in any territory of the United States.

9. That we brand the recent reopening of the African slave trade, under the cover of our national flag, aided by perversions of judicial power, as a crime against humanity and a burning shame to our country and age; and we call upon Congress to take prompt and efficient measures for the total and final suppression of that execrable traffic.

10. That in the recent vetoes, by their Federal Governors, of the acts of the legislatures of Kansas and Nebraska, prohibiting slavery in those territories, we find a practical illustration of the boasted Democratic principle of Non-Intervention and Popular Sovereignty, embodied in the Kansas-Nebraska Bill, and a demonstration of the deception and fraud involved therein.

11. That Kansas should, of right, be immediately admitted as a state under the Constitution recently formed and adopted by her people, and accepted by the House of Representatives.

12. That, while providing revenue for the support of the general government by duties upon imports, sound policy requires such an adjustment of these imports as to encourage the development of the industrial interests of the whole country; and we commend that policy of national exchanges, which secures to the workingmen liberal wages, to agriculture remunerative prices, to mechanics and manufacturers an adequate reward for their skill, labor, and enterprise, and to the nation commercial prosperity and independence.

13. That we protest against any sale or alienation to others of the public lands held by actual settlers, and against any view of

the free-homestead policy which regards the settlers as paupers or suppliants for public bounty; and we demand the passage by Congress of the complete and satisfactory homestead measure which has already passed the House.

14. That the Republican party is opposed to any change in our naturalization laws or any state legislation by which the rights of citizens hitherto accorded to immigrants from foreign lands shall be abridged or impaired; and in favor of giving a full and efficient protection to the rights of all classes of citizens, whether native or naturalized, both at home and abroad.

15. That appropriations by Congress for river and harbor improvements of a national character, required for the accommodation and security of an existing commerce, are authorized by the Constitution, and justified by the obligation of Government to protect the lives and property of its citizens.

16. That a railroad to the Pacific Ocean is imperatively demanded by the interests of the whole country; that the federal government ought to render immediate and efficient aid in its construction; and that, as preliminary thereto, a daily overland mail should be promptly established.

17. Finally, having thus set forth our distinctive principles and views, we invite the co-operation of all citizens, however differing on other questions, who substantially agree with us in their affirmance and support.

READING NO. 33

SOUTH CAROLINA DECLARATION OF CAUSES OF SECESSION[33]

The first state to secede, South Carolina adopted a statement, interpreting the nature of the Union, reviewing slaveholding states' grievances, and fixing the blame for disunion on the North and the Republican Party.

γ   γ   γ

The people of the State of South Carolina in Convention assembled, on the 2d day of April, A.D. 1852, declared that the frequent violations of the Constitution of the United States by the Federal Government, and its encroachments upon the reserved rights of the States, fully justified this State in their withdrawal from the Federal Union; but in deference to the opinions and wishes of the other Slaveholding States, she forbore at that time to exercise this right. Since that time these encroachments have continued to increase, and further forbearance ceases to be a virtue.

And now the State of South Carolina having resumed her separate and equal place among nations, deems it due to herself, to the remaining United States of America, and to the nations of the world, that she should declare the immediate causes which have led to this act.

In 1787, Deputies . . . appointed by the States recommended, for the adoption of the States, the Articles of Union, known as the Constitution of the United States.

. . . Thus was established by compact between the States, a Government with defined objects and powers, limited to the express words of the grant. . . . We hold that the Government thus established is subject to the two great principles asserted in the Declaration of Independence; and we hold further, that the mode of its formation subjects it to a third fundamental princi-

---

[33]Frank Moore, ed, *The Rebellion Record* (New York, 1862), I, 3*ff*.

ple, namely, the law of compact. We maintain that in every compact between two or more parties, the obligation is mutual; that the failure of one of the contracting parties to perform a material part of the agreement, entirely releases the obligation of the other; and that, where no arbiter is provided, each party is remitted to his own judgment to determine the fact of failure, with all its consequences.

In the present case, that fact is established with certainty. We assert that fourteen of the States have deliberately refused for years past to fulfil their constitutional obligations, and we refer to their own statutes for the proof. . . .

In many of these States the fugitive is discharged from the service of labor claimed, and in none of them has the State Government complied with the stipulation made in the Constitution. . . . Thus the constitutional compact has been deliberately broken and disregarded by the non-slaveholding States; and the consequence follows that South Carolina is released from her obligation. . . .

We affirm that these ends for which this Government was instituted have been defeated, and the Government itself has been destructive of them by the action of the nonslaveholding States. Those States have assumed the right of deciding upon the propriety of our domestic institutions; and have denied the rights of property established in fifteen of the States and recognized by the Constitution; they have denounced as sinful the institution of Slavery; they have permitted the open establishment among them of societies, whose avowed object is to disturb the peace of and eloin the property of the citizens of other States. They have encouraged and assisted thousands of our slaves to leave their homes; and those who remain, have been incited by emissaries, books, and pictures, to servile insurrection.

For twenty-five years this agitation has been steadily increasing, until it has now secured to its aid the power of the common Government. Observing the *forms* of the Constitution, a sectional party has found within that article establishing the Executive Department, the means of subverting the Constitution itself. A geographical line has been drawn across the Union, and all the States north of that line have united in the election of a man to the high office of President of the United States whose opinions and purposes are hostile to Slavery. He is to be intrusted with the administration of the common Government, because he has declared that "Government cannot endure permanently half slave, half free," and that the public mind must rest in the belief that Slavery is in the course of ultimate extinction.

This sectional combination for the subversion of the Constitution has been aided, in some of the States, by elevating to citizenship persons who, by the supreme law of the land, are incapable of becoming citizens; and their votes have been used to inaugurate a new policy, hostile to the South, and destructive of its peace and safety.

On the 4th of March next this party will take possession of the Government. It has announced that the South shall be excluded from the common territory, that the Judicial tribunal shall be made sectional, and that a war must be waged against Slavery until it shall cease throughout the United States.

The guarantees of the Constitution will then no longer exist; the equal rights of the States will be lost. The Slaveholding States will no longer have the power of self-government, or self-protection, and the Federal Government will have become their enemy.

Sectional interest and animosity will deepen the irritation; and all hope of remedy is rendered vain, by the fact that the public opinion at the North has invested a great political error with the sanctions of a more erroneous religious belief.

We, therefore, the people of South Carolina, by our delegates in Convention assembled, appealing to the Supreme Judge of the world for the rectitude of our intentions, have solemnly declared that the Union heretofore existing between this State and the other States of North America is dissolved, and that the State of South Carolina has resumed her position among the nations of the world, as a separate and independent state, with full power to levy war, conclude peace, contract alliances, establish commerce, and to do all other acts and things which independent States may of right do.

READING NO. 34

PRESIDENT BUCHANAN'S FOURTH
ANNUAL MESSAGE TO CONGRESS[34]

*In his final annual message—today called the State of the
Union message—President James Buchanan criticized Northern
interference with slavery, claimed the slavery question could
easily be settled, and examined the question whether either the
president or the Congress could prevent secession.*

γ   γ   γ

WASHINGTON CITY, *December 3, 1860. Fellow-Citizens of the
Senate and House of Representatives:*
    . . . The long-continued and intemperate interference of the
Northern people with the question of slavery in the Southern
States has at length produced its natural effects. The different
sections of the Union are now arrayed against each other, and the
time has arrived, so much dreaded by the Father of his Country,
when hostile geographical parties have been formed. . . .
    It can not be denied that for five and twenty years the agitation
at the North against slavery has been incessant. . . .
    In order to justify secession as a constitutional remedy, it must
be on the principle that the Federal Government is a mere
voluntary association of States, to be dissolved at pleasure by
any one of the contracting parties. If this be so, the Confederacy
is a rope of sand, to be penetrated and dissolved by the first
adverse wave of public opinion in any of the States.
    Such a principle is wholly inconsistent with the history as well
as the character of the Federal Constitution. . . .
    It was intended to be perpetual, and not to be annulled at the
pleasure of any one of the contracting parties. . . . Secession is
neither more nor less than revolution. It may or it may not be a
justifiable revolution, but still it is revolution.

[34]Richardson ed., *Messages and Papers*, V, 626*ff.*

Apart from the execution of the laws, so far as this may be practical, the Executive has no authority to decide what shall be the relations between the Federal Government and South Carolina. . . .

The question fairly stated is, Has the Constitution delegated to Congress the power to coerce a State into submission which is attempting to withdraw or has actually withdrawn from the Confederacy? If answered in the affirmative, it must be on the principle that the power has been conferred upon Congress to declare and to make war against a State. After much serious reflection I have arrived at the conclusion that no such power has been delegated to Congress or to any other department of the Federal Government. . . .

The fact is that our Union rests upon public opinion, and can never be cemented by the blood of its citizens shed in civil war. If it can not live in the affections of the people, it must one day perish. Congress possesses many means of preserving it by conciliation, but the sword was not placed in their hand to preserve it by force. . . .

READING NO. 35

CRITTENDEN PEACE RESOLUTIONS[35]

The Crittenden Peace Resolutions presented the last best hope of compromise in the secession crisis. In regard to slavery, they proposed a series of constitutional amendments, which could never be amended.

γ   γ   γ

Whereas, serious and alarming dissensions have arisen between the Northern and Southern States, concerning the rights and security of the rights of the slave-holding States, and especially their rights in the common territory of the United States; and whereas it is eminently desirable and proper that these dissensions which now threaten the very existence of this Union, should be permanently quieted and settled, by constitutional provision, which shall do equal justice to all sections, and thereby restore to the people that peace and good will which ought to prevail between all the citizens of the United States: Therefore,

Resolved by the Senate and House of Representatives of the United States of America in Congress Assembled, That the following articles be, and are hereby, proposed and submitted as amendments to the Constitution of the United States, . . .

Article 1. In all the territory of the United States now held, or hereafter acquired, situate North of Latitude 36° 30′, slavery or involuntary servitude, except as a punishment for crime, is prohibited while such territory shall remain under territorial government. In all the territory south of said line of latitude, slavery of the African race is hereby recognized as existing, and shall not be interfered with by Congress, but shall be protected as property by all the departments of the territorial government during its continuance. And when any Territory, north or south of said line, within such boundaries as Congress may prescribe,

---

[35]Edward McPherson, *Political History of the Great Rebellion* (Washington, 1865), 64–65.

shall contain the population requisite for a member of Congress according to the then Federal ratio, of representation of the people of the United States, it shall, if its form of government be republican, be admitted into the Union, on an equal footing with the original States, with or without slavery, as the constitution of such new State may provide.

Art. 2. Congress shall have no power to abolish slavery in places under its exclusive jurisdiction, and situate within the limits of States that permit the holding of slaves.

Art. 3. Congress shall have no power to abolish slavery within the district of Columbia so long as it exists in the adjoining States of Virginia and Maryland, or either, not without the consent of the inhabitants, nor without just compensation first made to such owners of slaves as do not consent to such abolishment. . . .

Art. 4. Congress shall have no power to prohibit or hinder the transportation of slaves from one State to another, or to a Territory in which slaves are by law permitted to be held, whether that transportation be by land, navigable rivers, or by the sea. . . .

Art. 6. No future amendment of the Constitution shall affect the five preceding articles . . . and no amendment shall be made to the Constitution which shall authorize or give to Congress any power to abolish or interfere with slavery in any of the States by whose laws it is, or may be, allowed or permitted.

And whereas, also, besides these causes of dissension embraced in the foregoing amendments proposed to the Constitution of the United States, there are others which come within the jurisdiction of Congress, and may be remedied by its legislative power; Therefore 1. Resolved. . . . That the laws now in force for the recovery of fugitive slaves are in strict pursuance of the plain and mandatory provisions of the Constitution, and have been sanctioned as valid and constitutional by the judgment of the Supreme Court of the United States. . . .

2. That all State laws which conflict with the fugitive slave acts of Congress, or any other Constitutional acts of Congress, or which, in their operation, impede, hinder, or delay, the free course and due execution of any of said acts, are null and void by the present provisions of the Constitution of the United States. . . .

3. That the Act of the 18th of September, 1850, commonly called the fugitive slave law, . . . the last clause of the fifth section of said act, which authorizes a person holding a warrant for the

arrest or detention of a fugitive slave, to summon to his aid the *posse comitatus*, and which declares it to be the duty of all good citizens to assist him in its execution, ought to be so amended as to expressly limit the authority and duty to cases in which there shall be resistance or danger of resistance or rescue.

4. That the laws for the suppression of the African slave trade, and especially those prohibiting the importation of slaves in the United States, ought to be made effectual, and ought to be thoroughly executed: and all further enactments necessary to those ends ought to be promptly made.

READING NO. 36

LINCOLN'S FIRST INAUGURAL ADDRESS[36]

In his first inaugural address Abraham Lincoln explained his view of the nature of the Union, his policy toward slavery and the seceded states, his faith in popular government, and his lack of intention to start a war.

γ   γ   γ

FELLOW-CITIZENS OF THE UNITED STATES:—In compliance with a custom as old as the Government itself, I appear before you to address you briefly, and to take in your presence the oath prescribed by the Constitution of the United States to be taken by the President "before he enters on the execution of his office." . . .

Apprehension seems to exist among the people of the Southern States that by the accession of a Republican administration their property and their peace and personal security are to be endangered. There has never been any reasonable cause for such apprehension. Indeed, the most ample evidence to the contrary has all the while existed and been open to their inspection. It is found in nearly all the published speeches of him who now addresses you. I do but quote from one of those speeches when I declare that "I have no purpose, directly or indirectly, to interfere with the institution of slavery in the States where it exists. I believe I have no lawful right to do so, and I have no inclination to do so." . . .

I now reiterate these sentiments; and, in doing so, I only press upon the public attention the most conclusive evidence of which the case is susceptible, that the property, peace and security of no section are to be in any wise endangered by the now incoming administration. I add, too, that all the protection which, consistently with the Constitution and the laws, can be given, will be cheerfully given to all the States when lawfully demanded, for whatever cause—as cheerfully to one section as to another. . . .

[36]Richardson, ed., *Messages and Papers*, V1, 5*ff*.

I take the official oath to-day with no mental reservations, and with no purpose to construe the Constitution or laws by any hypercritical rules. And, while I do not choose now to specify particular acts of Congress as proper to be enforced, I do suggest that it will be much safer for all, both in official and private stations, to conform to and abide by all those acts which stand unrepealed, than to violate any of them, trusting to find impunity in having them held to be unconstitutional. . . .

A disruption of the Federal Union, heretofore only menaced, is now formidably attempted.

I hold that, in contemplation of universal law and of the Constitution, the Union of these States is perpetual. Perpetuity is implied, if not expressed, in the fundamental law of all national governments. It is safe to assert that no government proper ever had a provision in its organic law for its own termination. Continue to execute all the express provisions of our national Constitution, and the Union will endure forever—it being impossible to destroy it except by some action not provided for in the instrument itself.

Again, if the United States be not a government proper, but an association of States in the nature of contract merely, can it as a contract be peaceably unmade by less than all the parties who made it? One party to a contract may violate it—break it, so to speak; but does it not require all to lawfully rescind it?

Descending from these general principles, we find the proposition that in legal contemplation the Union is perpetual confirmed by the history of the Union itself. The Union is much older than the Constitution. It was formed, in fact, by the Articles of Association in 1774. It was matured and continued by the Declaration of Independence in 1776. It was further matured, and the faith of all the then thirteen States expressly plighted and engaged that it should be perpetual, by the Articles of Confederation in 1778. And, finally, in 1787 one of the declared objects for ordaining and establishing the Constitution was "to form a more perfect Union."

But if the destruction of the Union by one or by a part only of the States be lawfully possible, the Union is less perfect than before the Constitution, having lost the vital element of perpetuity.

It follows from these views that no State upon its own mere motion can lawfully get out of the Union; that resolves and ordinances to that effect are legally void; and that acts of violence, within any State or States, against the authority of the United States, are insurrectionary or revolutionary, according to circumstances.

I therefore consider that, in view of the Constitution and the laws, the Union is unbroken; and to the extent of my ability I shall take care, as the Constitution itself expressly enjoins upon me, that the laws of the Union be faithfully executed in all the States. Doing this I deem to be only a simple duty on my part; and I shall perform it so far as practicable, unless my rightful masters, the American people, shall withhold the requisite means, or in some authoritative manner direct the contrary. I trust this will not be regarded as a menace, but only as the declared purpose of the Union that it will constitutionally defend and maintain itself.

In doing this there needs to be no bloodshed or violence; and there shall be none, unless it be forced upon the national authority. The power confided to me will be used to hold, occupy, and possess the property and places belonging to the Government, and to collect the duties and imposts; but beyond what may be necessary for these objects, there will be no invasion, no using of force against or among the people anywhere. Where hostility to the United States, in any interior locality, shall be so great and universal as to prevent competent resident citizens from holding the Federal offices, there will be no attempt to force obnoxious strangers among the people for that object. While the strict legal right may exist in the government to enforce the exercise of these offices, the attempt to do so would be so irritating, and so nearly impracticable withal, that I deem it better to forego for the time the uses of such offices.

The mails, unless repelled, will continue to be furnished in all parts of the Union. So far as possible, the people everywhere shall have that sense of perfect security which is most favorable to calm thought and reflection. The course here indicated will be followed unless current events and experience shall show a modification or change to be proper, and in every case and exigency my best discretion will be exercised according to circumstances actually existing, and with a view and a hope of a peaceful solution of the national troubles and the restoration of fraternal sympathies and affections. . . .

All profess to be content in the Union if all constitutional rights can be maintained. Is it true, then, that any right, plainly written in the Constitution, has been denied? I think not. Happily the human mind is so constituted that no party can reach to the audacity of doing this. Think, if you can, of a single instance in which a plainly written provision of the Constitution has ever been denied. If by the mere force of numbers a majority should deprive a minority of any clearly written constitutional right, it might, in a moral point of view, justify revolution—certainly would if such a right were a vital one. But such is not our case. All the vital rights of minorities and of individuals are so plainly assured to them by affirmations and negations, guaranties and prohibitions, in the Constitution, that controversies never arise concerning them. But no organic law can ever be framed with a provision specifically applicable to every question which may occur in practical administration. No foresight can anticipate, nor any document of reasonable length contain, express provisions for all possible questions. Shall fugitives from labor be surrendered by national or by State authority? The Constitution does not expressly say. *May* Congress prohibit slavery in the Territories? The Constitution does not expressly say. *Must* Congress protect slavery in the Territories? The Constitution does not expressly say.

From questions of this class spring all our constitutional controversies, and we divide upon them into majorities and minorities. If the minority will not acquiesce, the majority must, or the Government must cease. There is no other alternative; for continuing the Government is acquiescence on one side or the other.

If a minority in such case will secede rather than acquiesce, they make a precedent which in turn will divide and ruin them; for a minority of their own will secede from them whenever a majority refuses to be controlled by such minority. For instance, why may not any portion of a new confederacy a year or two hence arbitrarily secede again, precisely as portions of the present Union now claim to secede from it? All who cherish disunion sentiments are now being educated to the exact temper of doing this.

Is there such perfect identity of interests among the States to compose a new Union as to produce harmony only, and prevent renewed secession?

Plainly, the central idea of secession is the essence of anarchy. A majority held in restraint by constitutional checks and limitations, and always changing easily with deliberate changes of popular opinions and sentiments, is the only true sovereign of a free people. Whoever rejects it does, of necessity, fly to anarchy or to despotism. Unanimity is impossible; the rule of a minority, as a permanent arrangement, is wholly inadmissible; so that, rejecting the majority principle, anarchy or despotism in some form is all that is left.

I do not forget the position assumed by some, that constitutional questions are to be decided by the Supreme Court; nor do I deny that such decisions must be binding, in any case, upon the parties to a suit, as to the object of that suit, while they are also entitled to a very high respect and consideration in all parallel cases by all other departments of the government. And, while it is obviously possible that such decision may be erroneous in any given case, still the evil effect following it, being limited to that particular case, with the chance that it may be overruled and never become a precedent for other cases, can better be borne than could the evils of a different practice. At the same time, the candid citizen must confess that if the policy of the government, upon vital questions affecting the whole people, is to be irrevocably fixed by decisions of the Supreme Court, the instant they are made, in ordinary litigation between parties in personal actions, the people will have ceased to be their own rulers, having to that extent practically resigned the government into the hands of that eminent tribunal. Nor is there in this view any assault upon the court or the judges. It is a duty from which they may not shrink to decide cases properly brought before them, and it is no fault of theirs if others seek to turn their decisions to political purposes.

One section of our country believes slavery is right, and ought to be extended, while the other believes it is wrong, and ought not to be extended. This is the only substantial dispute.

The fugitive slave clause of the Constitution and the law for the suppression of the foreign slave trade are each as well enforced, perhaps, as any law can ever be in a community where the moral sense of the people imperfectly supports the law itself. The great body of the people abide by the dry legal obligation in both cases, and a few break over in each. This, I think, cannot be perfectly cured; and it would be worse in both cases after the separation of the sections than before. The foreign slave trade, now imperfectly suppressed, would be ultimately revived, without restriction, in one section, while fugitive slaves, now only partially surrendered, would not be surrendered at all by the other.

Physically speaking, we cannot separate. We cannot remove our respective sections from each other, nor build an impassable wall between them. A husband and wife may be divorced and go out of the presence and beyond the reach of each other; but the different parts of our country cannot do this. They cannot but remain face to face, and intercourse, either amicable or hostile, must continue between them. Is it possible, then, to make that intercourse more advantageous or more satisfactory after separation than before? Can aliens make treaties easier than friends can make laws? Can treaties be more faithfully enforced between aliens than laws can among friends? Suppose you go to war, you cannot fight always; and when, after much loss on both sides, and no gain on either, you cease fighting, the identical old questions as to terms of intercourse are again upon you.

This country, with its institutions, belongs to the people who inhabit it. Whenever they shall grow weary of the existing government, they can exercise their constitutional right of amending it, or their revolutionary right to dismember or overthrow it. . . . I understand a proposed amendment to the Constitution—which amendment, however, I have not seen—has passed Congress, to the effect that the Federal Government shall never interfere with the domestic institutions of the States, including that of persons held to service. To avoid misconstruction of what I have said, I depart from my purpose not to speak of particular amendments so far as to say that, holding such a provision to now be implied constitutional law, I have no objection to its being made express and irrevocable. . . .

Why should there not be a patient confidence in the ultimate justice of the people? Is there any better or equal hope in the world? In our present differences is either party without faith of being in the right? If the Almighty Ruler of nations, with his eternal truth and justice, be on your side of the North, or on yours of the South, that truth and that justice will surely prevail by the judgment of this great tribunal of the American people. . . .

My countrymen, one and all, think calmly and well upon this whole subject. Nothing valuable can be lost by taking time. If there be an object to hurry any of you in hot haste to a step which you would never take deliberately, that object will be frustrated by taking time; but no good object can be frustrated by it. Such of you as are now dissatisifed still have the old Constitution unimpaired, and, on the sensitive point, the laws of your own framing under it; while the new administration will have no immediate power, if it would, to change either. If it were admitted that you who are dissatisfied hold the right side in the dispute, there still is no single good reason for precipitate action. Intelligence, patriotism, Christianity, and a firm reliance on Him who has never yet forsaken this favored land, are still competent to adjust in the best way all our present difficulty.

In your hands, my dissatisfied fellowcountrymen, and not in mine, is the momentous issue of civil war. The government will not assail you. You can have no conflict without being yourselves the aggressors. You have no oath registered in heaven to destroy the government, while I shall have the most solemn one to "preserve, protect, and defend" it.

I am loath to close. We are not enemies, but friends. We must not be enemies. Though passion may have strained, it must not break, our bonds of affection. The mystic chords of memory, stretching from every battle-field and patriot grave to every living heart and hearthstone all over this broad land, will yet swell the chorus of the Union when again touched, as surely they will be, by the better angels of our nature.

READING NO. 37

PHOEBE CARY, "VOICE OF THE NORTHERN WOMEN"[37]

Phoebe Cary, Boston poetess, voiced the patriotic fervor felt by many Northerners after the fall of Fort Sumter and Lincoln's appeal to arms.

γ   γ   γ

ROUSE, freemen, the foe has arisen,
  His hosts are abroad on the plain;
And, under the stars of your banner,
  Swear never to strike it again!

O, fathers, who sit with your children,
  Would you leave them a land that is free?
Turn now from their tender caresses,
  And put them away from your knee.

O, brothers, we played with in childhood,
  On hills where the clover bloomed sweet;
See to it, that never a traitor
  Shall trample them under his feet.

O, lovers, awake to your duty
  From visions that fancy has nursed;
Look not in the eyes that would keep you;
  Our country has need of you first.

And we, whom your lives have made blessed,
  Will pray for your souls in the fight;
That you may be strong to do battle
  For Freedom, for God, and the Right.

[37]*Lyrics of Loyalty*, edited by Frank Moore, (New York, 1864), 325–326.

We are daughters of men who were heroes;
   We can smile as we bid you depart;
But never a coward or traitor
   Shall have room for a place in our heart.

Then quit you like men in the conflict,
   Who fight for their home and their land;
Smite deep, in the name of Jehovah,
   And conquer, or die where you stand.

READING NO. 38

ALEXANDER H. STEPHENS'S
"CORNERSTONE" SPEECH[38]

Alexander H. Stephens, vice president of the Confederacy, made his famous "cornerstone speech" in March 1861. Historians have sometimes misconstrued this speech as saying slavery was the Confederate cornerstone, whereas a close reading shows Stephens saying racial inequality—from which slavery followed —was the cornerstone.

γ γ γ

. . . The new constitution has put to rest, *forever,* all agitating questions relating to our peculiar institution, African slavery as it exists among us,—the proper status of the negro in our form of civilization. This was the immediate cause of the late rupture and present revolution. Jefferson, in his forecast, had anticipated this as the "rock upon which the old Union would split." He was right. What was conjecture with him is now a realized fact. But whether he fully comprehended the great truth upon which that rock *stood* and *stands* may be doubted. The prevailing ideas entertained by him and most of the leading statesmen at the time of the formation of the old Constitution were that the enslavement of the African was in violation of the laws of nature; that it was wrong in *principle*, socially, morally, and politically. It was an evil they knew not well how to deal with, but the general opinion of the men of that day was that somehow or other, in the order of Providence, the institution would be evanescent and pass away. This idea, though not incorporated in the Constitution, was the prevailing idea at the time. The Constitution, it is true, secured every essential guaranty to the institution while it should last, and hence no argument can be justly used against the constitutional guaranties thus secured, because of the common sentiment of the day. Those ideas, however, were fundamentally

[38]Moore, ed., *Rebellion Record*, I, 44–45.

wrong. They rested upon the assumption of the equality of races. This was an error. It was a sandy foundation, and the idea of the government built upon it; when the "storm came and the wind blew, it *fell*."

Our new government is founded upon exactly the opposite idea; its foundations are laid, its corner-stone rests, upon the great truth that the negro is not equal to the white man; that slavery—subordination to the superior race—is his natural and normal condition.

READING NO. 39

JEFFERSON DAVIS, SPECIAL MESSAGE TO THE CONFEDERATE CONGRESS[39]

A fortnight after Fort Sumter fell, President Jefferson Davis in a special message to the Confederate Congress explained his view of the nature of the Union and of slavery, and how the threat to black slavery had impelled Southerners to secede and form a new government.

γ   γ   γ

Gentlemen of the Congress. . . .

The declaration of war made against this Confederacy by Abraham Lincoln, the President of the United States, in his proclamation issued on the 15th day of the present month, rendered it necessary, in my judgment, that you should convene at the earliest practicable moment to devise the measures necessary for the defense of the country. The occasion is indeed an extraordinary one. It justifies me in a brief review of the relations heretofore existing between us and the States which now unite in warfare against us and in a succinct statement of the events which have resulted in this warfare, to the end that mankind may pass intelligent and impartial judgment on its motives and objects. During the war waged against Great Britain by her colonies on this continent a common danger impelled them to a close alliance and to the formation of a Confederation, by the terms of which the colonies, styling themselves States, entered "*severally* into a firm league of friendship with each other for their common defense, the security of their liberties, and their mutual and general welfare, binding themselves to assist each other against all force offered to or attacks made upon them, or any of them, on account of religion, sovereignty, trade, or any other pretense whatever." In order to guard against any misconstruction of their compact, the several States made explicit

[39]*Ibid.*, 168*ff.*

declaration in a distinct article—that "*each* State *retains its* sovereignty, freedom, and independence, and every power, jurisdiction, and right which is not by this Confederation *expressly delegated* to the United States in Congress assembled."

Strange, indeed, must it appear to the impartial observer, but it is none the less true that all these carefully worded clauses proved unavailing to prevent the rise and growth in the Northern States of a political school which has persistently claimed that the government thus formed was not a compact *between* States, but was in effect a national government, set up *above* and *over* the States. An organization created by the States to secure the blessings of liberty and independence against *foreign* aggression, has been gradually perverted into a machine for their control in their *domestic* affairs. . . . In addition to the long-continued and deep-seated resentment felt by the Southern States at the persistent abuse of the powers they had delegated to the Congress, for the purpose of enriching the manufacturing and shipping classes of the North at the expense of the South, there has existed for nearly half a century another subject of discord, involving interests of such transcendent magnitude as at all times to create the apprehension in the minds of many devoted lovers of the Union that its permanence was impossible. When the several States delegated certain powers to the United States Congress, a large portion of the laboring population consisted of African slaves imported into the colonies by the mother country. In twelve out of the thirteen States negro slavery existed, and the right of property in slaves was protected by law. This property was recognized in the Constitution, and provision was made against its loss by the escape of the slave. . . .

As soon, however, as the Northern States that prohibited African slavery within their limits had reached a number sufficient to give their representation a controlling voice in the Congress, a persistent and organized system of hostile measures against the rights of the owners of slaves in the Southern States was inaugurated and gradually extended. A continuous series of measures was devised and prosecuted for the purpose of rendering insecure the tenure of property in slaves. . . . Emboldened by success, the theatre of agitation and aggression against the clearly expressed constitutional rights of the Southern States was transferred to the Congress. . . . Finally a great party was organized for the purpose of obtaining the administration of the Government, with the avowed object of using its power for the total exclusion of the slave States from all participation in the benefits of the public domain acquired by all the States in common, whether by conquest or purchase; of surrounding them entirely by States in which slavery should be prohibited; of those rendering the property in slaves so insecure as to be comparatively worthless, and thereby annihilating in effect property worth thousands of millions of dollars. This party, thus organized, succeeded in the month of November last in the election of its candidate for the Presidency of the United States.

In the meantime, the African slaves had augmented in number from about 600,000, at the date of the adoption of the constitutional compact, to upward of 4,000,000. In moral and social condition they had been elevated from brutal savages into docile, intelligent, and civilized agricultural laborers, and supplied not only with bodily comforts but with careful religious instruction. Under the supervision of a superior race their labor had been so directed as not only to allow a gradual and marked amelioration of their own condition, but to convert hundreds of thousands of square miles of the wilderness into cultivated lands covered with a prosperous people; towns and cities had sprung into existence, and had rapidly increased in wealth and population under the social system of the South; the white population of the Southern slave-holding States had augmented from about 1,250,000 at the date of the adoption of the Constitution to more than 8,500,000, in 1860; and the productions in the South of cotton, rice, sugar, and tobacco, for the full development and continuance of which the labor of African slaves was and is indispensable, had swollen to an amount which formed nearly three-fourths of the exports of the whole United States and had become absolutely necessary to the wants of civilized man. With interests of such overwhelming magnitude imperiled, the people of the Southern States were driven by the conduct of the North to the adoption of some course of action to avert the danger with which they were openly menaced. With this view the Legislatures of the several States invited the people to select delegates to conventions to be held for the purpose of determining for themselves what measures were best adapted to meet so alarming a crisis in their history. Here it may be proper to observe that from a period as early as 1798 there had existed in *all* of the States of the Union a party almost uninterruptedly in the majority based upon the creed that each State was, in the last resort, the sole judge as well of its wrongs as of the mode and measure of redress. . . .

. . . In the exercise of a right so ancient, so well-established, and so necessary for self-preservation, the people of the Confederate States, in their conventions, determined that the wrongs which they had suffered and the evils with which they were menaced required that they should revoke the delegation of powers to the Federal Government which they had ratified in their several conventions. They consequently passed ordinances resuming all their rights as sovereign and independent States and dissolved their connection with the other States of the Union.

Having done this, they proceeded to form a new compact amongst themselves by new articles of confederation, which have been also ratified by the conventions of the several States with an approach to unanimity far exceeding that of the conventions which adopted the Constitution of 1787. They have organized their new Government in all its departments; the functions of the executive, legislative, and judicial magistrates are performed in accordance with the will of the people, as displayed not merely in a cheerful acquiescence, but in the enthusiastic support of the Government thus established by themselves; and but for the interference of the Government of the United States in this legitimate exercise of the right of a people to self-government, peace, happiness, and prosperity would now smile on our land. . . .

Jefferson Davis.

SELECTED BIBLIOGRAPHY AND SUGGESTIONS FOR FURTHER READING

An excellent general history of the period is David M. Potter, *The Impending Crisis, 1848–1861* (New York, 1976). *The Political Crisis of the 1850s* by Michael F. Holt (New York, 1978) is an able analysis of party politics. William J. Cooper, Jr., *Liberty and Slavery. Southern Politics to 1860* (New York, 1983), interprets Southern politics as a means to secure the blessings of liberty to the South. *The Coming of the Civil War* by Avery Craven (New York, 1942) is sympathetic with the South and critical of the injection of right and wrong into politics, making conflict irrepressible.

Roy F. Nichols, *The Disruption of American Democracy* (New York, 1948) traces the breakup of the Democratic Party in the late 1850s. *Ordeal of the Union* (2 vols., New York, 1947) and *The Emergence of Lincoln* (2 vols., New York, 1950) by Allan Nevins form part of an eight-volume magisterial set on the period, 1846–1865. Eric Foner, *Free Soil, Free Labor, Free Men: The Ideology of the Republican Party before the Civil War* (New York, 1970) contrasts the North's ideas and goals with the South's. *The Origins of the Republican Party, 1852–1856* (New York, 1987) by William Gienapp is a sophisticated and detailed study, using election returns. Three standard works on economic development are: George R. Taylor, *The Transportation Revolution, 1815–1860* (New York, 1951); Paul W. Gates, *The Farmer's Age: Agriculture 1815–1860* (New York, 1960); and Douglass C. North, *The Economic Growth of the United States, 1790–1860* (New York, 1961).

The best biography of Douglas is Robert W. Johannsen, *Stephen A. Douglas* (New York, 1973) and of Lincoln Stephen B. Oates, *With Malice toward None. The Life of Abraham Lincoln* (New York, 1977). Charles G. Sellers, "Who Were the Southern Whigs?", *The American Historical Review*, LIX, 335–346 describes a Whig ascendancy in the Old South; and Fletcher Green, "Democracy in the Old South," *The Journal of Southern History*, XII, 2–23 sees the Whig and Democratic Parties shifting back and forth, 1836–1852.

The literature on the secession crisis is abundant; good studies exist for every Southern state. Though old, *The Secession Movement 1860–1861* (New York, 1931) by Dwight Lowell Dumond is a scholarly study emphasizing constitutional and political matters. Steven A. Channing, *Crisis of Fear. Secession in South Carolina* New York, 1970) analyzes race relations and politics in a key state. *The Secessionist Impulse. Alabama and Mississippi in 1860* (Princeton, 1974) by William L. Barney examines parties and alignments, using census returns to help explain divergent ideologies. J. Mills Thornton, Jr., *Politics and Power in a Slave Society. Alabama, 1800–1860* (Baton Rouge, 1978) takes a long view of Alabama politics and its relation to black slavery. *And the War Came. The North and the Secession Crisis, 1860–1861* (Baton Rouge, 1950) by Kenneth M. Stampp is a thoughtful study. Ralph Wooster, *The Secession Conventions of the South* (Princeton, 1962) closely examines the subject.

The New York Tribune and *The Charleston Mercury* provide contrasting views of the period. Debates and votes may be found in *Congressional Globe*, 1833–1873 (Washington, 1834–1873). Essential materials are in U.S. Bureau of the Census, *Seventh Census of the United States, 1850* (Washington, 1854) and *Eighth Census of the United States, 1860* (Washington, 1865).

INDEX